READING/WRITING CONNECTIONS IN THE K–2 CLASSROOM

READING/WRITING CONNECTIONS IN THE K–2 CLASSROOM

Find the Clarity and Then Blur the Lines

LEAH MERMELSTEIN

Independent Literacy Consultant

<small>FOREWORD BY LUCY CALKINS</small>

Boston   New York   San Francisco
Mexico City   Montreal Toronto   London   Madrid   Munich   Paris
Hong Kong   Singapore   Tokyo   Cape Town   Sydney

Senior Series Editor: *Aurora Martínez Ramos*
Series Editorial Assistant: *Kevin Shannon*
Senior Marketing Manager: *Krista Clark*
Production Editor: *Janet Domingo*
Editorial Production Service: *Walsh & Associates, Inc.*
Composition Buyer: *Andrew Turso*
Manufacturing Buyer: *Andrew Turso*
Electronic Composition: *Publishers' Design and Production Services, Inc.*
Cover Administrator: *Joel Gendron*

For related titles and support materials, visit our online catalog at www.ablongman.com.

Between the time website information is gathered and then published, it is not unusual for some sites to have closed. Also, the transcription of URLs can result in typographical errors. The publisher would appreciate notification where these errors occur so that they may be corrected in subsequent editions.

Library of Congress Cataloging-in-Publication Data
Mermelstein, Leah.
  Reading/writing connections in the K–2 classroom: find the clarity and then blur the lines/Leah Mermelstein; foreword by Lucy Calkins.
    p.   cm.
    Includes bibliographical references and index.
    ISBN 0-205-41277-7
    1. Language arts (Primary) 2. Reading (Primary) 3. English language—Composition and exercises—Study and teaching (Primary) I. Title.
    LB1528.M47 2005
    372.6—dc22   2005051807

Printed in the United States of America

10 9 8 7 6 5 4 3   09 08 07 06

Photo Credits: All photos by Angela Jimenez

To Brenda Steele: a brilliant educator and mentor

CONTENTS

CHAPTER FIVE

The Components of Balanced Literacy 54

CHAPTER SIX

Units of Study 73

CHAPTER NINE

Minilessons   112

CHAPTER TEN

Conferences   131

CHAPTER ELEVEN

Small Group Work   158

FOREWORD

Over the past decade, I have often stood on the stage at Teacher's College, waiting for the audience to quiet, and then, when I have people's attention, I've said, "It is my privilege today to introduce our speaker, Leah Mermelstein." As I write this introduction, I feel as if you, the teachers of America, are spread before me, and I am again taking my place at the podium to introduce Leah Mermelstein to you. I wonder, when you hear me say, "It is my privilege . . . " how I can help you to understand the weight and significance of those words, for it truly is an awesome, beautiful honor to be able to introduce Leah to you.

The joy is particularly great on this occasion because I know that by reading *Reading/Writing Connections in the K–2 Classroom*, you will come to know all sides of this extraordinary woman. Leah's book reveals "Leah, the classroom teacher"; "Leah, the staff developer"; "Leah, the budding scholar"; and "Leah, the woman." But first of all and most of all, *Reading/Writing Connections in the K–2 Classroom* gives you "Leah, the classroom teacher."

And what a teacher she is! I wish, in this introduction, that I could put you on a magic carpet and bring you to the classrooms across New York City where Leah has taught children while dozens of us watch in awe. I wish you could come, sit with us at the edge of the meeting area, listening for a moment to this magnetic, magical teacher. You would see that Leah's teaching is spunky, full of verve and delight. You would listen with rapt attention as Leah's voice crescendos, sweeping the room into its enthusiasm and then, suddenly, goes quiet. In a whisper, she shares a secret about what grown-up readers do; "Do you think that maybe, even though you are kids, you guys could try those grown up strategies?" she asks.

You would see the youngsters wiggle with delight at the prospect, and after Leah has said, "Let's try it," and the class has dispersed like dandelion seeds, you would watch and listen as she pulls her chair alongside children—watching, questioning, nodding. Children talk with animation, practically spiraling out of their chairs in crescendos of enthusiasm. And then you would see that Leah has stopped listening to the children and that she is, instead, talking to them, telling them what she has noticed. She talks to these six-year-olds about their metacognitive strategies with as much enthusiasm and simplicity as if she was talking about centipedes and earthworms found under a rotting log. In just a few minutes of watching, she has seen so much. A researcher once said, "There is never a time when I sit beside a child when a miracle doesn't appear," and listening to Leah, you would know she, too, has the eyes to see miracles.

How I wish, in this introduction, that I could put you on a magic carpet and take you to a summer institute or an afterschool workshop, so that you could peak in on "Leah, the staff developer." I wish you could slip in among the teachers who study with her and sense their great satisfaction at having the chance to study with someone who knows teaching so intimately and well, and yet who can also step back just a bit from the hurly burl of classroom life to illuminate the great principles and patterns that underlie that complexity. Leah, the staff developer, always remembers the idiosyncratic, vibrant, human pulse of classroom life, and yet she allows her ideas on teaching to be guided by beliefs and principles.

Leah's enthusiasm, her brilliance, her breadth of knowledge, and her strong principles are contagious, leaving teachers with whom Leah works more brilliant more knowledgeable, and more principled in their own beliefs. They want to observe more, understand more, and in the end do more because they've had the privilege of working with Leah. In fact, Leah supports the teachers that she works with in the same ways that she does her students—by observing carefully, asking thoughtful questions, and making astute observations about their teaching. Leah, the staff developer, helps teachers take complicated ideas and create clear reading and writing curriculum for their students.

How I wish I could take you to Leah's crowded office in her home, her local library, or perhaps the coffee shop down the road so that you could also understand "Leah, the researcher." In her office you would find overflowing bookcases and piles of student work. In the library or coffee shop, you would most likely find Leah off in a corner hunkered down with books and articles on the teaching of reading and writing, a connection that has consumed her research over the past three years.

Leah was adamant that she write a book that was not only steeped in practical classroom experiences but also was based upon in-depth research and theory. And that she has done just that! She carved out time in her life to read and study the works of others. She listened to others' ideas and understandings and let these ideas help her refine her own. She spent time in countless classrooms watching exceptional teachers connecting reading and writing in their classrooms. Throughout all of this, she's asked questions and continually revised her thinking in order to deepen her understanding of the reading/writing connection. She's found an extraordinary range of reading/writing connections, and also had the courage to name ways in which reading and writing are not connected.

And through all of this there is of course "Leah, the woman." Wherever Leah goes, there is sure to be a strong and loving community. Leah pays attention to the tiny details of life. She's quick to laugh and make others laugh. She carefully brings out quiet voices and puts all in her company at ease. All who know her yearn to spend more time in her company. Whether it is friends, family, or colleagues, she is always surrounded by the people she loves. She finds the beauty in every situation and shares this beauty with others.

Leah's exquisite book *Reading/Writing Connections in the K–2 Classroom* is a result of all of these Leahs. In *Reading/Writing Connections in the K–2 Classroom* Leah Mermelstein invites you into her schools, her workshops, her summer institutes, and most importantly, she invites you into her mind. She demonstrates throughout the book that she cares that you and your students not only use the reading/writing connection but that you also understand it. Every word, every sentence is carefully crafted towards this understanding.

It is my great pleasure to invite you to join Leah in these pages and discover the magic of the reading/writing connection.

Lucy Calkins
Columbia University

Research shows that reading and writing develop concurrently and interrelatedly (Langenberg, 2000; Sulzby and Teale, 1991). Throughout my teaching career I have seen that many, many students read and write with an instinctive understanding that what they do in reading relates to what they do in writing (and vice versa). Because they have this instinctive understanding, their reading and writing do in fact develop concurrently, or at the same time, just as this research suggests.

However, I've seen just as many students who do not have this instinctive understanding. In the same way that two toddlers might sit side by side playing in the playground unaware that they could interact, we have students in our classroom who see reading and writing side by side on their classroom schedules and are completely unaware of the relationship between the two. These students' reading and writing skills do develop concurrently as supported by the research; however, I find that their reading and writing skills do not develop nearly as quickly as those students who do understand the relationship between reading and writing.

I decided to write this book because I believe that through careful, explicit assessing, planning, and teaching we can help every student understand the relationship between reading and writing. And once students understand this relationship, we can then show them how to quickly put this understanding to use, letting their writing skills improve and add to their reading skills, and vice versa. In that way every student can develop reading and writing skills concurrently and quickly, thus learning more in a smaller period of time. Marie Clay defines this phenomenon as the "pleasant ring of a two-for-one bargain" (2001, p. 11). This book will provide both new and veteran teachers with specific ways to get a "two-for-one bargain" in their assessments, in their planning, and in their teaching of reading and writing so that they in turn can help their students learn more by using the reading/writing connection.

Writing this book has proved to be quite an endeavor. I wanted it to be rich in both theory and in research, but at the same time I wanted it to be practical, providing you with many ideas you could immediately try in your classroom. Different experiences over the past ten years have assisted me in trying to achieve both of these goals.

First, I brought my experiences as a primary level teacher. I can remember watching one of my students read during my first year of teaching. In the midst of reading the student looked up and said, "This author labeled her chapters rather than giving them good titles. She's such a good writer. I'm surprised she didn't work harder."

I laughed because earlier that day I had conducted a writing minilesson that focused on the differences between a label and a title. Even early on in my teaching career, I was fascinated by the ways in which the teaching of writing affected how students read. I was equally as fascinated by the ways in which the teaching of reading affected how students wrote.

This fascination with the reading/writing connection continued when I decided to leave the classroom and work as a staff developer for the Teacher's College Reading and Writing Project at Columbia University. I had the unique opportunity there to work under the mentorship of Lucy Calkins, author of *The Art of Teaching Reading* and *The Art of Teaching Writing*, among other publications. Lucy structured our work at the project so that once a week we were not working in schools, but rather studying in daylong think tanks. In these think tanks my colleagues and I read professional literature, conducted classroom-based research, and continually refined and added to our understanding of what it meant to teach reading and writing to young students.

It was here during these weekly think tanks where I learned the value and payoff of vigilantly studying one idea in depth. That idea for me was, of course, the reading/writing connection. I took the ideas that were developed during our weekly think tanks and tried them out with hundreds of New York City school teachers and their students. It was only in the day-to-day, nitty-gritty reality of working side by side with both the teachers and their students when I could closely study the ideas developed in our think tank, noticing which ones worked and which needed to be revised.

Now, as an independent literacy consultant I work with teachers, principals, curriculum specialists, and teachers not only in New York City but also nationwide. Wherever I go, there is a keen interest in studying the reading/writing connection. A common question I get in my travels is, How do we fit in all that we know about quality reading and writing instruction into a day? a month? a year?

I have found that when teachers understand the relationship between reading and writing, and then use that understanding to move between the two, they fit more into a day than they ever dreamed possible. While on the road, I've also been fortunate enough to try out different chapters of the book as presentations and have received both positive feedback and thoughtful and constructive critique.

Finally, I refined my understandings on the teaching of reading, the teaching of writing, and the connection between the two. I read the work of authors and researchers such as Lucy Calkins, Ellin Keene, Stephanie Harvey, Frank Smith, Marilyn Adams, Marie Clay, Susan Zimmerman, Debbie Miller, Katherine and Randy Bomer, Carl Anderson, Ken and Yetta Goodman, Richard Allington, and Michael Pressley, to name a few, to refine my understanding of the teaching of reading and writing. I also read work by Andrea Butler, Jan Turbill, Don Graves, Jane Hansen, Robert Tierney, David Pearson, Frank Smith, Julie Jensen, Sandra Stotsky, James Squire, and Marie Clay, among others, to refine my understanding of the ways in which reading and writing connect. While writing this book, I felt the presence of these brilliant educators. I'm sure you'll feel their presence while reading it, too.

Bringing the reading/writing connection to your classroom will be exciting but it will not be easy. It will not always look like the neatly organized charts or Curriculum Calendars you'll find inside the pages of this book. What you do in reading might not always gracefully move writing or vice versa. When I was a first grade teacher, I spent five years learning with Isoke Nia, founder of All Write Literacy Consultants. Whenever we studied something new, we would first look at it in simple and clear ways so that later on we could complicate it.

Throughout this book you'll find charts, transcripts of minilessons and conferences, and Curriculum Calendars where the reading/writing connection is crystal clear. When you bring this work to your classroom it will be a bit messier, a bit more complicated. My hope is that the layout of this book helps you to approach the reading/writing connection in an organized fashion, but it also gives you the courage to complicate it and mess it up in your own classroom.

READING/WRITING CONNECTIONS IN THE K–2 CLASSROOM

Reading/Writing Connections in the K–2 Classroom is divided into three parts, each part building on the part before it. Part I, "Building," explores some of the essential understandings you need in order to use the reading/writing connection in powerful and lasting ways. Part II, "Planning," helps you to use the reading/writing connection in your daily, monthly, and yearly planning. Part III, "Teaching," explores how to use the reading/writing connection to strengthen your everyday encounters with students.

Every chapter has some consistent features that hopefully will assist you in your day-to-day teaching, your curriculum planning, and your own long-term professional development. One feature, "Putting the Reading/Writing Connection into Action," will suggest practical ways to use the reading/writing connection in your classroom. Another feature, "For Further Study," was created especially for staff developers, literacy leaders, principals, and/or members of a study group. Here you'll find tips on how to use this book as a starting point for further conversations, along with ideas for research you might conduct in your classroom. The appendix includes lists of professional literature, additional examples, and helpful assessment tools.

As you read, you'll notice that assessment is woven into every chapter. Beverly Falk reminds us that "assessment should always be in the service of student learning" (1998, p. 58). I've integrated assessment into each of the chapters because I wanted to give you a clear image of what it looks like to assess in the midst of your teaching so that you can quickly use your assessments to help students learn. Additionally, Chapter 3 will provide you with particular thinking strategies and qualities of writing that you can assess for throughout the year.

You'll also notice that word study (including phonics, phonemic awareness, and spelling) is woven into many of the chapters. The National Reading Panel (National Institute of Child Health and Human Development, 2000) emphasized the importance of "integrating the teaching of phonemic awareness and phonics with reading real books and with written and oral expression" (p. 2-137). Throughout this book, I will show you how to do just that. You'll see ways to integrate phonemic awareness, phonics, word study, and spelling into both your planning and teaching of reading and writing. In that way you'll get a sense of how these important skills fit into *real reading and writing experiences*.

It is also imperative that word study is addressed as a separate component. Doing this ensures that you have a systematic approach to teaching these important topics. There are many approaches to teaching word study. I recommend reading books like *Spelling K–8* by Diane Snowball and Faye Bolton, *Phonics They Use* by Patricia M. Cunningham, and Marilyn Adams's *Beginning to Read* to further your understanding of how to plan and teach word study in your classroom.

Anne Lamont, author of *bird by bird*, says all good stories are out there waiting to be told in a fresh, wild new way (1994, p. 183). I've read many stories about teaching young children to read and write—each story authored by a brilliant teacher or researcher, each story offering a new perspective on how to be more thoughtful about the craft of your teaching. And now, I tentatively put my own story out there, next to so many brilliant others, and hope that I tell my own story in a fresh, wild new way.

Leah Mermelstein

ACKNOWLEDGMENTS

Since the start of my career, my ultimate dream has been to write a book. Because of this dream, I have lived differently. I've taught students, coached teachers, attended professional conferences, and met with colleagues not just as a teacher, but also as a hopeful writer. I am honored to finally be able to thank everyone who has helped me make my dream of writing a book a reality.

My passion for teaching began when I was a graduate student at the University of Massachusetts. I met many people while studying there who made this experience a unique and lasting one. First, I will forever be grateful to Sharon Edwards for being a model of the quintessential teacher, and for showing me through example that good teachers are lifelong learners. Sharon also introduced me to two brilliant professors, Robert Maloy and Byrd Jones, and I instantly became a part of their professional team. The three of them included me in any and all of their professional endeavors, whether it was facilitating workshops, conducting classroom-based research, or writing professional texts. I am grateful to them for showing me early on how to let this type of work impact the work I did with the students in my classroom. I also thank Sonia Nieto, my advisor at the time, who helped me to design a graduate program that combined a wide array of practical experiences alongside rich research and theory. I thank Peter Elbow, both a professor and writer, who graciously agreed to pair up his college students with my first grade students. It was through conversations with Peter that I first began to learn the power in letting writers talk to one another. I also thank Jodi Bornstein, my thought companion throughout graduate school. Together, we learned how to take good ideas and transform them into powerful teaching practices.

After graduate school, I was lucky enough to get a job at PS 11 in Manhattan. Before I got there, I had heard that PS 11 had a reputation for being an incredibly collaborative community. Once I got there, I learned just how true that statement was. I am grateful to every colleague I met while working there for including me in the school community, and most importantly, for giving me tremendous amounts of love and support. There are a few people from PS 11 that I would like to thank personally. First, I want to thank Lesley Gordon, my first principal, for not only having faith in such a rookie but also being wise enough to surround that rookie with quality staff development. I also want to thank Brenda Steele, to whom I have dedicated the book. Brenda became the principal of PS 11 after Leslie left. I thank Brenda for her gentle but firm way of reminding my colleagues and I that there was always more to learn. I thank Hindy List, Susan Radley, and Peter Sinclair, my staff developers while I worked at PS 11. They pushed me to move forward when I was ready and listened quietly when I was frustrated.

After teaching at PS 11, I left the classroom to work as a staff developer at the Teacher's College Reading and Writing Project. I want to begin by of course thanking Lucy Calkins, the founding director of the project, who has so graciously written the foreword to my book. I will forever be grateful to Lucy for all the ways that she has supported me professionally. I thank her for asking me to join her in the work at the project and for allowing me to be part of a community of learners who continually searched for the best ways to teach reading and writing. I also want to thank Lucy for asking me to join her in co-authoring the book *Launching the Writing Workshop* from the First Hand Series at Heinemann. What an honor is was to write side by side with Lucy! Her thoughtful critique and her dazzling writing style helped me to have both the courage and skill to undertake the huge task of writing a book on my own. I also thank Laurie Pessah, the co-director of the Project, for her constant support while I was at the project and her continued friendship now that I've left. I thank Isoke Nia, who was one of my mentors while I worked at the Project and continues to be my mentor to this day. I am inspired by her unbelievable brilliance, her hard questions, and her commitment to all students. Miriam Swirksi-Lubin, Linda Chen, Mary Ann Colbert, Kathy Collins, Lydia Bellino, Liz Phillips, Marjorie Martinelli, and Cheryl Tyler were my constant Primary Writing and Reading thought companions, and I thank them for sharing their ideas with me and continually pushing my thinking about reading and writing. I also thank Carl Anderson, Gaby Layden, Janet Angelillo, and Kathleen Tolan for their constant support in the writing of this book. While working at the project, I had the opportunity to learn from many literacy educators. I thank Nancy Anderson, Andrea Butler, Brian Cambourne, Richard Allington, Kathy Short, Katie Wood Ray, Katherine and Randy Bomer, Elizabeth Sulzby, Diane Snowball, and Patricia Cunningham for graciously sharing their thinking at workshops and in study groups.

Most of my days over the past five years have been spent working side by side with principals, staff developers, teachers, and students. This book is graced with their brilliant work. I thank everyone from PS 1 in Manhattan, Lowerlab in Manhattan, PS 295 in Brooklyn, PS 87 in Queens, PS 94 in Queens, PS 261 in Brooklyn, Levy Lakeside School in Merrick, The Guilderland Elementary Schools, The Bethel Elementary Schools, The Prosser Elementary Schools, The Nooksack Valley Elementary Schools, Lake George Elementary School, Roxbury Elementary School, The Center School in Litchfield, Julian Curtiss Elementary School in Greenwich, and Skano Elementary School in Albany. I thank Judi Aronson, the extraordinary principal of PS 261, who always made sure that her school was my home away from home. I also thank her for allowing me to take photographs of the beautiful students from her school for the book. A special thanks goes to Shawn Brandon, Millie DeStefano, Adele Cammarata, Marissa Dechiara, Ellen Dillon, Chrissy Koukiotis, Marcy Mattera, and Jennifer Moore, all extraordinary teachers, who over the years have graciously opened up their classrooms and their teaching to me. I was lucky enough throughout these years to convince many of the teachers that I worked with to join me in evening study groups and in fact many of the ideas inside of this book were born during these long evening meetings. I thank all of you (you know who you are) for taking risks in your teaching and having faith that our often messy process would eventually yield positive results.

There were many people who took time out of their busy lives to read my book and offer me thoughtful critique. Lucy Calkins, Laurie Pessah, Katherine Bomer, and Erica Denman all read my book at critical junctures. Their wise feedback always reenergized me to keep searching for the clearest way to explain complicated ideas. Lisa Burman, Cheryl Tyler, Ellen Dillon, Shawn Brandon, and Norman Stiles read earlier drafts of my book and I thank them for reading it gently, while at the same time offering me critical feedback. I thank Jennifer Moore, Chrissy Koukiotis, and Marcy Mattera, for not only reading different parts of the book, but also offering constant support throughout the entire process. I thank Tara Azwell, Emporia State University; Lucy Calkins, Teacher's College, Columbia University; Sherri Phillips Merrit, University of North Carolina at Greensboro; and Carol Wickstrom, University of North Texas for reading and reviewing my book.

I thank the entire team at Allyn and Bacon for their support in writing this book, especially Kevin Shannon, Janet Domigo, Elizabeth Grell, and Marey Leif. I of course thank Aurora Martínez Ramos, my editor at Allyn and Bacon, who skillfully helped me revise while continually reminding me to never lose my voice. I want to also thank Kathy Whittier and the wonderful team at Walsh & Associates for devoting such time and care to the production of my book. I thank Angela Jimenez, who took the beautiful photographs for this book.

Finally, I also thank my parents and first teachers, Terry and Lothar Mermelstein, who continue to teach me important lessons about living and learning.

READING/WRITING CONNECTIONS IN THE K–2 CLASSROOM

BUILDING

You've probably come to this book hoping to gain a better understanding of the reading/writing connection. You're probably hoping to see transcripts of minilessons, conferences, and Units of Study all geared toward that. All of the above is important, but it's not enough.

If you want to assess, plan, and teach differently because of the reading/writing connection, then you must ask yourself, "What essential understandings must I have in order to do that?" Part I, "Building," will support you in understanding what's essential in order to connect reading and writing effectively in your classroom.

First, you must build a powerful community of learners. Ralph Peterson reminds us in his groundbreaking book, *Life in a Crowded Place*, that "Well-formed ideas and intentions amount to little without a community to bring them to life" (1992, p. 2). Chapter 1 will help you to bring ideas to life in your classroom by suggesting ways to create powerful relationships.

Also, in order to make effective reading/writing connections, you must understand the relationship between reading and writing. In Chapter 2, I will bring clarity to this relationship by comparing reading and writing, highlighting both the similarities and differences.

Once you understand the similarities and differences between reading and writing, you must also understand how to use that knowledge to deliberately move between the teaching of reading and the teaching of writing. In Chapter 3, I will show you how to do this. First, I will outline thinking strategies that both readers and writers use and suggest that one way you can blur the lines between reading and writing is to teach those thinking strategies at the same time. Then, I'll show you how to study student writing, once again blurring the lines, using student writing samples to aid you in teaching not just writing but reading as well.

Take your time reading these chapters. Discuss them in study groups. Agree. Disagree. Write in the margins. But most importantly, let your understanding of the reading/writing connection help your students read and write with intention, clarity, and depth.

CHAPTER 1

POWERFUL RELATIONSHIPS

The child sitting in front of you is more important than reading—more important than writing.

—Donald Graves

Recently, I visited a first grade classroom with a group of teachers to study what we should teach the next day. My pen was racing madly, writing down all the teaching possibilities for this class. The very next day, I gathered the same students on the rug for a mini-lesson. The question wasn't what to teach, but which teaching point to choose from all the ideas I had.

But before I could begin Jose stood up and said, "You know it's kind of funny, but sometimes I like to write about playing with Barbies." As you can expect, the class erupted into laughter. What was my reaction? I said, "That's enough. Let's move on." And I continued to teach. At that moment, I was thinking about what I wanted to teach Jose and his classmates about reading and writing, but I wasn't thinking about what those students were learning.

Psychologist Dr. Thomas Gordon states, "Teaching is a process that is carried out by one person, while the process of learning goes on inside another" (1974, p. 3). I taught some wonderful things that morning in that first grade classroom, but when I said, "Let's move on," the students learned one thing I never intended on teaching: Don't talk or write about things in this classroom that seem different.

I had a golden opportunity to develop a relationship with Jose and the entire class that would have led to deeper learning. Unfortunately, I missed it.

In this chapter I will examine how to develop the kinds of relationships that facilitate student learning. Often, we do many of these things in the beginning of the year to build classroom community. But then October arrives, and we abandon community building to get to the "real" business of teaching reading and writing. Relationships suffer and that interferes with students' learning.

I'm talking about relationships first because, frankly, without them, I don't think anything else is possible. It is at the heart of all that we do.

INTRODUCE ENGAGING TOOLS

First, you must plan for your students' relationship to reading and writing. Of course, you want it to be a powerful one. You want them to feel, in Frank Smith's words, "part of the Literacy Club" (1985, p. 123). One way that you can do this is to introduce them to engaging tools. Sharon Edwards, a first grade teacher, and Robert Maloy, a university professor, discuss an incredibly powerful concept in their book *Kids Have All the Write Stuff*. They created Writing Boxes for all of the students in Sharon's first grade classroom.

Inside of these boxes were colorful, child-sized items—tools for writing such as scented markers, pencils, rulers, scissors, tape, and different sizes and colors of paper. Sharon's students brought the writing boxes home and what Sharon, Bob, and the families found was literally an "explosion of writing" (1992, p. xviii). The engaging tools inside the Writing Boxes helped the students develop a relationship with writing.

When we outfit our students with the real tools of readers and writers, it is more than just a beginning of the year activity. It will connect your students throughout the year into the world of literacy. These tools don't have to be big fancy ones: a bookmark, a freshly sharpened pencil, a black flair pen, sticky notes, a colored pencil for revision. Their writing and reading will become crisper, stronger. They will have the tools of the trade.

EMPHASIZE HOW STUDENTS TREAT ONE ANOTHER

We also need to develop students' relationships with one another. In the beginning of the year, we are bombarded with enough organizational realities to make our mind spin.

- What will our Units of Study be?
- How will we arrange our classrooms?
- How will we record conferences?
- How will students get their supplies?

We need to pay attention to these realities, but if we want all of our students to have successful learning experiences, we also need to pay attention to how our students interact with one another.

- What will we do when a student rolls her eyes at another student's attempt to spell *beautiful?*
- What will we do when a student does what Jose did—announces that he likes to play with Barbies—and our class erupts with laughter?
- What will we do when a student announces that she thinks Kenya is the worst reader in the class?

These interactions happen in a split second. Because of that, they are easy to ignore in the hecticness of our day-to-day teaching. But they are in no way small, and we cannot ignore them. These small things and how we react to these small things teach students the ways in which they will have relationships with one another. Ralph Fletcher says in his book *What a Writer Needs:* "The best writing classes I visit are taught by teachers who work hard at creating an environment where children can put themselves on the line when they write" (1992, p. 26).

You'll want to help the students in your classroom feel comfortable putting themselves on the line in your classroom. When I first began teaching, I wanted my students to like me, and it somehow felt wrong to reprimand them. Over time, I realized that being kind was important at times, but so was being strict. I became quite strict about certain things—one of them being how students treated one another. I knew if I wasn't strict about that, my students wouldn't put themselves on the line in the classroom.

GET TO KNOW YOUR STUDENTS

Donald Graves believes in order to teach writing well you need to learn five details about every student in your classroom. When you get to know the details of your students' lives, you're equipped when a students says she has nothing to write about. You'll know better.

You'll know that she has stories, poems, and letters living inside of her, and you'll be able to guide her to write from her own experiences. And when a student says there is nothing he wants to read, you'll be able to help him choose a book based upon your knowledge of that student.

When I taught first grade, I used to watch Adam out of the corner of my eye, and I worried about how his writing partnership was going. It took all of my energy just to get him to say good morning to me at the start of the day, and I couldn't imagine him talking with his partner about anything. One day I sent home a note asking parents to tell me about their children. The next day, Adam came in with a crumpled up piece of paper. He handed it to me, carefully avoiding my eyes.

When I opened the letter, it simply stated Adam loves the Beatles. I thought perhaps he liked beetles as in insects, but no, Adam liked "The Beatles." The moment I brought this up to Adam, I saw the first smile emerge. Many more smiles, many more shared conversations—many more read-alouds, many more published pieces—emerged from the relationship that grew out the information I learned about his life.

PUTTING THE READING/WRITING CONNECTION INTO ACTION

- Have students share their lives as readers and writers.
  1. Where are their favorite places to read at home/school?
  2. Where are their favorite places to write at home/school?
  3. What kinds of books do they like to read? (topics, genres)
  4. What kinds of books do they like to write? (topics, genres)
- Have storytelling circles where students share the details of their lives with one another. Have them share their hobbies and interests.
- Send letters home to parents or guardians asking them for information about their children. You might ask about their hobbies, their interests, their favorite places to read and write.

LET YOUR STUDENTS GET TO KNOW YOU

Your students must also get to know you. I'm not saying every intimate detail, but they must know you in order for you to get to know them. I remember going into Shawn Brandon's brilliant kindergarten classroom. When I introduced myself to the students, there was a flurry of conversation as the students raised their hands in excitement. "Yes," I said as I pointed to Derrick. He said, "Are you the Leah Mrs. Brandon eats sushi with?"

Shawn thinks about the relationships that she develops with her students. She thinks about how they will get to know her. When Shawn models in her minilessons, she does not choose a safe, easy topic and write it simply. She writes about topics that truly matter to her and writes about these topics in beautiful and eloquent ways, even in kindergarten. She also shares the books she reads. She understands that unless she puts herself on the line, and shares her reading and writing life, her students never will.

START WITH STRENGTH

Sister Judy Hayes, a participant at the Reading and Writing Project's Summer Institute at Columbia University, said once during my section that starting with strength allowed her students to trust her. "Once they trust me," she said, "They are putty in my hands. It feels like we are dancing together, the student and I, gracefully dancing when I sit down for a conference." "Of course," she says, "We step on each other's feet once in a while, but we figure it out and we dance again."

Her words reminded me of the day that I worked with Taras, a first grade student in my class, on his writing. He was working on a piece about his uncle's funeral. On page one he described how beautiful a particular scene was at the funeral. On the next page he said he didn't care about that because his uncle was dead. His entire book seesawed between this scene and his feelings.

It was beautifully organized. I was so proud of him. I wanted to hug him and a part of me wanted to stop right there and simply revel in his strengths.

"Taras," I begin, "You've got it. You helped me as a reader understand that even though the funeral was beautiful, all you could think about was how your uncle died." "Yes," he said, "I did it because that's what I wanted people to know how much I missed my uncle." Taras looked up and smiled. He knew he had done something smart.

"Taras," I said, "You've got the organization of your whole piece. Let's take a look at the some of the words inside your piece. You know," I said, "As I read your piece I felt like I needed more words on these pages," I said, pointing to the pages where he had described the scenes. "I don't quite see it yet." Taras's eyes filled up with tears.

"But that's too hard. I can't do it." he said.

"Taras," I said, "I know it's hard, but I want you to try it—you are writing about something so important. I know you can do it." Taras nodded okay as he wiped the tears off his face. I left him so he could compose himself. And sure enough, he tried it and did it beautifully.

Taras was aware of his strengths as a writer and so was I. He was certainly engaged, and I knew enough about him that, although he was right—it would be hard—I knew he could do it. I could sit there when tears welled in his eyes and push a little more (yes, it was hard) because I knew it wouldn't destroy him, but rather it would enable him to grow in his abilities as a writer. I could say some harder things to him. And that's what starting with strength does. It develops a relationship with a student that allows you to teach rigorously on a regular basis.

As we begin our journey of studying the reading/writing connection, don't forget that powerful relationships are what create powerful teaching and learning. Without relationships in our classrooms, all else suffers. Develop relationships across your year—so that students can learn what you teach.

I wish I could return to that first grade classroom, back to that moment when I said, "Let's move on." I can't, but I know that very soon you'll have a day when you have a lot to teach. And on that day, you'll have a Jose in your classroom who will say something quickly. He'll open up a golden opportunity for you to deepen your relationship with your class, which will lead to deeper learning.

Don't miss this golden opportunity. Don't move on.

FOR FURTHER STUDY

- Ask a colleague to observe a student you're struggling with, writing down all of the strengths that she sees. Have her share her notes with you and then discuss ways that these reflections can influence your relationship with that particular student.
- Make a class list.
  1. Try to write down five details about every student in your classroom.
  2. Note which students you could do this for and which you couldn't.
  3. Gather more information about the students that you could not do this for.
  4. Discuss how those details could influence how you teach reading and writing.

CHAPTER 2

FIND THE CLARITY . . .

Reading and writing are both acts of composing. Readers, using their background of knowledge and experience, compose meaning from the text; writers, using their background of knowledge and experience, compose meaning into text.

—Andrea Butler

How can we connect reading and writing in our classrooms? This is the question I posed to a group of teachers one Tuesday evening early in September. And then just as always, we talked and talked. Most of those teachers had read Katie Wood Ray's wonderful book *Wondrous Words* and had taught their students to read text in order to help them write text. We talked about minilessons and conferences and how those were great places to connect reading and writing. We talked and talked and before we knew it, it was time to leave.

I left school that day with a weird, something isn't quite right, feeling. As fruitful as the conversation was, in my heart of hearts (even though I was scared to admit it) I knew that I hadn't asked the right question. I realized that before we could study *how* to connect reading and writing in our classrooms, we first had to understand the relationship between reading and writing. What I should have asked that evening was, *How are reading and writing both the same and different?*

The answer to that question—How are reading and writing both the same and different?—became the heart of my work that year and is the focus of this chapter.

HOW ARE READING AND WRITING THE SAME?

While I worked at the Reading and Writing Project, Lucy Calkins, founding director, took on the awesome responsibility of helping thousands of New York City teachers simultaneously launch Reading and Writing Workshops. We spent many Thursdays in think tanks discussing how to keep both the integrity and depth of this work intact, while quickly moving teachers toward conducting both Reading and Writing Workshops in their classrooms. We found that teachers were most successful in doing this when we helped them understand the similarities between reading and writing.

Robert J. Tierney and David Pearson state that "at the heart of understanding reading and writing connections one must begin to view reading and writing as essentially similar processes of meaning construction" (1983, p. 5). The similarities between reading and writing will, of course, affect the ways in which you assess, plan for, and teach your students. These implications will be explored in depth in subsequent chapters, but for now, lets simply look at what the similarities are.

Both reading and writing are purposeful activities.

Katherine and Randy Bomer remind us in their book *For a Better World: Reading and Writing for Social Justice* just how important it is for students to read and write for authentic, purposeful reasons: "You don't just sit down to write a letter of complaint; the need arises in life, and the genre is always and only tied to that reason" (2001, p. 4). A considerable amount of the reading and writing that I do in my own life arises because of particular reasons or needs that I have. I read recipes because I'm cooking something new and I don't want to mess up. I write notes to remind myself to pick up the laundry. (I often forget.) It's crucial that we encourage our students to read and write in authentic and purposeful ways just as Bomer and Bomer suggest so that they also can see the power that reading and writing have for solving problems and getting things accomplished in their lives.

Both reading and writing are a process.

Calkins, when describing the writing process, said, "Just as researchers often follow a scientific method, writers follow a process of craft when they work" (1994, p. 70). I would say the same is true for readers. They also follow a process of craft when they read. Experienced readers and writers understand that their ideas grow over time as they plan, read and/or write, rethink, review, and revise. Time and attention always bring deeper meaning to both reading and writing.

James Squire says, "Our failure to teach composing and comprehending as process impedes our efforts not only to teach children to read and write, but our efforts to teach them how to think" (1983, p. 23). Often, I'll suggest to teachers that they reread books to their students and encourage their students to talk about these books over time. I used to worry that students would find rereading books boring or that after a while they would have nothing else to say about those books. What I've found, however, is the complete opposite. Students tend to do their best thinking with the books they have read more than once. Reading these books over time. I've found, not only helps them view reading as process, but it also helps them to think inside of this process just as Squire suggested.

The average 5- to 8-year-old cannot draw on past experiences to help him understand the reading and writing process. He needs us (experienced readers and writers) to demonstrate how to revise and rethink our own reading and writing. Figure 2.1 shows a possible way that you might compare the reading and the writing process with your students. It won't always make sense to align these reading and writing processes, but hopefully seeing the processes side by side will help you align them in your classroom when it makes sense to do so.

Readers and writers use similar sources of information (cueing systems).

Researchers such as Marie Clay and Ken and Yetta Goodman have taught us that readers use meaning (or semantic), structure (or syntactic), and visual (or graphophonic) sources of information while reading. These sources of information influenced the ways in which I taught reading as a classroom teacher. I modeled how to use these sources of information while reading, and then observed students to see which ones they used independently. Finally, I taught them how to integrate the ones they weren't using independently into their repertoire.

Over time, I wondered if writers also used meaning, structure, and visual sources of information. What I found was that just as these sources of information influenced the ways in which I taught reading, they also had the potential to influence the ways in which I taught writing. Figure 2.2 outlines some of the strategies that you'll want to teach students to use while reading and writing. It also points out that different strategies support students in utilizing different sources of information. You'll see many of these strategies in action next when we examine students in the midst of reading and writing.

Meaning.   The first source of information is meaning (or semantics). Both readers and writers need to ensure that first and foremost their reading and writing make sense. They

FIGURE 2.1   The reading and writing processes.

WRITING PROCESS	READING PROCESS
REHEARSAL	**REHEARSAL**
■ Drawing before you write.	■ Looking at pictures before you read.
■ Reading before you write (their own writing, other students' writing, and published writing).	■ Reading the blurb on the back of the book.
■ Talking (often storytelling) before you write. This talk will help students use prior knowledge to compose new texts.	■ Talking before you read. This talk will help students use prior knowledge to comprehend new texts.
■ Set goals (I want to write my grandma a poem for her birthday).	■ Set goals (I want to read this chapter to examine Frog and Toad's friendship).
DRAFT	**DRAFT**
■ Using meaning, structure, and visual sources of information to compose meaning into both the pictures and the words.	■ Using meaning, structure, and visual sources of information to compose meaning from both the pictures and the words.
■ Write a beginning.	■ Read a beginning.
REVISE/EDIT	**REVISE/EDIT**
■ Getting closer to meaning (adding or deleting from both the pictures and words) by:	■ Getting closer to meaning (adding or taking away from your thinking) by:
Talking to a partner. Rereading writing. Reading other texts.	Talking to a partner. Rereading the text. Writing about what you read. Drawing about what you read.
Changing your mind about a word you wrote. Changing your mind about what you want your text to be about.	Changing your mind about what a word says. Changing your mind about what a text means.
PUBLISH	**PUBLISH**
■ Getting your writing ready for the world by: Adding color. Making a cover. Practicing reading (so others can enjoy listening).	■ Getting your reading ready for the world by: Practicing reading (so others can enjoy listening).
CELEBRATE	**CELEBRATE**
■ Put your writing into the world.	■ Put your reading out into the world.
REFLECT	**REFLECT**
What did I learn while writing that I could now always use when composing text?	What did I learn while reading that I could now always use when comprehending text?

FIGURE 2.2   Strategies that support the different sources of information.

	MEANING	STRUCTURE	VISUAL
	Does it make sense?	*Does it sound right?*	*Does it look right?*
Reading	Think about the book. Did what I read make sense? If it didn't, I could:	Did what I read sound right? If it didn't, I could:	Did what I read look right? If it didn't, I could:
	Reread. Look at the picture. Ask myself what's happened in the book so far. Talk to someone.	Reread. Use the pattern of the book (if there is one) to help me. Try to make what I read sound like talk. Ask myself if there is another word that would fit.	Reread. Look at the first letter and then get my mouth ready for the corresponding sound. Look for parts of the word that I know. Ask myself if I just know that word *or* if there is a word that I do know that would help me.
Writing	Think about my writing. Did what I write make sense? If it didn't, I could:	Did what I write sound right? If it didn't, I could:	Did what I write look right? If it didn't, I could:
	Rewrite. Look at my picture. Ask myself, What's happened in my story so far? Talk to someone.	Rewrite. Remember the pattern of my writing (if there is one). Try to make my writing sound like talk. Ask myself if there is another word that would fit.	Rewrite. Listen to the first sound and then write the corresponding letter. (Then middle sound, and end sound). See if there are parts of the word I know how to write. Ask myself if I just know that word *or* if there is a word I know that would help me.

need to keep this in mind before, during, and after reading and writing. Making meaning (comprehension) and creating meaning (composition) are precisely what reading and writing are about, but what does it look like when our youngest readers and writers use meaning at its simplest, most basic level? When readers use meaning, they ask themselves if what they read makes sense, and when it doesn't, they'll do something so it does.

Ciprian, for example, a first grade student, was recently reading a poem. When I observed him, he seemed to be having difficulty figuring out what the poem was about. He looked at the picture that accompanied the poem, but still he was confused. He then began to read the words of the poem. After he read the first two lines, he went back and looked at the picture. "Oh," he said, "It's about firemen." Then he continued reading.

Ciprian started off by looking at the picture. At first, the picture didn't help him make meaning, but then he began reading and looked at the picture once again. That's when it came together for him. He not only read the words, but also looked at the picture. He used meaning here as a source of information; that is, he knew right from the beginning that his reading needed to make sense and he persevered until it did.

Writers, like readers, also use meaning as a source of information. When writers use meaning, they ask themselves if what they are writing (or about to write) makes sense. If it doesn't they will do something to ensure that it does make sense. Later on in the day I watched Ciprian write. Ciprian was attempting to write a poem and this time, he looked less than thrilled. He opened and closed his folder a few times, fiddling with some paper in it. Then he stared into space. When he saw Millie, his teacher, coming, he grabbed his pencil and appeared to be deep in thought.

"Ciprian," she said dramatically as she approached him, "I can't believe you haven't gotten started. What's going on?" Ciprian's eyes filled up with tears and he said, "I don't know how to write poetry. I don't know how to make it rhyme."

Millie then went on to explain to Ciprian that not all poems have to rhyme, but the most important thing that poets do is start by writing about something that matters to them. "What do you want your poem to be about?" she asked him. "My family," he said. "They make me feel happy and safe." "Gosh, that sounds like you've already got the start of a poem. Get going." And once Millie left him, he did (see Figure 2.3).

Ciprian didn't begin by thinking that his poem had to make sense. Rather, he began by trying to think of rhyming words. Millie helped him begin with meaning by asking him to think and talk about something that mattered to him. Ciprian, with his teacher's assistance, began his writing as he did his reading, ensuring that it made sense.

Structure.   The second source of information is structure (or syntax). *Structure* refers to the grammatical aspects of language. It can refer to the internal structure (how an individual sentence is organized). For example, "She goed to the store" is not a structurally correct sentence. It can also refer to the external structure (how the entire text is organized). The genre of poetry, for example, often has an external structure of repeating lines. It's important that readers pay attention to the structure or structures presented in their texts. They must continually read, asking themselves, *Does what I'm reading sound right?*

Recently I watched Isaiah, a kindergarten student, read. The text he was reading said "Time to get up," but he read the text as "Time to got up." I asked him if he thought what he was reading "sounded right." He shook his head. Then, I asked him to go back and "make it sound right." This time he went back and read the text correctly. Isaiah made his reading "sound right" by going back and rereading and changing the tense of *got* to "get" (one of the structure strategies in Figure 2.2).

Later on in the day, I watched Isaiah reread his writing. As he reread, he came to a sentence he wrote that said, "The party is 3:00." He continued rereading, not noticing that

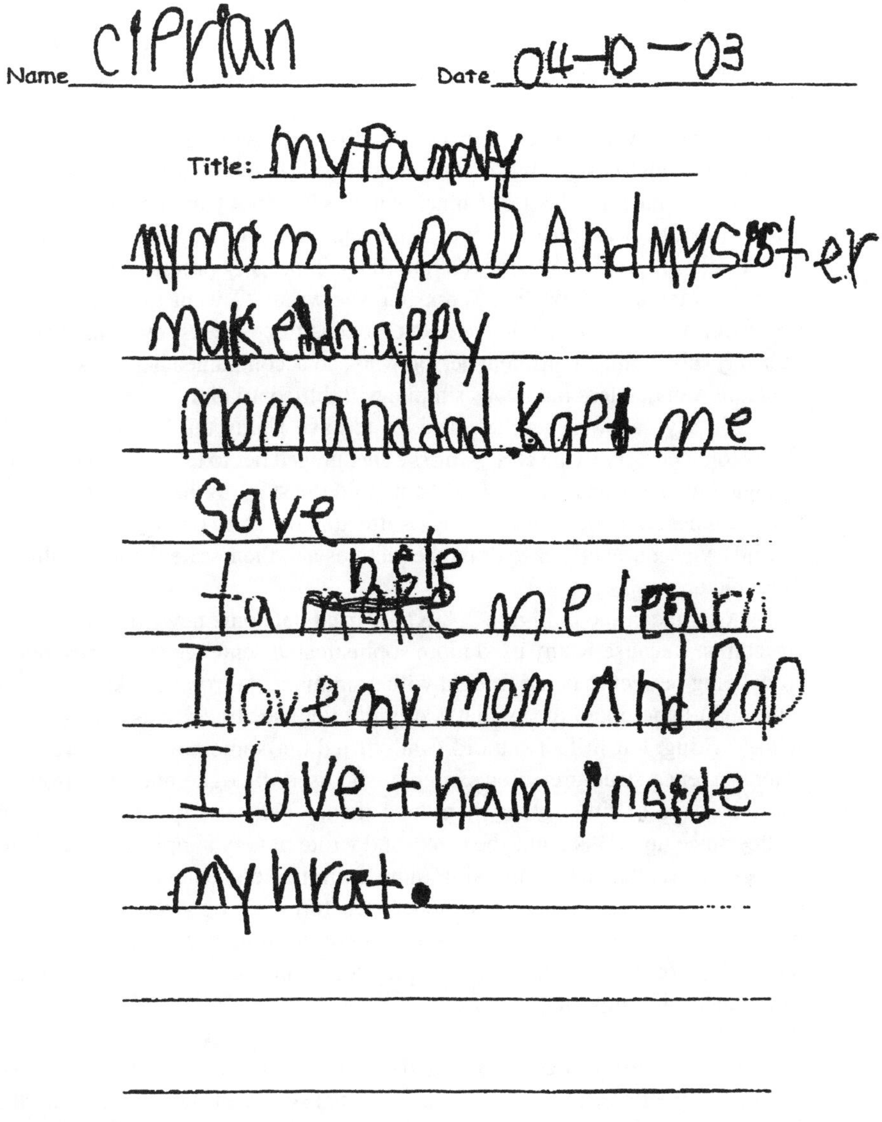

Name cIPrIan   Date 04-10-03

Title: myfamily

mymom mypaD Andmysister makeehappy

momanddad.kept me save

ta help me learn

I lovemy mom And Dad

I love tham inside

my hrat.

FIGURE 2.3   Ciprian talked before he wrote this poem, therefore using meaning as a source of information when he ran into trouble.

his writing didn't sound right. "The party is 3:00," I said. "Does that sound right to you?" He nodded yes. "'The party is 3:00,' or 'The party is *at* 3:00.' Which one sounds right?" I asked him. "The party is at 3:00," he said, and quickly wrote the word *at* above his original sentence.

   In this instance, I prompted Isaiah to read his writing in the same way that he had read his independent book, asking himself if his own writing "sounded right." At first, he thought his sentence sounded fine. It was only when I gave him another option of how it might sound did he decide to rewrite. Isaiah used structure as a source of information while both reading and writing. In both instances he reread making sure that the text "sounded right."

While we want writers to make sure that their writing sounds right, we also want to encourage them to use increasingly sophisticated sentence structures. For example, Kathy, a first grade student at PS 1 in Chinatown in New York City, began first grade speaking a limited amount of English. She was in the silent stage of English acquisition (Cary, 1998). As the year progressed, she moved into Stage 2, or early production.

One day during Writing Workshop she wrote, "I went to the park with my sister." Proud of this accomplishment she spent the next three weeks rewriting this same sentence, each day substituting a different person who had accompanied her to the park. Her sentence structure was flawless but it was simple, with little variation.

Chrissy, her wise teacher, decided to have Kathy tell her one of her stories. Once Kathy told her story to the class, Chrissy encouraged her to tell the same story over and over again to anyone who would listen. Kathy told the story to the principal, to her family, and to the teacher next door. Finally, after Kathy told her story enough times to fall in love with it, Chrissy encouraged her to draw the pictures and then write the words that accompanied those pictures.

As you can see in Figure 2.4, Kathy tried out some new and sophisticated sentence structures. Because Kathy used more sophisticated sentence structures, her writing went from being perfect to being fraught with grammatical errors. Looking at Kathy's writing, you might be tempted to say that Kathy did not use structure as a source of information while writing, but in fact she did. Kathy tried out some new and increasingly sophisticated sentence structures. For example, she used dialogue and also used new words to show passage of time, other than "and then." This was quite an accomplishment for Kathy, since up to this point she spoke and wrote in very simple sentence structures. Having Kathy practice speaking using more complicated sentence structures helped her to write using more complicated sentence structures. Using structure as a source of information while writing sometimes produces correct sentence structures, as it did with Isaiah, and it sometimes produces complicated sentence structures, as it did with Kathy. Both are vitally important.

Visual.   The third source of information is the visual sources of information (or graphophonic). Sometimes teachers confuse the visual source of information with the strategy of looking at the picture (which is a meaning-based strategy), but *visual* (or graphophonic) refers to the relationship between sounds and letters. Visual is primarily a phonics or a decoding or encoding strategy; that is, in order for readers and writers to use the visual sources of information they must connect letters and sounds.

Readers use the visual sources of information in a few different ways. One way they do this is by looking at (and then recognizing) a letter or a group of letters. Then they get their mouth ready for the sounds of those letters in order to help them read the text. They might also recognize a word in its entirety and therefore be able to "read it quickly" without paying attention to the individual letters or sounds.

FIGURE 2.4 **Kathy told the glasses story many times. This oral retelling helped her to use the "structure source of information" by writing using more complicated sentence structures.**

Next, let's watch Evan, a kindergarten student, read. Notice how he used the visual source of information to help him read and understand a text.

Evan: Time to wake up. (The text says *Time to get up.*) He points to each word. He does this on every page of the book. (I watch him, note that he does it, but do not stop him until he has finished reading the book.)

> **Leah:** Evan, you read "time to wake up." Does that look right? (I point to the word *get.*)
>
> **Evan:** No.
>
> **Leah:** Could you reread and get your mouth ready for that word so it does look right?
>
> **Evan:** Time to get up.
>
> **Leah:** Time to get up. (I point to the words and pause on the word *get.*) Does it look right now?
>
> **Evan:** Yes.
>
> **Leah:** How did you know that this was *get* and not *wake?*
>
> **Evan:** Because there is a *g.*
>
> **Leah:** Oh, so you got your mouth ready for the word.

Evan read the text expecting it to make sense. He made a meaningful substitution when he read the word *wake* for *get.* His reading also "sounded right" because *wake* and *get* are both verbs. When prompted, Evan reread getting his mouth ready for the word. The strategy "getting your mouth ready for the word" is in fact a visual strategy.

Writers also use the visual sources of information, but they use them a bit differently. Readers start with the letters on the page and then try and match those letters to the corresponding sounds in order to read a text. Writers start by listening to the sounds and then try and record the corresponding letters on the page in order to help them write a text. Writers (like readers) might also recognize a word in its entirety and therefore be able to "write it quickly."

Later on, I watched Evan as he tried to write the sentence *Mom went to school.* First, he quickly wrote the word *Mom.* Then he said the word *went* and wrote a *w.* Then he said the word again slowly and recorded *an.* Finally, he said the word one more time and recorded the *t.*

In this instance Evan used the visual sources of information in two distinct ways. First, he wrote the word *Mom* quickly. He didn't listen to any of the individual sounds; rather, it seemed like he knew this word in its entirety. When he got to the word *went* he listened to the beginning, medial, and end sounds in *went* and was able to record onto the page what he thought the corresponding letters were.

PUT THE READING/WRITING CONNECTION INTO ACTION

Observe students in the midst of reading and writing. Assess for which sources of information they use (or don't use).

1. Do they use the meaning source of information in reading? in writing?

2. Do they use the structure source of information in reading? in writing?

3. Do they use the visual source of information in reading? in writing?

Figure 2.5 sums up the similarities differences between reading and writing.

FIGURE 2.5   Comparing reading and writing.

SIMILARITIES	DIFFERENCES
Both reading and writing are purposeful activities.	Writers express text for a purpose. Readers access text for a purpose.
Both reading and writing are a process.	Writers always produce a product. Readers sometimes produce a product. Writing is a slower process. Reading is quicker process.
Both readers and writers use similar sources of information.	
Meaning	Writers must choose their topic. Readers must read about the topic that the writer chose.
Structure	Writers choose their own structures. Readers are introduced to new structures.
Visual	Writers go from sound to print. Readers go from print to sound.

HOW ARE READING AND WRITING DIFFERENT?

I found enormous comfort in discovering the similarities between reading and writing. But like any worthwhile and complicated idea in teaching I soon found it wasn't that simple. "Yes, I understand they are similar," Eileen, a teacher I worked with, commented one day. "But what about Taina in my class? She's a strong reader, but she struggles to write no matter what I do. The two acts must be different for her." There were enough "what abouts" to convince me that although reading and writing are similar, inside of those similarities there are also some distinctive differences.

Julie Jensen states, "We can feel certain that some features of composing and comprehending are shared by all media; others are unique to a particular medium" (1984, p. 1). Figure 2.5 points out that although reading and writing are similar, they both have unique features. Millie, a first grade teacher from PS 261, said it best: "Reading and writing are not identical twins. They're more like brother and sister."

Next, we'll explore the uniqueness of reading and writing. Just as the similarities will have tremendous impact upon our assessing, planning, and teaching, so will the differences. These implications will be examined in depth in Part II and Part III. But for now, let's simply examine what those differences are.

Writers express text for a purpose.
Readers access text for a purpose.

We've already established that it's important to encourage students to read and write in purposeful ways. Students will do this in slightly different ways across reading and writing.

Writers might start with a purpose and then express a text because of that purpose. They compose meaning into a text. Recently, while visiting a kindergarten classroom, I had the opportunity to listen in to a group of students. They were upset because their classmates were inadvertently walking in on one another in the bathroom. "I have an idea," one student said. "Why don't we make a sign that says 'Please knock.'?" Off they went to get the paper. Then they made the sign and hung that sign on the bathroom door. These writers started with a purpose and then expressed that purpose by writing words.

Readers also start with a purpose, but then they access text because of that purpose. They compose meaning from a text. In my classroom, I used to have a ritual entitled "question of the day." Every day a different student thought of a question that she wondered about. The student then perused our nonfiction books in the classroom in search of the answer to that question. Once the student found the answer, she shared what she had learned with the rest of the class. My students began with a purpose in the exact way that writers do, but they accessed that purpose by reading text. You're sure to notice as you work with your students that some will have an easier time expressing themselves in writing, while others will have an easier time with accessing text in reading.

Writers always produce a product.
Readers sometimes produce a product.

Recently, while cleaning out my parent's basement, I found a letter I wrote to the tooth fairy when I was 10. Reading this letter instantly took me back to what I was thinking in that moment. I remembered that my sister had recently lost a lot of teeth and I had not. Although I didn't believe in the tooth fairy, I knew if I wrote a letter to him or her I would get money from my parents. It was amazing to find this piece of writing after all of these years, but what was more amazing was that simply by reading the writing I remembered my writing process. I remember that I started with purpose (to get money) and then I chose a genre suited to that purpose (a letter). This piece of writing was tangible evidence of some of the thinking I did in order to write that letter.

Writers as part of their process always produce a product, and that product reveals part of their thinking process. Readers, on the other hand, don't necessarily produce a product as part of their process and because of that, their thinking is at times harder to understand. In the next chapter, I'll offer strategies on how to look at student writing to help yourself understand not just the thinking your students do in writing, but also the thinking that your students do in reading.

Writing is a slower process.
Reading is quicker process.

Frank Smith said this about writing: "It is tiring physically and demands more concentration and it is slow—perhaps ten times slower than the speed at which we comfortably manage to read, speak, or listen to speech" (1983, p. 79). We've all seen students who find writing laborious. They cross out, check the alphabet chart, put their head down, and/or cry.

Let's consider all that these students are doing as they go through the writing process. When students write, they have to think about what to write and how to say it (written expression). At the same time, they have to say each word, listen for the sounds, and try and reproduce the letters that make up that word (spelling). In order to reproduce those letters, they must also know how to form each individual letter (handwriting). Because handwriting is a part of writing, we often are misled by how much students know because their eyes may perceive more than their hand can execute (Clay, 1975). Our youngest writers also draw as part of their writing process and they also must consider how to draw what it is that they are trying to write. This will also slow down their writing process.

Recently, I was in a kindergarten classroom and Monique called her teacher over to announce that she was making a lowercase *b* for the first time and she was a little nervous. Monique reminded me of how much our youngest writers must do in order to get the ideas in their heart onto the page.

Although the reading process can also at times be laborious, readers don't have to contend with handwriting or drawing. The fact that writers are slowed down has some positive aspects for them as readers. Marie Clay in her book *What Did I Write* said, "It is probable that early writing serves to organize the visual analysis of print" (1975, p. 71). When students are slowed down while writing, it gives them an opportunity to analyze what they're doing. This close-up analysis in writing will most certainly help those students while reading.

PUTTING THE READING/WRITING CONNECTION INTO ACTION

Have different-sized paper for different students. These different-sized papers might support those students who are finding writing laborious due to their fine motor issues in handwriting.

Writers must choose their topic.
Readers must read about the topic that the writer chose.

Leslie Abel, a literacy coach at Guilderland Elementary School, recently shared with me some of her son Nick's writing experiences. Nick had been writing about hockey ever since she could remember. In first grade he wrote a list book about hockey. In second grade he wrote a letter, a "how to," and a poem that also were about hockey. To this day (he's in fourth grade now), she said that he continues to write clear, cohesive pieces about hockey, each time writing about it differently. He loves writing and is quite skilled at it. Leslie has noticed that Nick doesn't have the same passion or skill for reading. She's wondered if perhaps he finds writing easier because he can choose a familiar topic and then write about that topic in ways that make sense to him. Although readers, of course, also have choices in what they read, in the end they are bound to the books available to them.

Randy Bomer, while conducting research in his wife Katherine's classroom, also noticed that many of her students were stronger writers. He believed like Leslie believed that writing was their strength because they chose to write about familiar topics and ideas. Whether they were writing about a day with grandma, or the class pet, or going to Big Lots, they found it easier to write when they were writing about very familiar topics. He believed those same students struggled more in reading because their books contained topics and ideas that they didn't have the same familiarity with. Because of that, they had a harder time making sense while reading.

This difference between reading and writing might have the exact opposite effect on some students. They might struggle in writing because they have to choose their own topics and may in fact find a certain comfort in the fact that in reading the text provides them with a topic.

PUTTING THE READING/WRITING CONNECTION INTO ACTION

- Encourage students to read books that contain familiar topics. Books about schools, fights with friends, or being scared or jealous are often good books because they all deal with familiar and appealing ideas to young students.
- When possible, introduce books to students that contain unfamiliar topics. Discuss the unfamiliar topics with your students so that they become familiar.

Writers choose their own structures.
Readers are introduced to new structures.

We've already established that both readers and writers use structure as a source of information. A writer must make decisions about how to structure her writing, while a reader is introduced to new structures in the midst of his reading. Caroline, for example, loves to reread stories, especially ones that her teacher has already read aloud to the class. She looks at the pictures and then at the same time retells the stories, remembering many of the words that her teacher previously used during the read-aloud. She has great success reading stories but she experiences difficulty writing stories. Specifically, she struggles with the structure of stories. While writing, she often leaves out parts of her story and/or writes more than one story. For Caroline having to choose her own structures in writing makes it more difficult. She experienced more success when the structure was presented to her in the books that she read.

Just like writers must structure their own texts, they must also make decisions about the specific words or vocabulary they will use inside of those structures. Will they choose to use the word *nice* or *considerate, bad* or *selfish, went* or *jumped?* Again for some writers, having choice in this vocabulary makes writing easier. They will choose to write using familiar and known vocabulary. For other writers, this choice makes it more difficult because they have a hard time coming up the vocabulary that will reveal their intended meaning.

Writers go from sound to print.
Readers go from print to sound.

Earlier in the chapter, I pointed out that both writers and readers use the visual (or graphophonic) sources of information, but they use these sources of information differently.

Specifically, writers start with the sound and move to the letter, whereas readers start with the letter and move to the sound. Marie Clay, in *Write Now, Read Later,* wondered why it was easier for most students to go from sound to print than vice versa (1977, p. 13). In my own experiences working with students, they often (but not always) will begin listening to sounds and recording letters in writing before they are recognizing letters and producing sounds in reading. Because many students are encoding print before they are decoding print, writing becomes an essential place for students to practice and internalize phonics concepts.

Curriculum planning, talking and listening, the components of balanced literacy, minilessons, conferences, and small group work—basically, the journey of this book—all of it is built upon understanding the similarities and differences between reading and writing. And although we'll always feel like we don't quite get it, as our clarity deepens and grows, we'll watch both our teaching and our learners soar.

FOR FURTHER STUDY

- Plan for how you can teach the reading and writing process side by side.
- Study your classroom libraries. Ask questions such as:
  1. Which books contain familiar topics? Which do not? Do I have enough of a balance between the two?

  2. How can I ensure that the unfamiliar topics and ideas in books become more familiar?
  3. Which books contain familiar internal and external structures? Which do not? Do I have enough of a balance between the two?
  4. How can I ensure that these unfamiliar internal and external structures become more familiar?

...AND THEN BLUR THE LINES

Reading and writing are so related. One reads best with a sense of writer;
and one writes best with a sense of the reader.

—Suzanne L. Holt and JoAnne L. Vacca

In Chapter 2 we explored one essential understanding of the reading/writing connection. If we want the reading/writing connection to be accessible to all of our students then we ourselves must find the clarity. We must assess, plan, and teach with a clear understanding of how reading and writing are both the same and different. In Chapter 3, we will explore another essential understanding of the reading/writing connection. If we want the reading/writing connection to be accessible to all of our students, then we must also understand how to blur the lines. We must understand how to deliberately move between reading and writing letting the similarities *enhance* or improve one another and the differences *complement* or add to one another.

Renowned educator Marie Clay states, "Two meager bodies of tentative knowledge can combine as a larger resource for problem solving" (1998, p. 137). These two bodies of knowledge that she's referring to are reading and writing. The idea that reading can help writing and that writing can help reading is defined as reciprocity. This chapter will give you a crystal-clear image of what reciprocity looks like in action.

First, I'll explore the similar types of thinking that both readers and writers utilize as they go through the reading and writing process in order to compose meaning into and from texts. I'll suggest that once you're aware of these similar types of thinking, you can teach them at similar times letting the thinking in the writing process *enhance* the thinking in the reading process (and vice versa). Then I'll explore one difference, which is this: Writers always produce a product, whereas readers only sometimes produce a product. I'll show you how to look at students' writing products in ways that will *complement* or add to your understanding of those students in *both* writing and reading. My hope is that by seeing the reciprocity between reading and writing in action you'll continue discovering brand new ways to deliberately and thoughtfully blur the lines between reading and writing.

WHAT COMMON THINKING STRATEGIES DO READING AND WRITING SHARE?

In Chapter 2, I made the argument that reading and writing are both a process and that both of these processes involve thinking. Next, I'm gong to outline the types of thinking that readers and writers might use as they go through the reading/writing process. After I've shown you a particular thinking strategy, I'll suggest that you can pair that thinking strategy with a quality of writing to look for in students' work.

Readers and writers make decisions independently.

Both readers and writers must continually make decisions on their own. Recently, I watched Ellen Dillon conduct a writing minilesson. She said, "Yesterday a lot of you came to me when you were finished and said, 'I'm finished. What do I do now?' Today I want to teach you that when you think you are finished, you have an important decision to make. You can reread and add to your present piece of writing or you can start a new piece."

Ellen was working on developing her students' abilities to make decisions independently in writing. Similarly, readers also need to develop their abilities to make decisions.

independently. Ellen would be wise to conduct a similar minilesson in reading in which she showed her students how they also had an important decision to make when they thought they were finished reading. They would have to decide whether they were going to start a new book or reread their present book.

Her students' abilities to make decisions independently would be far greater if she taught this concept in both reading and writing, rather than just reading or just writing. If she taught her students how to make decisions in both reading and writing at similar times, she would be in essence *enhancing* or improving the work in both.

Now, that you've see the thinking strategy of making decisions independently in action, let's imagine what evidence we could look for in our students' writing samples that would help us understand whether a student was thinking in those ways. One day while visiting Ellen's classroom, I opened up Grace's folder and looked inside. In just forty-five minutes, Grace had written one story about going to her grandma's house, and she also had written a three-page nonfiction book about bears.

Grace certainly had *stamina* in writing because she had written independently for a long period of time. We can speculate (although we're never sure) that in order to produce that much writing in a short period of time, Grace made some decisions independently. She probably made a decision about what to write about (topic choice). She also probably made a decision about what genres to write in (story and nonfiction) and she also made a decision about what to do when she finished one piece of writing. Sometimes stamina is the ability to sustain writing for a long period of time, as it was with Grace, and sometimes stamina is the ability to stay with one writing piece for an extended period of time.

When I'm trying to figure out whether my students are using (or are capable of using) the thinking strategy of making decisions independently, I can look at the amount of writing they complete in any given day. If Grace isn't making decisions independently in her reading, her writing reveals that she is capable of doing so. Just as I suggested that you could use the common thinking strategies to enhance one another across reading and writing, I am also suggesting that you can look at student writing as a way to complement or add to your understanding of a student's reading.

PUTTING THE READING/WRITING CONNECTION INTO ACTION

Here are some of the types of decisions that readers and writers must make independently.

READING	WRITING
What should I do when I'm finished reading?	What should I do when I'm finished writing?
How do I choose a book for reading?	How do I choose a topic for writing?
Where do I sit in the room to read?	Where do I sit in the room to write?
What can I do when I don't know how to read a word?	What can I do when I don't know how to write a word?
How do I get my supplies for reading?	How do I get my supplies for writing?
How do I clean up my supplies for reading?	How do I clean up my supplies for writing?

Readers and writers activate relevant prior knowledge.

Another common way that both readers and writers think is that they activate relevant prior knowledge. Lucy Calkins, when describing why students should choose their own writing topics, says, "We care about writing when we write with, for and about the people that matter to us and when we write about or 'off of' the issues and experiences that matter to us" (1994, p. 14). Lucy reminds us that we are more effective writers when we use our prior knowledge to compose.

Reading is no different. Debbie Miller, in her book *Reading with Meaning,* defined the thinking strategy of activating prior knowledge to her students by saying that it is "all the stuff that's already inside your head, like places you've been, things you've done, books you've read—all the experiences you've had that make up who you are and what you know to believe to be true" (2002, p. 57).

Let's take a look inside a classroom, so you can see what it looks like when students are activating relevant prior knowledge. One day early in September, I walked into a second grade classroom in the midst of a heated discussion. The class had recently learned that they were not scheduled for art until the second half of the year. They asked their teacher if they could write a letter to the principal letting her know their feelings about this decision and also offering her possible ways to alter the schedule so that she could fit art in for their class.

After the conversation, the class composed a letter together to the principal. The heated discussion enabled them to activate relevant prior knowledge. During the conversation, they talked about a familiar topic (art class), and then they chose an appropriate and familiar form to write in (a letter). By activating relevant prior knowledge through talk, they more easily and more effectively composed a letter to the principal. The letter was so effective that the principal in fact did alter the schedule so that the class would receive art immediately.

Again, this teacher would be wise to enhance her students' abilities to utilize this thinking strategy by showing her students how to activate prior knowledge in reading to help them comprehend, just as they had activated prior knowledge in writing to help them compose.

What could we look for in our students' writing as evidence that they were activating relevant prior knowledge? We could look at the types of *topics* that our students choose. For example, recently I watched Sara begin a writing session by writing, "I love Rosh Hashanah. I'm so excited. It makes me want to scream." We can speculate by her choice in words that Rosh Hashanah is a familiar and important topic to her. More than likely, she would be able to write stories, poems, and information pieces all about Rosh Hashanah. Her writing sample gives us some tangible evidence that she is probably activating relevant prior knowledge in her writing and is capable of doing the same thing in her reading (if she's not doing so already).

Readers and writers determine importance.

Effective readers and writers both read trying to determine the most important ideas and themes in a text (Afferback and Johnston, 1986; Baumann, 1986; Tierney and Cunningham,

1984; Winograd and Bridge, 1986). Readers determine importance in the texts they're reading, while writers determine importance in the texts they're writing. Ellin Keene and Susan Zimmermann, in their brilliant book *Mosaic of Thought,* state that students determine importance by "using evidence from the text, their own knowledge and their beliefs" (1997, p. 80).

Let's visit a classroom so we can see what it looks like when students are in the midst of determining importance. Once in a first grade classroom I watched a teacher reading aloud a nonfiction book about frogs. After she had read a few pages, she turned to her students and said, "Turn to your partner and talk about what you think is important to remember about frogs from these pages."

The teacher deliberately set up a situation in which the students could practice the thinking strategy of determining importance. If she wanted to enhance her students' ability to utilize this thinking strategy, she could teach them how to reread their own writing, also trying to determine the most important parts.

What could we look for in our students' work as evidence that they were determining importance in writing? We could look for writing samples that were *focused.* In Figure 3.1, Uzziah has written a story about fracturing his toe. He focused his writing on how painful this experience was. He focused this piece of writing by choosing to include some details, while also choosing not to include other details.

We can speculate that in order to write this piece he determined what was important about his experience and then focused his writing on those important parts. Looking at Uzziah's writing helps us understand him not only as a writer, but as a reader as well. I can deliberately take the types of thinking that I think are happening for him in writing and cross them over into reading (if he has not already crossed them over himself).

Readers and writers infer.

Readers and writers also develop ways of thinking that let them linger longer on the important parts of a text. One way they can do this is by inferring. When students infer, they use their prior knowledge and textual information to draw conclusions, make critical judgments, and form unique interpretations from text (Anderson and Pearson, 1984).

Once while watching a class listen to the book *A Letter to Amy* by Ezra Jack Keats, I heard a student say, "I think Peter is a good friend to Amy. He invites her to his party even though she is a girl. He mails a letter to her all by himself." This student is inferring. She made this inference by not only paying attention to Peter's actions in the story, but also using her own prior knowledge about what makes someone a good friend. Both of these pieces of information helped her to form her own unique interpretation of Peter.

This teacher would be wise to think about how she could enhance this strategy by showing her students how to do something similar in their own writing. She might, for example, during a realistic fiction Unit of Study say to her students, "Think about what the main character in your story is going to be like. Will she be bossy? Will he be helpful? Will she be quiet? Or will he be loud? Once you're decided what your character is like, write your story including details about some of the things that your character might do, say, or think."

In the reading example, the student inferred by paying attention to the details in the text as well as by using her own prior knowledge. In the writing example, the students

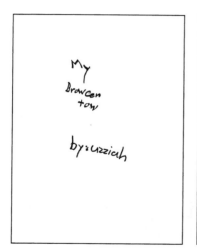

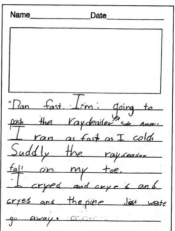

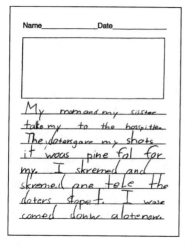

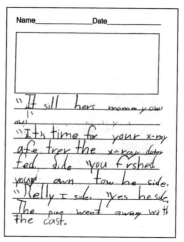

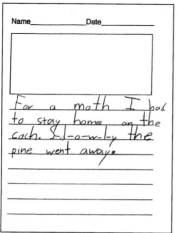

FIGURE 3.1   Uzziah has focused his writing. "Run fast. I'm going to push the radiator." Said Amer. I ran as fast as I could. Suddenly the radiator fall on my toe. I cried and cried and cried and the pain just wouldn't go away. My mom and my sister take me to the hospital. The doctors gave me shots. It was painful for me. I screamed and screamed and told the doctors to stop it. I was calmed down a lot now. "It still hurts Mommy yow ow!" "It's time for your x-ray." After the x-ray the doctor said, "You fractured your toe." "Really" I said. "Yes" he said. The pain went away with the cast. For a month I had to stay home on the couch. Slowly the pain went away.

FIGURE 3.2   Nkosi elaborated in his writing.
One winter night me and my sister went outside to
play snow ball fight. "Come on Tiffany I'm gong to
get you." I said. After that we went inside to rest.
We played a video game. I said "I'm going to win."
Then we had hot chocolate. My mom made it. I said,
"Thank you."

would have begun writing with an idea (my character is going to be bossy), and then would
have to think about the details that might go with that idea.

What might we look for in a piece of writing for evidence that a student has inferred?
We might look for elaboration. Simply put, we look for writing that has been expanded
upon at the important parts. In Figure 3.2, Nkosi has expanded upon himself as a character
by adding dialogue. As a matter of fact, before he wrote this piece he told me that he didn't
understand why he was so mean to his sister and so nice to his mother. His writing gives us
evidence that he shifts between the details of his writing and the unique idea of himself that
he is trying to present. I can use his writing as evidence that he is inferring in writing and

that he is ready to infer in reading (if he is not already doing so). Once again, I can let his writing complement or add to my understanding of him as a reader.

Readers and writers envision.

Another way that readers and writers linger on the important parts of a text is that they envision. When readers envision, they create images from the text both during and after reading. These images may include visual, auditory, and other sensory connections to the text (Keene and Zimmermann, 1997, p. 22). Writers envision in the same way, but they have to *compose* creating images *into* a text, rather than *comprehend*, creating images *from* a text.

Let's see what it looks like when a student envisions. Once, while conferring with Tony during reading I said to him, "Tony, close your eyes and try and picture this scene. What do you see? What do you hear? What do you smell?" After he answered, I let him know that it is often helpful when reading to slow down and picture the scene. If I wanted to enhance that thinking for Tony, I would be wise to show him how he could ask himself those very same questions while writing.

If we wanted to look at a student's writing for evidence of the thinking strategy of envisioning, we could notice whether a student included *descriptive writing* in her text. In Figure 3.3 we see a poem that Leah, a first grade student, composed. We see quite a bit of descriptive writing. We see that she used a lot of sound works such as "plop splash and

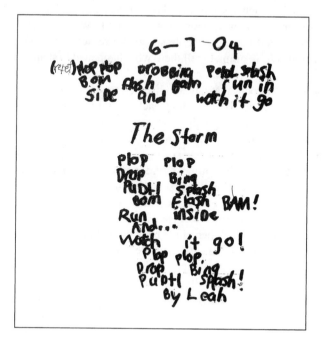

FIGURE 3.3   Leah used descriptive writing. (Repeat) Plop, plop dribble, plop, splash/Boom, flash, boom, running inside and watch it go. The Storm/Plop plop/Drop bing/Puddle splash/Boom flash bam/Run inside/And. . . ./Watch it go!/Plop plop/Drop bing/Puddle, splash

boom." We can imagine that Leah envisioned what a storm looked like in order to help her compose this text. She is showing us through her writing that she is most certainly ready to begin envisioning while reading (if she's not doing so already). Once again, we've used the reciprocity between reading and writing, letting Leah's writing complement, or add to, our understanding of her reading.

Readers and writers synthesize.

Ellin Keene and Susan Zimmermann define synthesis as "the process of ordering, recalling, retelling, and recreating into a coherent whole. It is the ability to collect a disparate array of facts and connect them to a central theme or idea" (1997, p. 169). Readers must take all of the parts of a text and use the parts of the text to understand the whole. One common example of synthesizing is retelling.

Writers also synthesize, and they do so in a few different ways. Just as readers might retell a book they're reading, writers might retell the story they're writing. They also might start with an idea and then ask themselves how they will connect the parts of their text to reveal that idea. They may, for example, start off by saying their sister is bossy and then create a text in which the different parts of the text connect in such a way that the idea of being bossy is highlighted. Either way, writers, as they compose, must be able to order, recall, and retell their texts into a coherent whole in very similar ways to readers.

Recently, I watched a teacher say to her class, "Every day before we write we are going to close our eyes and think of the story that we want to write. Then, we are going to turn to our partners and tell them the whole story. We're not just going to tell them what we're writing about. We're going to tell them what happened first and then next and then next."

As I walked around the room that day and listened to stories of times at grandma's house and fights with friends, I realized that this teacher set up a situation where students could synthesize their stories in order to help them compose their stories. First, they came up with their topic ideas, and then they recalled and recorded their thoughts to create the parts that went with that original idea.

What could we look for in their writing as evidence that they synthesized? We could look for writing that was *structured.* Sean, a first grade student, was writing about the day that his mom told him that his Nana Fanny died. Before he began writing, he knew he wanted to structure it with a "circle structure." He wanted to start with an image of his face before he knew that his Nana died and then circle back to the same image of his face at the end of the text once he knew that his Nana had died. He structured his text this way because he wanted his readers to see how the expression on his face changed with this painful news. As you can see in Figure 3.4, he successfully executed his plan.

Sean structured his writing carefully, ordering each of his parts to reveal his central idea. He worked on both the internal and external structures in his writing. I can speculate that because Sean's writing is well structured, that he probably synthesized his idea in order to do this. If he can synthesize while writing, he's probably ready to synthesize while reading.

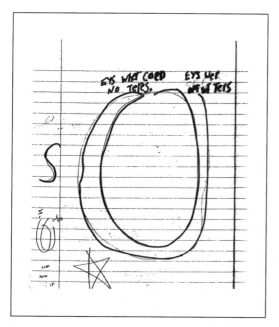

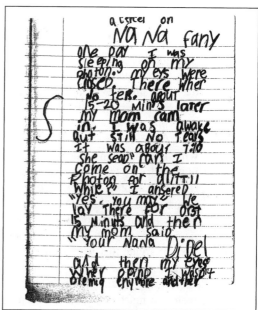

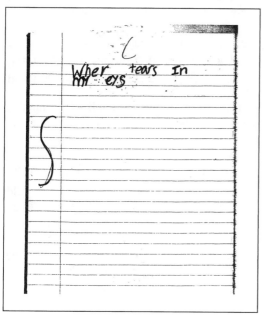

FIGURE 3.4 **Sean structured his writing.** One day I was sleeping on my futon. My eyes were closed. There were no tears. About fifteen to twenty minutes later my mom came in. I was awake but still no tears. It was about 7:10. She said, "Can I come on the futon for a little while?" I answered, "Yes you may." We lay there for about fifteen minutes and then my mom said, "Your Nana died!" And then my eyes were opened. I wasn't dreaming anymore and there were tears in my eyes.

Readers and writers ask questions of themselves and the writers and readers of their texts.

Both readers and writers ask questions to more effectively comprehend and compose. Readers ask questions not only of themselves, but also of the imagined writers of the text they're reading. Writers ask questions not only of themselves, but also of the imagined readers of their text. Often when I'm working with writers I'll ask them, *What's the most important part of your story?* When I ask that question, they often answer me with something that is not even yet on the page. I ask this question of students in the hopes that they will internalize my question and ask themselves that same question while writing independently.

Just as often when I'm conferring with writers, I'll say, "As a reader of your writing. I have some questions. I don't understand what happened after your sister left the park." Just as I want them to ask questions of themselves while writing, I also want them to anticipate the questions that a reader might have.

It's vital that we encourage our youngest students to anticipate the questions their readers might have. Donald Graves, in his research with young writers, concluded that "children generally ignore audience at first, then gradually include them and then take them too much into consideration and finally get back to a balance between their own voices and their audience" (1985, p. 194). Because it is not in young students' nature to pay much attention to audience, we must give them writing opportunities in which they have to keep an authentic audience in mind.

It would be wise of me to take the questions that I ask students in writing and bring them to reading. I could enhance the work that I do in writing by asking my students to slow down their reading, asking themselves questions such as, *What is the writer trying to tell me here?* or *What do I really think about this part?*

What evidence might we see in the writing of a student who had utilized the thinking strategy of asking questions? We might see a student who had *revised* his or her writing. In Figure 3.5 Lucie revised her writing. She added the words "It went all the way up to the ceiling. It went up, up, and up." We cannot be sure if she added this because she asked herself *What details would the reader need here?* or *What do I think is the most important part of my story?* or some combination of both. But we can speculate from looking at her revision that she did in fact ask questions while writing. Clearly, she should also be asking questions while reading.

PUTTING THE READING/WRITING CONNECTION INTO ACTION

Here are some questions that readers and writers might ask as they compose and comprehend.

READERS	WRITERS
What is the writer trying to tell me here?	What else would my reader need to know?
Why did the writer write this?	Why am I writing this?
What is the most important part?	What is the most important part?

FIGURE 3.5   Lucie revised and edited her work.
I went to the movies. I liked it there because they
gave me a balloon. It was a pink balloon. We went
to the bar. My balloon flew away. It went up, up, up.
It went all the way up to the ceiling. "I want it." I
said. Mommy said I could get another one. I got a
new pink balloon. I felt happy to have a new
balloon.

Readers and writers monitor their reading and writing processes.

In Chapter 2, I spoke of how readers and writers both use different sources of information. These sources of information are meaning (or semantics), structure (or syntactic), and visual (or graphophonic). Readers and writers monitor their reading and writing, putting one source of information against another to reread and rewrite.

It is imperative that our students monitor their reading and their writing. Many students, if left to their own accord, will continue reading and writing even if what they read or wrote doesn't make sense, doesn't sound right, or doesn't look right. If they continue doing this, they run the risk of developing bad habits and may come to believe that their own reading and writing at times just won't make sense.

In the book *Breaking Ground: Teachers Relate Reading and Writing in the Elementary School,* Heather Hemming researched how to get the writers in her first grade classroom to monitor what they wrote. She felt that "if writers could become aware of the factors that affect their composing, such as the monitoring role of reading, they could move towards a position of control over their writing" (1985, p. 56). Writers, in order to monitor their writing, *must reread,* asking themselves three questions simultaneously: *Does my writing make sense? Does my writing sound right? Does my writing look right?* If it doesn't, they need to rewrite.

If I wanted to enhance the thinking strategy of monitoring, I could ask my readers to also monitor their reading. I could remind them that when they read they also must ask themselves three questions: *Does it make sense? Does it sound right? Does it look right?* If the answer to any of those questions is no, then they must reread and select appropriate fix-up strategies (Garner, 1987).

What evidence might you see in a student's writing if he were utilizing the thinking strategy of monitoring? You would see evidence that a student had *edited* his writing. Looking back at Lucie's writing, not only did she revise her piece, but she also edited her piece. In the first sentence she added the words "to the." We can surmise that she reread her writing and when she read "We went to bar" she said, "My words look right, but they don't sound right." Then she then edited her writing. Because her writing is edited, we can speculate that she monitored while writing. It also gives us a glimpse of what she is capable of in reading. More than likely, she can also monitor while reading.

Readers and writers activate their knowledge of letters and sounds.

Both readers and writers compose and comprehend by activating their knowledge of letters and sounds. I saw this in action recently while visiting a classroom. I walked into this classroom in the middle of a teacher's demonstration. She was writing in front of her students. "I want to write the word 'today,' " she said. "Hmmm, is there a part of that word that I know? I know the word 'to' and the word 'day.' Both of those words will help me write the word 'today.' " This teacher could again enhance this work by providing a similar demonstration in reading, showing them how to look for parts of words that they know to help them read new words.

What evidence would I look for in students' writing that would reveal that they have activated their knowledge of letters and sounds? I would look at their *spelling* or their *use of phonics.* If we look at Figure 3.6 we see that Deianeira has made a list of what the class needs for the Halloween party. Looking at her print helps us to see that she has in fact activated her knowledge of letters and sounds. She has recorded both the beginning and end sounds, which helps me to know that she is utilizing her knowledge of phonics. From looking at her writing, we can surmise that she is probably ready to read some simple-level texts. While reading with her, I more than likely would help her activate her knowledge of phonics, encouraging her to look at both the beginning and end sounds in words.

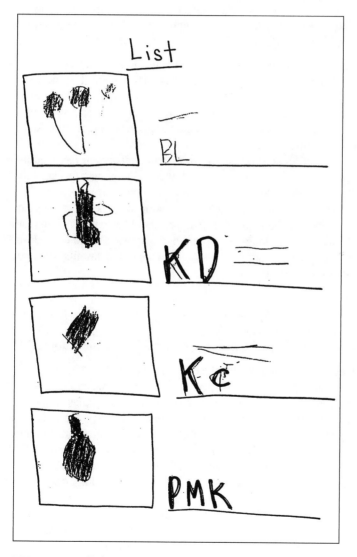

FIGURE 3.6 **Deianeira used print strategies.** List/Balloons/Candle/Cake/Pumpkin.

HOW CAN I USE THIS INFORMATION?

So far in this chapter I've shown you how to link thinking strategies up with qualities of writing. It makes sense for us to now explore how to use this information to assess our students across both reading and writing. But before I do this, I want to remind you that unless your students have *daily opportunities to read and write* your assessments across reading and writing will amount to very little. Moffett and Wagner explain further why it's so vital that students read and write side by side every single day:

> The best way for the receiver to learn to comprehend is to compose. To play well, you have to play all roles in it. You cannot be a good fielder in baseball if you are not also a base runner, because to know which teammate to throw the ball to you must know what the runner is most likely to do. (1983, pp. 10–11)

In order for our students to play well in the game of literacy they must also take on all of the roles of a literate person. They must read. They must write. But most important, they must be doing both side by side every single day in the classroom. Only then will they be able write from the perspective of a reader and read from the perspective of a writer. And only then can we get a true assessment of them not just as a reader, not just as a writer, but as a literate person who reads and writes.

Once you've set up your classroom so that students are in fact reading and writing every day, then you'll be ready to assess your students' moving between reading and writing. Next, I'll introduce you to Jason and show you a piece of his writing. Together, we'll look at Jason's writing. Then, we'll use what we noticed to speculate the kinds of thinking he is doing in writing and the kinds of thinking he should also be doing in reading. Finally, we'll think about which thinking strategy might be appropriate to teach Jason to do next while he reads and writes. Hopefully, this careful analysis of Jason's writing will help you do the same with your own students.

What qualities of writing do you see?
What can you speculate about the type of thinking Jason is doing?

Jason is a second-grade student from Bethel, Connecticut (see Figure 3.7). He has written a story about one time when he played a baseball game and got hurt. He was quite disappointed, but in the end he cheered up because he hit a homerun for the team. When I asked him what the most important part of this story was, he said that it was how his mood changed from sad when he got hurt to happy when he got the homerun.

One quality in Jason's writing that particularly struck me was that Jason had clearly organized his writing in a sequential order. Specifically, he told what happened first and then next and then next. Because he has structured his story in order, he more than likely did some sort of synthesizing while writing. More than likely, he thought of all of the parts of his story and then in his mind put those parts together in sequential order. I can blur the lines here and make sure that, just as he retells his story in his mind to help him write, he also retells while reading to help him comprehend. If I were Jason's teacher, I might check up on this by asking Jason to retell a text that he had read.

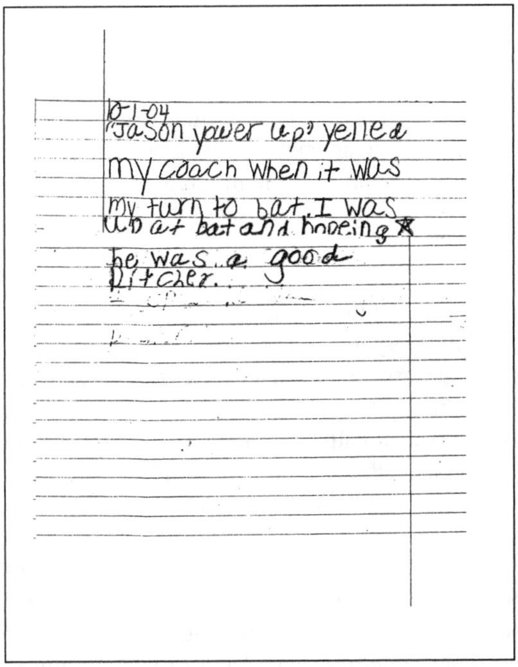

10-1-04
"Jason your up" yelled
my coach when it was
my turn to bat. I was
up at bat and hopeing
he was a good
pitcher.

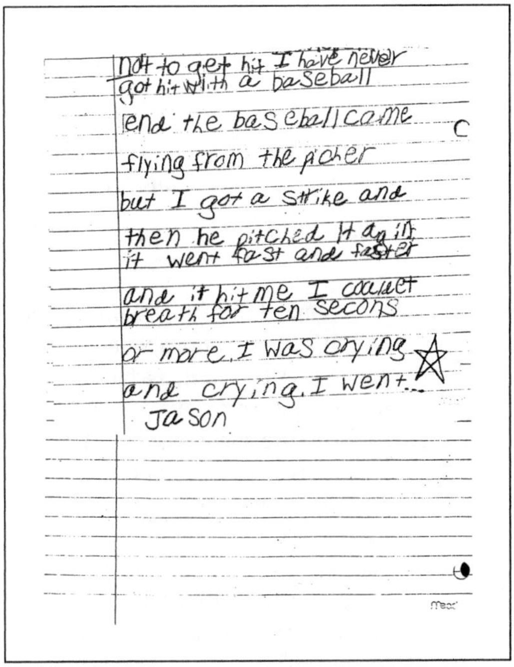

not to get hit I have never
got hit with a baseball
end the baseball came
flying from the picher
but I got a strike and
then he pitched it agin
it went fast and faster
and it hit me I couldt
breath for ten secons
or more. I was crying
and crying. I went...
Jason

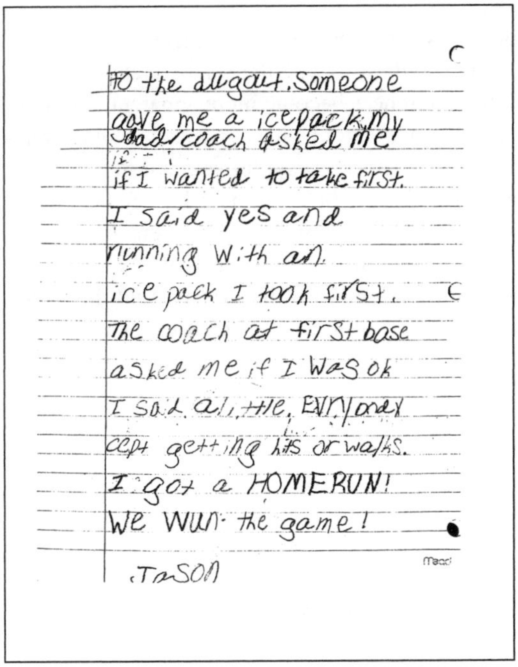

to the dugout. Someone
gave me a icepack. My
dad/coach asked me
if I wanted to take first.
I said yes and
running with an
ice pack I took first.
The coach at first base
asked me if I was ok
I said a little. Evryoney
cept getting hits or walks.
I got a HOMERUN!
We wun the game!
Jason

FIGURE 3.7 Jason organized his writing in sequential order. "Jason, you're up," yelled my coach when it was my turn to bat. I was up at bat and hoping he was a good pitcher so that I wouldn't get hit. I had never got hit with a baseball. Then, the baseball came flying from the pitcher but I got a strike and then he pitched it and it went fast and faster and it hit me. I couldn't breathe for ten seconds or more. I was crying and crying. I went to the dug out. Someone gave me an ice pack. My dad/coach asked me if I wanted to take first. I said yes and running with an ice pack I took first. The coach at first base asked me if I was okay. I said a little. Everybody kept getting hits of walks. I got a HOMERUN. We won the game.

Jason also had some parts of his story that were both focused and elaborated upon. For example, when he was hit with the ball, he said, "I couldn't breathe for ten seconds or more. I was crying and crying." Because his writing is at times both focused and elaborated upon, I can also speculate that he is both determining importance and inferring while writing. Again, I could blur the lines and check up on this in reading. I could make sure that Jason, while reading, also determined importance and inferred.

What thinking strategy might I teach Jason next?

One of the things I noticed about Jason is that although he retold his story in order, he had a difficult time connecting one part of his story to another part. For example, at the end of his story, he had a hard time connecting the last part, when he got a homerun and was happy, to the previous part of his story, when he was in pain and unhappy. I decided that he could use some more work on synthesizing, specifically learning how to connect each part of his story together to create a coherent whole, rather than just simply placing the parts together in sequential order. I might teach him how to ask himself while writing, *What can I write next that would help people know how this part connects to this part?* I could enhance this work by teaching him how to synthesize in similar ways while reading. I might teach him to ask himself while reading, *How does this part of the story connect to the previous part?* There are many ways I could have looked at Jason's writing, but what I want to emphasize is that I let Jason's writing influence not just what I would do with him in writing, but in reading as well.

The best relationships we have in our lives, whether they're with friends, family, or coworkers, are ones in which we share not only similarities with the person, but differences as well. Things seem to go perfectly until the differences become more apparent. At times, these differences might scare us and our first instinct might be to disconnect from the relationship. But I've found that when I embrace these differences, I learn the most.

The relationship between reading and writing is no different. You'll more than likely find great comfort in the similarities, much you like you do with another person, but soon enough the differences between reading and writing will become apparent and you might be tempted at those times to separate reading and writing. But if you first find the clarity and then blur the lines between reading and writing, you'll find yourself teaching in ways that you never dreamed possible.

FOR FURTHER STUDY

- Assess your students' writing as a way to plan both writing and reading curriculums. While assessing writing, you'll want to ask:
  1. What qualities of writing do I see? What qualities are missing?

2. What can I speculate about the kinds of thinking my students are doing in writing and are capable of doing in reading?

3. What thinking strategy might I teach next? What will this look like in writing? What will this look like in reading?

PLANNING

In Part I, I tried to build your understanding of the reading/writing connection. Understanding this connection, however, is only the first step. If you want the reading/writing connection to truly impact how your students learn, then you must take your knowledge and put it to use. In Part II, I'll show you how to use your understanding of the reading/writing connection to plan thoughtful reading and writing curriculum.

Planning for a comprehensive reading and writing program is a monumental task. Across a year you need to plan both yearly curriculum and Units of Study that meet the needs of all of your students. Across a day, you need to plan for Read Aloud, Shared Reading, Shared Writing, Interactive Writing, Word Study, Small Group Work, and Reading and Writing Workshops, once again trying to meet the needs of all of your students. The list of what you need to plan goes on and on. I'm sure that if you're like me, you often yearn for just a little more time to plan. Randy Bomer in his book *Time for Meaning* says, "More time is a meaningless idea, when you think about it. How could there be more of time? Time just is. What we are really complaining about is our difficulty in both controlling and choosing what to do with the time we have" (1995, p. 2).

The next few chapters will serve as a resource for helping you *control and choose* how to plan reading and writing curriculums. It will argue that you don't necessarily need more time, but rather, you need to use your knowledge of the reading/writing connection to make the planning that you do more efficient. Chapter 4 will help you plan for ways to connect speaking, listening, reading, and writing. Chapter 5 will help you plan for the components of balanced literacy. Chapter 6 will help you plan for one Unit of Study, and Chapter 7 will help you plan a Curriculum Calendar for the year.

LISTENING, SPEAKING, READING, AND WRITING

The cognitive processes involved in composing meaning from (listening, reading) and through (talking, writing) language are similar, but realized in different ways.

—Brian Cambourne and Jan Turbill

W hen I decided to write this book, I called my friend Katherine Bomer for some writing advice. As always, her advice was brilliant. "Plan workshops," she said. "Take the chapters that you're imagining and then plan those chapters as workshops for teachers."

I took Katherine's advice and planned a weeklong course for The Reading and Writing Project's Summer Institute, each day presenting a possible chapter for my book. First, I *spoke,* and then I asked the participants to reflect and ask questions. I *listened* for the places they seemed excited and/or bored. The following week when I sat down to write, my workshop notes were by my side and I referred to them constantly. I found myself at times writing the exact words I had said one week prior during the institute.

Although writing is never easy, the chapters that I presented as workshops weren't too painful to write. But soon, I started to write chapters that I had not presented as workshops. And those were more difficult to compose. One day in the middle of a particularly hard chapter it hit me why I was having so much difficulty. Talking and listening were no longer part of my writing process and I realized I was missing both desperately. Once I realized this, I tried again to do what Katherine had suggested in the first place. I planned lots of workshops where I would have opportunities both to speak and to be listened to. When I brought talking and listening back to my writing process, I settled back into my writing and found more success, along with more sanity.

This story seems especially pertinent to tell now as I begin to write a chapter that examines speaking and listening. I'll begin first by suggesting that speaking and listening are deeply connected to reading and writing. We'll visit some classrooms so that we can see these connections in action. I'll also suggest that when you understand this connection, you can plan ways for your students to speak and listen in more efficient and effective ways. Then, we'll explore reading and writing partnerships as a structure where students can blur the lines between speaking, listening, reading, and writing in order to compose and comprehend in more powerful ways.

HOW DOES SPEAKING CONNECT TO WRITING?

Both speakers and writers *compose meaning into* text. They do this using similar sources of information. Both use their experiences and knowledge to make meaning. Both also compose meaning by paying attention to the internal and external structures of language. A speaker must produce the sounds of language to compose meaning, whereas a writer must produce the appropriate letters to compose meaning. Because the act of speaking is so similar to the act of writing, both can easily be brought together so that speaking improves writing and writing improves speaking. Next we'll visit Chrissy Koukiotis's first grade classroom so that you can see this in action. It is Monday morning and Chrissy's students have just arrived in the classroom. They begin their morning by sharing weekend stories.

Chrissy: As we came up the stairs this morning, Jade and Peggy started to tell me weekend stories. Peggy told me quickly that her cousin got married. Can you tell all of us the whole story?

Peggy: Well, my cousin got married. We went to the wedding and then we got our picture taken with the bride and then we danced. My sister wasn't brave enough to dance, but I was. I even got to dance with the bride.

Chrissy: Who did you go to the wedding with?

Peggy: My mom and dad and older sister Donna.

Chrissy: That reminded me of my weekend story. I went to a wedding also. Ms. Diane, one of the first grade teachers, got married this weekend. I danced all night long. Jade, you quickly told me you got a new book bag. Could you tell all of us the whole story now?

Jade: Well, my Titi took me to the store and she said that I could buy a new book bag. It was hard because there were two I liked. I finally decided on this blue book bag.

Chrissy: How did you decide?

Jade: Well, I looked at each one for a while and thought and then finally I choose the blue one because it was bigger and I could fit all of my school stuff in it.

Chrissy: I bet you and Peggy will write those stories today during Writing Workshop. Did Peggy and Jade's stories remind any of you of stories that you want to tell? (Chrissy then had two or three more children share their stories in the same fashion as Jade and Peggy did.)

While Jade and Peggy spoke, Chrissy listened carefully and asked clarifying questions to get them to say more. Finally, she told Jade and Peggy that they could write those exact stories during Writing Workshop. Later on in the day, Peggy and Jade did write those stories. As a matter of fact, both of them used many of the words in their writing that they had used while telling their story. They experienced what I experienced when I talked before I wrote. It helped them —just as it helped me—to discover and practice some of the words they wanted to use while writing. Their speaking in fact enhanced or improved what they ended up writing that day.

To an observer, this encounter may have looked casual—a spur of the minute teaching decision that Chrissy made—but there was nothing casual about what she did. This teaching moment was carefully planned out and deliberate. Chrissy knows that casual hallway conversations are powerful because they are student initiated. When she picks her students up every morning, she *plans* to listen to her students' stories and then incorporate those stories into her teaching so that she can use their speaking to improve their writing.

HOW DOES SPEAKING CONNECT TO READING?

We've just established the connection between speaking and writing. Now, let's examine the connection between speaking and reading. Speaking tends to complement, or add to, the reading process. When you speak while you're reading, it slows you down helping you to deepen or revise your comprehension. We've all experienced daydreaming through a text, only to realize that we've "read" three pages, and don't understand a word. This is less apt to occur if you're speaking while you're reading.

To help you see the speaking/reading connection in action, I want to bring you back to Chrissy's classroom, where two students were reading the book entitled *Will I Have a Friend?* As they read, they stopped at different parts and spoke to one another. At one point in the beginning they spoke about the main character Paul and what they thought he was like. As they were discussing this, they went back to the text pointing out things in both the pictures and the words that supported what they were saying. Later, they predicted what they thought might happen next, again going back to the text to support their thinking. It was clear from watching them that not only did their talk slow down their reading of this text, but it also added to their comprehension of the text.

HOW DOES LISTENING CONNECT TO READING?

Both listeners and readers *compose meaning into* a text. Pauline Gibbons states, "The process of listening is in many ways similar to the process of reading. Both involve comprehension rather than production. And both involve the active construction of meaning" (Gibbons, 2002, p. 102). Listeners and readers must use what the text is about to help them comprehend. Both need to pay attention to the internal and external structures presented in the text. A listener must recognize the sounds of the language, while a reader must recognize particular letters in a text. Because listening and reading are so similar, they also have the potential to enhance or improve one another.

Once again, we'll visit Chrissy's classroom to see the listening/reading connection in action. Now, Chrissy is reading aloud a poem entitled "In Autumn" to her class. Chrissy reads the poem one line at a time, asking them to try and make a picture of each sentence in their minds. For example, after she reads, "They're coming down in showers. The leaves all yellow and gold," she asks the students to stop and make a picture in their minds of what the leaves might look like. She was deliberately teaching her students how to listen using the thinking strategy of envisioning, knowing full well that later she was going to teach her students to read their own texts also using the thinking strategy of envisioning. The envisioning work that her students did while listening to the poem will most certainly improve the envisioning work they will do when they read their own texts.

HOW DOES LISTENING CONNECT TO WRITING?

Listening also plays an important role in writing, as it can add to a student's writing process. There are a few different ways that this might happen. First, when a student listens to other texts, he or she can listen to those texts for potential writing ideas. Earlier in the chapter Chrissy asked her students if Peggy's and Jade's stories reminded them of their own stories. Here, Chrissy was pointing out to her students that if you listen to what other stories are about, you can get ideas on what your story might be about. You also, when you listen, can get ideas on *how* to write your story. Recently, I watched Abel, a kindergarten student, share his writing: "Once upon a time," he began, "there was a boy named Abel. He was playing in the kitchen and suddenly a plate of macaroni fell on the floor." Listening to other texts had certainly added to Abel's writing process. He had placed literary language such as "once upon a time" and "suddenly" in his writing probably because he had listened to how other stories went.

Writers also benefit from having other people listen to their writing. Don Graves, from his research with young writers, says, "What authors of any age need is attentive listeners" (Graves, 1994, p. 133). Just recently I listened to Jose, a second grade student, share his writing with the class. He was reading his story about one time when his dad played a trick on his mom. It was unclear from listening to his writing what the trick had actually been. When he asked for questions, Daphne, another student in the class, raised her hand and asked Jose what trick his dad had played on his mom. Daphne's careful listening not only added to Jose's writing process but it also benefited Daphne. Specifically, she practiced how to listen carefully, questioning a text when confused (an important reading comprehension strategy).

This example of a share session highlights how crucial it is for students to listen to each other's writing during share sessions. Some teachers, however, have confided to me that they don't conduct share sessions because their students, during these share sessions, struggle to listen to one another. Many of our students will not listen the way that Daphne listened to Jose unless we explicitly teach them how to do so. I recently watched Chrissy teach her students how to listen to one another during a share session by comparing the listening that they should do in a writing share to the listening they already did during a Read-Aloud session. That is what she said:

> When you listen to your friends share their writing, I want you to listen in the same ways that you listen when I read aloud. Do you listen for your favorite parts when I read aloud? Of course you do. You'll do the same thing when your friends share their writing. You'll listen thinking about your favorite parts of their writing.
>
> Do you listen and ask questions when you don't understand a part of the Read-Aloud? Of course you do. You'll do the same things when your friends share their writing. You'll listen, letting the author know if you don't understand a part. Do you ask questions when you want to know more about a part of the Read-Aloud? You'll do the same thing when your friends share their writing. You'll listen carefully and then you'll ask questions so that you can learn more.

SUPPORTING SPEAKING AND LISTENING THROUGHOUT YOUR DAY

As important as it is for students to speak and listen while reading and writing, it's also crucial that you provide students with opportunities across the day to speak and listen to one another, so that they acquire more oral and literary language. Oral language is language that is dependent upon the context. For example, a student in the block area who turns to a friend and says "Put this one here and that one there" is using oral language. His friend understood the words "Put this one here and that one there" because he was pointing to the blocks in the block area as he said it. If the two students weren't in the block area, the words would not have made sense.

Literary language, on the other hand, is language that is able to stand on its own. Earlier in this chapter Jade, one of Chrissy's students, said while sharing her story, "I looked at each book bag and couldn't decide which one to buy. Finally, I chose the blue one because it was bigger." This language is more literary because Jade does not need to be in a particular context for her words to make sense. Her words stood on their own. Next, I'll address some of the ways that you can help your students acquire both oral and literary language throughout your day.

PUTTING THE READING/WRITING CONNECTION INTO ACTION

- Help the students move from oral language to literary language by having them tell their stories as you turn the pages of a blank booklet. The blank booklet and the turning of the pages will serve as a reminder that they are creating a piece of literature and should use literary language. After students have become comfortable while you turn the pages of a blank booklet, you might laminate and give all of your students their own book to store in their writing folder and use whenever they are going to tell their story to a partner.

Choice time.

If you are blessed enough to have a choice time in your day, it's wise to use that time to build both students' oral and literary language. You'll want to try to create opportunities during choice time for students to use language to get things done. Students might collaborate in blocks, paint a picture, describe the class pet, pretend in dramatic play, or conduct a science experiment (among other things). All of these are powerful ways for students to talk and listen to one another in natural and unguarded ways. It's also helpful to have students share back what they did during choice time with the rest of the class. This reporting back gives students yet another opportunity to listen and speak with one another.

Sharing sessions.

Another way that you can build language skills is by asking students to bring in artifacts from home and then share these artifacts with one another. The artifact could be a picture, something from nature, a toy, anything that a student is passionate about. Students could talk about their artifacts with a partner. I recommend that you conduct these share sessions a bit differently than the typical "show and tell" so that their talk becomes increasingly more sophisticated. You'll probably want to model a variety of ways that your students could talk about their artifacts. For example, one day you might show the students how to describe what their artifact looks like, while on another day you might show students how to tell a story about their artifact. All of these ways will again help your students to become more articulate speakers and more thoughtful listeners.

Informal conversations.

A lot of the talking and listening that adults do is informal. We greet each other in the morning. We talk about our hobbies with friends. We gossip. Most of us love that kind of talk. Why wouldn't we? We've initiated the conversation so it's bound to be exciting and engaging. Just as informal conversation is powerful for us as adults, it is also powerful for our students.

Many of the schools that I work in, especially the schools with a high ELL population, have been thinking about ways to bring more informal conversation into their classrooms. Some teachers have been using snack time as an informal time to encourage students to talk about whatever they would like to with their friends. Others, such as the teachers at PS 1 in Chinatown, have initiated a schoolwide café called "Chit Chat Café." For a half hour on Friday afternoons the whole school turns into a café. Students move from one classroom to another. They sit down with a cup of tea and literally chit-chat with a friend or friends. The students at PS 1 are largely English language learners, and these teachers understand that informal conversations are one powerful way to help students to become more comfortable and adept at speaking and listening to the English language.

Another way you can encourage informal conversation is through survey and graphs. In many elementary math programs there are activities in which students are asked questions and then their answers are compiled into a survey or graph. Later, the teacher uses the completed survey or graph to teach important math skills or concepts. Recently, I watched a group of students having conversations about one of these questions, and I was amazed at the amount of natural and unguarded talk that was occurring.

READING AND WRITING PARTNERSHIPS: A POWERFUL STRUCTURE

So far, we've examined how speaking, listening, reading, and writing can both enhance and add to one another. Now, we're going to bring this understanding to reading and writing partnerships. I want to begin the conversation of partnerships by first highlighting some of the benefits you'll find if you encourage students to read and write not only by themselves, but also in partnerships. When students are engaged in reading and writing partnerships, they must speak, listen, read, and write, often all at the same time; thus, partnerships become an ideal structure in which students can blur the lines between speaking, listening, reading, and writing in ways that help them better compose and comprehend.

Another benefit of reading and writing partnerships is that they enable students to see reading and writing as a process, rather than a one-shot deal. Usually, partners begin by first working independently and then coming together to collaborate on that same reading or writing work. More than likely, this collaboration will cause them to revise and rethink their reading and writing because not only will they regularly talk with others about their reading and writing, but they also will know that they have a daily audience.

Finally, if you launch reading and writing partnerships at the same time in your classroom, your planning for them will become much more efficient. You will have the opportunity to teach similar things at similar times. For example, if you teach students on Monday to sit knee to knee in their reading partnerships, you can also teach them how to sit knee to knee in their writing partnerships. More than likely, they'll catch on quickly in writing because they will be able to use what they previously learned in reading to help them. Thus, once again, we're seeing how reading enhances writing and writing enhances reading.

Launching partnerships.

It's often tempting to jump into reading and writing partnerships without thinking much about how they'll go. But if we begin by first thinking through wise ways to launch them, we're more likely to be happy with the results. Next, I'm going to suggest some of the things you'll want to think about and plan for as your students begin working in reading and writing partnerships so they do in fact read, write, speak, and listen in these partnerships in deep and eloquent ways.

Model language in whole group sessions.   Often, the ways in which our students speak and listen to one another in partnerships without our assistance is dazzling. When I see this, I'm reminded not to become too heavy handed and teach my students out of the brilliant things they are already doing. There are times, however, when our students do need our assistance in their partnerships. One way we can support them is to provide them with language during our whole class teaching that they can use in their own partnerships later on.

Recently, for example, I was in a first grade classroom in Guilderland, New York, during their writing share. Andrew, one of the students in the classroom, was sharing a story about going on an airplane. After he finished he took questions from his classmates. One student asked him if he got any food on the airplane. Another student asked him how long the trip was. Then, Andrew's teacher, April, said, "I'm wondering which part of your airplane story was the most important."

"When we went up in the air," he answered quickly. "It was fun and scary all at once!" "Wow," said April. "That's not even in your piece. Listen to this. The plane went up in the air. It was fun and scary all at once. I love those words. I think you should add that! Who else thinks he should add that?" she asked the class. Almost every hand went up. "Well," said April as she turned to Andrew, "It's up to you. You're the author. Do you think you'll add that?" He nodded yes.

Then April turned to the class. "Do you see what I just asked Andrew?" she said. "I asked him what the most important part of his story was. Then I suggested that he could add that part. This is a question you all can ask your partners when you're working in reading and writing partnerships."

Here, April deliberately highlighted that she asked, "What's the most important part?" Then she told her students they also could ask that same question in their own partnerships.

PUTTING THE READING/WRITING CONNECTION INTO ACTION

Here is some language that you might model for your students to support them in listening and speaking to one another.

READING	WRITING
What do you think is going to happen next in the story?	What happened next in your story?
I don't understand the part when . . .	I don't understand the part when . . .
The part I really understood was . . .	The part I really understood was . . .
What does _____ mean?	What does _____ mean?
Could you say more about . . .	Could you say more about . . .
I think the most important part of this was . . .	What's the most important part in your story?
	You should add that into your story.
I agree with what you said.	I agree with what you said.
I disagree with what you said.	I disagree with what you said.
I want to add on to what you said.	I want to add on to what you said.
I think _____ because . . .	I think _____ because . . .
I wonder _____ because . . .	I wonder _____ because . . .
My favorite part of the book is _____ because . . .	My favorite part of your writing is _____ because . . .

Plan for how you'll form partnerships.   You'll also want to think about how you will group students together in their partnerships. Often, teachers will ask me if I put like or unlike students together in a partnership. I can remember struggling with this same question as a classroom teacher. When I taught first grade, I worked with my colleague Katherine Bomer to create reading and writing partnerships among our students. The night before, Katherine and I talked on the phone so that we could form the partnerships. We discussed our students' personalities, who was shy, who was boisterous who liked baseball, and who liked Barbies. We compared their skills and strategies. It took quite a while to form these partnerships because every partnership was formed for a slightly different reason.

Once they began working together, we watched them carefully, noticing which were successful and which were not. In the end we switched one or two. Although I tend to put more like students together for reading and partnerships (although across my day I'll put unlike students together often), I must consider so much more than skill level.

Plan management lessons.   You'll also want to plan management lessons early on. Once, I naively asked kindergarten students to turn and talk. All the students literally turned their bodies around in a complete circle and then they started talking each facing the front of the classroom. This story reminds me of how important it is to plan partnership management lessons. You'll probably have to teach your students things such as how to sit facing one another, how to stay on topic, how to listen. This is time-consuming, but important. If you teach these management lessons early on, you'll later be able to focus on the more complicated comprehension and composition work.

It's often easier to begin by teaching partnerships in your whole-class lessons. Chrissy did just that earlier in the chapter during the shared reading of the poem "In Autumn." She asked the students during her whole-group lesson to turn and talk to a partner. Students practiced how to turn to a partner, how to listen to one another, and how to speak. They were doing all of this, though, in a highly structured manner. Later on Chrissy could point out to them that what they did together they could also do in their individual reading and writing partnerships.

What partnerships might look like early in the year.   Once you've carefully planned how to launch partnerships, you'll want to plan for ways that your students can use these partnerships to improve and add to their reading and writing. Next, we'll look at some simple ways that students can work in partnerships early on in the year.

- Partners might *talk before they read.* Together, they might look at the cover, the title, and the blurb on the back of the book. All of this will help them rehearse their reading.
- Similarly, partners might *talk before they write.* Rather than simply saying to their partner "I am writing about my mother today," you might teach them how to rehearse some of their language with their partners. You might teach them to say things to their partner such as, "One spring day I woke and my mom said we were going to bake peanut butter cookies. As soon as I heard that I jumped out of bed." In that way the words that they say become part of the words that they write.
- Partners might *reread* books together. They are many benefits to this. First, students build good reading habits; that is, they learn to sustain reading for a longer period of time. They will also build both their fluency and their comprehension.
- Similarly, partners might *reread* their writing together. Again, there are also many benefits to this. Students will also build good writing habits. They'll learn to sustain writing for a longer period of time. They will also develop fluency in their writing.

What partnerships might look like later in the year.   As the year progresses, you will most definitely want to lift the level of work that your students are doing in their partnerships. You'll want to make sure that your students are not only reading and writing together in their partnerships, but that they are also speaking and listening to one another.

- Partners might go to one another for support during Reading and Writing Workshop.
- Partners *can share* their writing, expecting that they'll *ask questions* and/or *give comments* to one another.
- Partners *can share* their thinking about books expecting that their *partner will ask questions and/or make comments* about their thinking. This is ideal if partners read the same book separately and then come together in their partnership and talk about what they read.

In order to write this chapter, I spent many days watching brilliant teachers in their classrooms. I paid special attention to the ways in which their students spoke and listened to one another. In all of these classrooms the lines were blurred all day long; that is, students talked, they listened, they read, and they wrote without clear delineations. What impressed me, though, was the deliberateness of it all. Even though the work looked blurry, it was anything but that.

These teachers not only understood talking, listening, reading, and writing, but they also understood the connection among the four. They watched how each improved and added to the other. Because of this they deliberately planned ways to put their students in listening, speaking, reading, and writing situations in which each act helped them to do the other better.

Students will blur the lines between reading, writing, talking, and listening every moment of every day, but we have the power to make this blurry work clear by using our knowledge of speaking, listening, reading, and writing and how they work together to help our students compose and comprehend in powerful and lasting ways.

FOR FURTHER STUDY

- Study different texts for their literary language and plan for how you will use those texts in your classroom.
  1. What do I notice about the vocabulary in this book? How does this writer begin her stories? (*One day, A long time ago, One rainy morning, She looked, She listened*)
  2. How does this writer continue her story? (*A few minutes later, After breakfast, Suddenly*)
- Examine activities that occur throughout your day seeing if you can plan to integrate more speaking and listening into them.

1. How can I bring more speaking and listening to my Read-Aloud?
2. How can I bring more speaking and listening to my morning meeting?
3. How can I bring more speaking and listening to my writing share?
4. How can I bring more speaking and listening to my Reading and Writing Workshop?
5. How can I bring more speaking and listening to my choice time activities?
6. How can I encourage more informal conversation among my students?

CHAPTER 5

THE COMPONENTS OF BALANCED LITERACY

Effective literacy learning programs are built not only on sound teaching-learning approaches, but also on a solid understanding of those approaches and how they interconnect.

—Andrea Butler

Last year I gave up running and started practicing what I thought would be a more sane form of exercise: Bikram Yoga. For those of you who don't know, Bikram Yoga is a form of yoga that's practiced in a room heated to 104 degrees. The same twenty-six poses are done every single time, each pose performed two times in a row. Although I was practicing three to five times a week, it never got easier—every day was as hard as the day before! The improvements I saw were minimal, if any at all. It's a wonder that I actually kept going, but I persevered, hoping that I would soon start to improve.

One day I brought my friend with me. She also was a runner and had never done yoga in her life; however, to my amazement (or my disappointment, I'm not sure), it looked like she had been practicing for longer than one day. She didn't struggle in the same way that I did. I thought perhaps it was my imagination but at the end of class she smiled and said it wasn't so bad. "What I especially loved," she said, "was the way that every pose got you ready for the next one. Like how Half Moon gets you ready for Awkward Pose, and Awkward Pose gets you ready for Eagle Pose. It just makes so much sense." I nodded in feigned agreement, but the reality was, I had never in my year of practicing yoga realized that the poses had any connection to one another.

I tell this story because I believe the same thing happens to us when we start planning for what we'll teach inside of the components of balanced literacy. Every day, I work with brilliant, dedicated, wonderful teachers who persevere with the components of balanced literacy as I did with yoga, trying to fit in as many components as possible in one day. But just as I struggled, they do also. They're so busy trying to fit it all in that they have never asked themselves how the different components connect together. I certainly didn't when I was a classroom teacher. I was also too busy trying to fit it all in.

This chapter will show you how to spotlight the reading/writing connection in the components of balanced literacy. You'll get a clearer sense on how "to do" each component, but more importantly, you'll learn how to connect the components across reading and writing so that your planning is more efficient and your teaching is more consistent, which in turn will help your students learn. Hopefully, it will bring the same ease and clarity to the components of balanced literacy that I have finally found in my yoga practice.

WHAT ARE THE COMPONENTS OF BALANCED LITERACY?

Units of Study (as will be discussed further in Chapters 6 and 7) are ever changing, but the components of balanced literacy are the reading and writing structures that go *across a year*. The beauty of the components lies in the predictability. Regardless of whether it is September or June, you still set time aside for Shared Reading, Interactive Writing, Read-Aloud, and others. Although the amount of time you will spend on each component and the teaching that you do inside of them will certainly change, the fact that you do them will not. Before I dive into each of the components and all of the teaching implications, I want to first simply name what I view as the components of a balanced literacy program. Here is my list:

- Shared Writing
- Read-Aloud
- Interactive Writing

- Shared Reading
- Writing Workshop (partnership and small group work)
- Reading Workshop (partnership and small group work)
- Word Study (which might include phonics, phonemic awareness, and/or spelling)

Depending upon whom you ask, there are many variations as to what the actual components of a balanced literacy program are. My list of components and how I define these components may in fact differ from lists you've seen in other texts. I've organized and defined them in this way in the hopes that it will help you understand not just which components to do, but also why you should be doing each component. Most important, I want you to clearly see how these components connect across reading and writing.

I want to also talk for a moment about how I will address the word study component in this chapter. Rather than address word study as a separate component, for the purposes of this chapter I'll show you ways to integrate word study into the other components of balanced literacy (see Figure 5.1). This way students will see how these important skills fit into real *reading and writing experiences.*

WHAT DOES BALANCED LITERACY ACTUALLY MEAN?

Often when I visit schools and ask teachers to describe their curriculum to me, they'll say that they do "balanced literacy." I often ask them what they mean by "balanced." The answers I get are varied. Their varied answers don't surprise me because as I worked on this chapter I discovered a variety of views as to what the word *balanced* in "balanced literacy" actually means.

One explanation of *balanced* I found was the idea that in balanced literacy you are balancing certain kinds of curricula with other kinds of curricula (e.g., Hiebert and Cole) 1989. Another definition emphasized the balancing of teacher-initiated activities with student-initiated activities (e.g., Spiegel, 1994) Balance has also been defined as equally weighing curriculum with instruction where the types of curriculum and instruction have been viewed before as antithetical (e.g., Baumann and Ivey, 1997). More recent definitions of balance have included much of the above but have also emphasized assessment as a key factor in planning for an appropriate balance (Raphael and Pearson, 1997).

Most recently, Spiegel has defined balance as a "decision making approach through which the teacher makes thoughtful choices each day about the best way to help each child become a better reader and writer" (Spiegel, 1998). Throughout this chapter, you'll see that I emphasize Spiegel's definition of balance. I believe in order to get the appropriate balance in balanced literacy, you must make thoughtful decisions each day about the best way to help your students become more skillful readers and writers.

The first question then is, *What reading and writing knowledge do our students need if they are to become skillful readers and writers?* In Chapter 2, I explored how both readers and writers use *meaning, structure, and visual sources of information.* These same sources of information can, of course, help us to understand what to plan for in the components of balanced literacy so that we make sure that our students are progressively becoming more skillful readers and writers.

FIGURE 5.1   The components of balanced literacy.

SHARED WRITING	READ-ALOUD
The teacher composes a variety of texts with her students. She often models her thinking as she writes. The students participate by listening to the teacher's thought process and then trying some strategies in order to help compose the text. The teacher writes the text, therefore taking away the visual sources of information, so that students can focus on using meaning and structure as they compose meaning into the text that is being written.	The teacher reads aloud various types of text. He often models his thinking aloud as he reads. The students participate by listening to the text and the teacher's thinking strategies, and then trying some of them out by talking with partners. The teacher reads the text, therefore taking away the visual sources of information, so that students can focus on meaning and structure.

✓ Shared Writing and Read-Aloud both focus on building up students' independence in the *meaning and structure* sources of information.

INTERACTIVE WRITING	SHARED READING
The teacher composes an enlarged text with the students. The students participate by writing parts of the text. The teacher writes what is too easy or too difficult for the students. The teacher builds the meaning and the structure up, so that students can bring in the visual sources of information as they compose meaning into a text.	The teacher reads an enlarged text aloud. The students participate by reading along, using strategies when they encounter difficulty. The teacher builds the meaning and structure up, so that students can bring in the visual sources of information as they compose meaning from a text.

✓ Interactive Writing and Shared Reading both focus on building up students' independence in the *visual* sources of information.

WRITING WORKSHOP	READING WORKSHOP
■ Minilesson	■ Minilesson
■ Work time	■ Work time
Students are working independently or in partnerships.	Students are working independently or in partnerships.
Teachers are working one on one, and with small groups, teaching them strategies that will improve the quality of their writing.	Teachers are working one on one, and with small groups, teaching them strategies that will improve the quality of their reading.
■ Share	■ Share

✓ Both have the same structure.

✓ In both, teachers work with individuals and small groups.

✓ In both, students are expected to use meaning, structure, and visual sources of information independently to compose meaning into and from texts.

The next question, then, is, *How do we use the components of balanced literacy to teach our students more about meaning, structure, and visual sources of information?* If we are to teach inside each of these components in powerful but different ways, then each component must be used to highlight a different source of information. When I practice yoga, different poses highlight different body parts. Half Moon Pose works on upper body strength. Awkward Pose works on leg strength, and Eagle Pose works on balance. My whole body is now strong because there is a particular pose that lets me work on just one area at a time.

Our students need the same scaffolds inside of the components that I had in yoga. They need components in which they work mainly on meaning and structure sources of information. They also need components in which they work mainly on visual sources of information. And finally, they need components that help them "put it all together." I've made clear delineations between the components, fully aware that in your classroom the lines might be a bit blurrier. Keep these delineations in mind, however, as they will focus your instruction.

Some teachers have wondered if it would make sense to start with some components of balanced literacy and, as the students grow in their knowledge, add more components. Marilyn Adams reminds us that this is not a wise idea. She states that "the parts of the reading system must grow together. They must grow to one another and from one another. In order for the connection and even the connected parts to develop properly they must be developed conjointly. They must be linked together in the very course of acquisition" (Adams, 1990, p. 6). As we look at the components of balanced literacy, keep in mind that your students will be most successful if they're practicing all of the components simultaneously.

LOOKING AT COMPONENTS THAT CONNECT

When Patricia Cunningham came to speak to an audience of teachers at the Teachers College Reading and Writing Project (2003), she talked about how people learn new things. "Learners," she said, "need to know *what* they are doing and *why* they are doing it. They need to have cognitive clarity." And although this doesn't surprise me, it is at the forefront of my mind as I write this chapter. You'll see that I'll describe each component so that you, the learner, will have cognitive clarity. You'll see what each component is and why you would do that particular component with your students—specifically, which sources of information are being addressed.

Teachers who have read this chapter suggested that I provide examples of strategies you might teach in different components. When I tried to make a list, I realized that everything we could teach students about reading and writing could be categorized underneath particular components. What I've tried to do instead is give you a short list of other strategies you might teach in different components, knowing that over time you'll add many new ideas to each of these lists. I also tried to match strategies across reading and writing components. For example, you'll see that Shared Writing and Read-Aloud share many similar strategies; however, Shared Writing will approach the strategy from a writing angle and Read-Aloud will of course approach the same strategy from a reading angle. Finally, you'll see the connection between the reading and writing components and how each component enhances and adds to the others. Hopefully, seeing this will help make your planning for the components of balanced literacy more efficient and more effective.

Shared Writing: Highlighting meaning and structure sources of information.

In Shared Writing, the teacher composes a variety of texts with her students. This is different from language experience in that the teacher is not simply acting as a scribe for her students, but is jointly composing the text with her students. The goal of Shared Writing is to help students develop composing strategies that will move them from using oral language to more literary language.

The teacher models her thinking aloud as she writes, so that the students see an experienced writer's thought process. The students participate by *listening* to the teacher's thought process. Then, they often *speak* (either in partnerships or in whole-class discussions), trying out those same strategies with the teacher's assistance. The teacher acts as a scribe; therefore, she is doing the visual (or graphophonic) work of writing so that students can focus on strengthening the ways in they use meaning and structure as they speak. This work will certain improve the ways in which the students use meaning and structure while writing independently.

Often when I describe Shared Writing in this manner, teachers look perplexed. "I've never used Shared Writing as a place to teach the composing process," they'll say. "I've used it to model spelling strategies. I've used it to model how what we say can be written down. I've used it to model capitals, lowercase, periods, commas, but never to just teach students how to write in detailed, structured ways."

Shared Writing is often described as a place to model spelling strategies; however, I believe that is the role of Interactive Writing (which we'll get to shortly). Next, we'll watch Maria, a second grade teacher, conduct a Shared Writing session with her class (see Figure 5.2). I've transcribed this session so that you can see the language that Maria used while teaching. I've also, in the italics, reflected upon Maria's teaching, extrapolating some of her insightful teaching moves. You'll see this structure throughout this chapter. I've done this in the hopes that it will help you apply similar concepts to your own teaching.

In Shared Writing, the teacher's job is to write the text for the students and scaffold what the students say. The students' job is to use both meaning and structure sources of information while speaking to compose meaning.

Read-Aloud: Highlighting meaning and structure sources of information.

Just as Shared Writing develops students' understanding of how to use meaning and structure when they write, Read-Aloud strengthens students' understanding of how to use meaning and structure when they read. Because these two components are so similar, they will enhance or improve one another. During Read-Aloud, the teacher reads aloud various types

FIGURE 5.2   You can plan Shared Writing sessions that focus on meaning and structure sources of information.

Writers, I know that we've been working on writing nonfiction, and we've been trying to use headings to put like sentences together. Today, I thought we could try it as a class.

(On a piece of chart paper, Maria had written the words "What snails look like.") The heading we're working on today is what snails look like. Watch me first. Hmm . . . what do snails look like? Snails have a hard white shell. Yes, that is what snails look like.

This Shared Writing session has one teaching point, which is that all of the sentences underneath a heading should go together. Maria modeled how her thinking process is also part of her writing process. Maria also chose the class's pet snail as the topic of the Shared Writing because all of the students could bring meaning to that topic. You'll want to make sure that like Maria, you also choose topics that are familiar to your students. You'll also want to show your students (like Maria did) how the thinking process is part of the writing process.

Snails need lots of water to survive. Wait a second. That's true. Snails do need lots of water, but that doesn't belong underneath the heading of what snails look like.

Did you see what happened? First, I said a sentence about what snails looked like. Then I said that snails need lots of water to survive. That sentence is true, but it doesn't belong underneath the heading of what snails look like.

Once again, Maria demonstrated how her thinking process is part of her writing process. This time Maria modeled making a mistake, the kind of mistake she has seen her students do countless times.

Could you talk to your partner about what else you think we should write underneath this heading?

The students now have a chance to practice what was just demonstrated. They are practicing how to use meaning and structure strategies while writing. Specifically, they are learning how to organize like sentences together. They are also trying out new vocabulary in the process.

(Maria took notes on what the students were saying and intervened when necessary. When the students talked about how to take care of snails or what snails do, she reminded them of the heading and how their goal was to write about what snails looked like.)

Maria takes notes on what the students say rather than trying to make a chart "on the spot." I highly recommend this for Shared Writing. I use Shared Writing to teach students how to improve the content of their writing (not the print work), so I tend not to model writing the actual words. There are other components that you'll see shortly when I most definitely model writing the print, but I find that if you do it in Shared Writing, it takes your attention away from building students' oral language. I recommend that you quickly write what you and the students compose. Later, you can make a chart of this without the students. Once the chart is made, I would read it with the students and then display it in the classroom.

---

of texts. She often models her thinking aloud as she reads. The students participate by *listening* to the text and the teacher's thinking strategies. They often talk about the book (either in partnerships or in whole-class discussions), trying out the similar types of thinking that their teacher previously modeled. The teacher reads the text; therefore, she is doing the visual (or graphophonic) work of reading. The students can then focus on listening using meaning and structure to help them comprehend the text. Next, let's take a look as Millie conducts a Read-Aloud with her first grade class (see Figure 5.3).

The teacher's job during Read-Aloud is to read the words of the text and extend what students say. The students' job is to listen and use talk to further their comprehension.

Shared Writing and Read-Aloud are similar because they both help develop students' understanding of how to use *meaning and structure as they read and write.* Because they are similar they have the potential to enhance or improve one another. For example, if Maria wanted to enhance the work that she did with putting like information together, she might conduct a Read-Aloud asking students to listen to like information and try to comprehend it. If Millie wanted to enhance the work that she did in her Read-Aloud, she might conduct a Shared Writing session in which they would work together to compose a text that was elaborated upon.

FIGURE 5.3   Read-Aloud, like Shared Reading, strengthens students' ability to use meaning and structure sources of information.

Readers, today I want to reread *A Letter to Amy* so that we can talk about Peter, the main character. We're going to talk about what Peter the character is like.

Often (but not always) it's helpful to talk about books that students have already heard. They are likely, on a second read, to delve more deeply into the text. It's also helpful that Millie gave the students a clear focus on what to listen for during the Read-Aloud. Sometimes she gives a focus, other times, the focus comes from what the students say.

(While Millie reads aloud, she stops and thinks aloud:) Gosh, I think Peter is so brave to invite a girl to his party.)

Just as Maria modeled how the thinking process was part of her writing process, Millie modeled how the thinking process was part of her reading process.

Could you all turn to your partner and talk about what you think Peter is like?

(The students turn and talk and Millie joins them as they talk. At times she listens and at times she joins their conversations.)

Let's listen in on one of the partnerships as they discuss the main character Peter.

   Virginia: I think Peter was brave because he did so much for one girl. He mailed the letter. He went out in the rain. All of this for just one girl.
   Alder: Yes, he was brave. He was brave to invite a girl to his party. I wouldn't be brave enough to invite a girl to my party. Everybody would laugh.

In this exchange, you clearly see that Virginia and Alder listened and comprehended more sophisticated meaning and structure. In the Shared Writing session the students composed using more sophisticated meaning and structure.

(Millie then brings them back and continues reading. She stops a few more times and asks the students to talk to a partner.)

PUTTING THE READING/WRITING CONNECTION INTO ACTION

Here are some possible skills and strategies that you can teach across Shared Writing and
Read-Aloud.

SHARED WRITING	READ-ALOUD
Ways to begin your writing (putting words down about your characters and/or your setting).	Paying attention to the beginning of a story (who are the characters, what is the setting).
Adding character actions, thoughts, and/or spoken words to your writing.	Paying attention to characters' actions, characters' thoughts, and/or characters' spoken words.
Choosing words to continue your story to signal a change in time (*a little while later, suddenly, after breakfast*).	Paying attention to words that signal a change in time (*suddenly, a few minutes later, after breakfast*).
Determining what's important in your story. Adding more details to the important part of your story.	Determining what's important in the text. How do you know that?
Writing your story over pages—keeping in mind what you wrote at the beginning of your story when you compose the end of your story.	Culminating the pages of a story. I keep in mind what happened at the beginning of the book when I learn what happens at the end of the book.
Looking at the details in your picture to help you put the details in your words.	Looking at the pictures to help you understand.
Telling details, drawing details, writing details.	Talking about the book, looking at the pictures, reading the book.

Interactive Writing: Highlighting visual sources of information.

Moira McKenzie, warden of the Inner London Education Authority, created an approach
that she called Shared Writing (now called Interactive Writing). McKenzie built on Hold-
away's work in Shared Reading by providing a similar structure for writing with students.
Typically in Interactive Writing, the teacher composes an enlarged text with the students.
The students participate by writing parts of the text. The teacher and student share the pen.
The teacher writes what is too easy or too difficult for the students.

The teacher begins an Interactive Writing session by building up the students' meaning and structure; that is, she brainstorms (or simply tells the students) what they're writing that day, so that students can more easily bring in the visual (or graphophonic) sources
of information as they compose meaning into a text. At the end, the teacher and the students
have produced a text that is conventional (the spelling and punctuation are correct). Because students are writing parts of the text, they will sometimes write something that is not
conventional. Many of the teachers that I work with use white masking tape to cover up the
error. They then give the students a chance to try again. Let's now watch Millie conduct an
Interactive Writing session with her students.

FIGURE 5.4 Interactive Writing sessions help students use visual sources of information while writing.

Writers, today we're going to write a letter to the principal asking her to come to our publishing party. We'll write a little bit of the letter every day so that by Friday we can give it to her. I thought we would start by saying, "Dear Brenda, Please come to our publishing celebration." Is there anything else we should say?

A little girl in the front says, "We should tell her that the celebration will be next Monday."

You're right. We should. Okay, let's get started writing the letter.

Because the focus of Interactive Writing is on the visual sources of information, Millie spends only a brief moment on the content of the letter. This is different from the previous Shared Writing session, where Millie and the students spent the entire session on the content. This letter will not be finished in one day. It will be worked on for short intervals over a couple of days.

Dear—that word is on our word wall. Where would we find the word *dear* on the word wall? Yes, Jack, you're right: underneath the *d*. Jack, could you find the word *dear* on our word wall?

(Jack comes up and points to the word *dear* on the word wall.)

Let's all learn the word *dear*. Let's look at the word *dear* together. What do you notice about the word?

>**Sam:** It has the word *ear* in it.
>**Millie:** You're right. Okay, let's spell the word *dear*.
>(Everyone chants the spelling of the word *dear* together.)
>**Millie:** Okay, now I'm going to cover up the word *dear*. I want you to write it yourself.
>(The students write the word *dear* on their small dry-erase boards.)

Now let's check it. (Millie uncovers the word *dear* so that the students can check what they've just done.)

Bill, could you come up to the front and write the word *dear?*

(Bill comes up to the front and writes the word *dear*.)

Now, let's imagine it's Writing Workshop. Let's say that Sam wanted to write a letter to his grandmother. He might start by saying "Dear Grandma." Would he know how to write that word?

(The class shouts out "Yes!" and they once again chant "d-e-a-r.")

Here, Millie was working on learning words. She did what Snowball and Bolton calls look, say, name, cover, write (1999, p. 256). This helps students not just write the word correctly today, but also hopefully learn the word and write (and read) it correctly always.

Okay, I'll write *Brenda*. (Millie quickly writes the name Brenda.)

Here is a great example of where the teacher chooses to write the word Brenda. She did not use this session to focus on blends, which would be more appropriate for a later session.

Okay, everyone say the word *will*. What do you hear at the start of that word? Whisper the letter that makes that sound to a partner. (The class says the word.)

Millie's hoping to get the entire class involved in this, which is why she had all of the students say the word and whisper the name of the letter to a partner.

(continued)

FIGURE 5.4 Continued

I heard a lot of you saying that *will* begins with the letter *w*. *Will* is just like *web* on our alphabet chart. Let's say those two words together. Listen: *will* and *web*. *Will* and *web* start the same way. Jose, will you come to the front and make the *w?*

(Jose comes to the front and makes the *w*.)

Let's say the word *will* again. (The class says the word.) What do you hear at the end of that word? Whisper the letter that makes that sound to a partner.

Here Millie is showing the students how to use phonics and phonemic awareness as tools in writing. She works on phonemic awareness by having the students say the words web and will and then listen to how they both start the same way. She works on phonics by having the students listen to the sounds in the word will and then record the corresponding letters.

(This session continues for a few more minutes as the teacher and the students compose the letter together.)

Sometimes a component has one clear teaching point and sometimes it doesn't. It's fine to do a component with many teaching points (as this one has). As a matter of fact, it is sometimes helpful so that students have an opportunity to integrate different strategies at once in a meaningful and purposeful context. You do want to make sure that when you do a component as a minilesson during Reading and Writing Workshop, it has only one teaching point.

Shared Reading: Highlighting visual sources of information.

Just as Interactive Writing focuses on the visual sources of information, so does Shared Reading. In Shared Reading, the teacher reads and rereads enlarged texts aloud. These texts could be big books, poems, and/or rhymes. You should of course choose different texts, for different reasons, but the text should be enlarged (just as in Interactive Writing) so that all students can follow the print.

Different Shared Reading sessions are for different purposes. Early sessions, which Don Holdaway calls *discovery* (1979, p. 71), feel more like Read-Aloud because most conversations focus on what the text is about, therefore just like in Read-Aloud, the students are focusing on the meaning and structure sources of information. What makes Shared Reading in this instance different from Read-Aloud is that the text is enlarged and the teacher is running a pointer underneath the words as she reads. The students (even in these early discovery sessions) might notice that there is a one-to-one relationship between oral language and written language.

Later Shared Reading sessions, which Don Holdaway calls *exploration* (1979, p. 72), focus on rereading these same texts. Because the meaning and structure have been built up, students can more easily bring in the visual sources of information. The students now participate by reading along, using meaning, structure, and visual strategies when they encounter difficulty. Any Shared Reading session could have elements of discovery and exploration in it—that is, the teacher might begin by reading a new text and focus on meaning and structure and then move on to an old favorite where they bring in the visual sources of information.

Let's now watch Shawn Brandon as she conducts a Shared Reading session. Shawn is rereading the book *The Monster Party;* therefore, the students are familiar with the meaning and structure in this text. Now she is trying to help her students also bring in the visual source of information by getting them to look at the first letter and get their mouths ready for the corresponding sound.

Interactive Writing and Shared Reading are similar because both are working on the visual sources of information. Because they are similar they can be used to *enhance* or improve one another. For example, if Millie wanted to enhance the work that she did during Interactive Writing, she might conduct a Shared Reading session in which she focuses on

FIGURE 5.5   A Shared Reading session is a good place for students to use the visual sources of information while reading.

Readers and writers, we have already read the book *The Monster Party*. We're going to read it again, but this time we're going to stop every time we get to a sticky note and think about what that word is. After we look at the picture we'll get our mouth ready for the sound to see if we were right.

(The students read along with Shawn as she points to the words. All eyes are on one text. The text reads, "What can this little monster do? He can . . ." She stops at the covered up word. The students yell out, "Sing!")

Of course they yell out "sing." They know this book by heart, but watch what Shawn does to focus them on the visual (or graphophonic) sources of information.

Shawn: How could we check to make sure we were right?
Billie: Well, he's singing.
Shawn: You're right, Billie. He is singing. We could check by looking at the picture. But it also looks like he could be yelling. The word could be *yell*. How else could we check? (The class yells out that they could look at the word also.)

You're right. We could look at the word. Let's read it again and look at the picture but this time I'm going to take the sticky note away so that you can get your mouth ready for the word to check if you are right. "What can this little monster do? He can . . ." (Shawn slows down now and puts the pointer right on the *s* in the word *sing*. She purposely points at the *s* so that the students focus on the *s* and get their mouth ready for the word.)

Shawn: Were we right? Is the word *sing?* (The class yells out "Yes!") How did you know that the word was *sing* and not *yell?*
Sam: It was *sing* because I saw an *s*.
Shawn: So you checked by looking at the picture and the first letter. Then you got your mouth ready for the first sound. If the word had been *yell* what would you have seen?
Tony: A *y*.
Shawn: You're right.

Students in this instance were not just making predictions on what the word might be based upon the picture. By taking the sticky note away and getting students to focus in on the word, they were in fact using phonics as a tool in reading (just as they used phonics as a tool during the Interactive Writing session). Here they had to look at the letter and then get their mouth ready for the corresponding sound.

skills such as being able to read a word quickly or looking at the ends of words to make sure they look right. If Shawn wanted to enhance the work that she did in Shared Reading, she might conduct an Interactive Writing session where she has the students say the word and listen for the first sound and then record the corresponding letter.

PUTTING THE READING/WRITING CONNECTION INTO ACTION

Plan for tools that will focus all of your students' attention on the visual sources of information.

1. In Shared Reading you might call attention to a word, a letter, or a part of a word with a pointer.
2. During Interactive Writing, you might give students their own individualized alphabet charts, word walls, or name charts.

PUTTING THE READING/WRITING CONNECTION INTO ACTION

Here are some other possible skills/strategies you might teach during Interactive Writing and Shared Reading.

INTERACTIVE WRITING	SHARED READING
Writing a word for every word that you say (one-to-one matching).	Reading a word for every word that you point to (one-to-one matching).
Return sweep (writing to the end of the line and knowing to return to the left).	Return sweep (reading to the end of the line and knowing to return to the left).
How to listen for a sound and then record the corresponding letter (beginning, medial, end).	How to recognize a letter and get your mouth ready for the first sound (end sound, chunks in the middle).
Using words or parts of words that you know to help you write unfamiliar words.	Finding words or parts of words that you know to help you read unfamiliar words.
Rereading what you wrote.	Rereading what you read.
Noticing that there are spaces between the words.	Paying attention to the spaces between the words.
Putting spaces between your words.	
Using the picture.	Using the picture.
Writing sight words quickly. I don't stretch out the word *have*. I just write it quickly.	Reading sight words quickly. I don't get my mouth ready for *have*. I just read that word quickly.
Writing fluently.	Reading fluently.
Using tools (alphabet chart, name chart, word wall, partner) to help you when you run into trouble.	Using tools (a strategy chart, partner) to help you when you run into trouble.

Reading Workshop and Writing Workshop: Putting it all together.

In Reading and Writing Workshop students are using *meaning, structure,* and *visual sources of information* all at once. When I practice yoga, I've come to realize that the first three poses (Half Moon, Awkward, and Eagle) are warm-ups for the Triangle Pose. Essentially, in Triangle Pose your body takes everything it learned during Half Moon, Awkward, and Eagle and puts it together into one pose. Reading and Writing Workshops have the same purpose in the components of balanced literacy. Shared Writing, Read-Aloud, Interactive Writing, and Shared Reading are essentially the warm-ups for Reading and Writing Workshop: In Reading and Writing Workshop students must use what they've learned in the other components and put it together. The teacher gets a chance during Reading and Writing Workshop to assess what the students have learned in the other components and where their confusions still lie.

Both Reading and Writing Workshop have the same structure. They begin with a short minilesson during which you teach one new skill or strategy. (In writing, it's a writing skill. In reading, it's a reading skill.) Then, there is a work time where students work independently or in partnerships. During this time teachers are conducting one-on-one conferences and small group instruction by carefully assessing their students and teaching based upon their individual needs. The teacher then closes up the workshop by conducting a share session in which both students and teachers share and reflect upon their reading and/or writing work.

Many teachers that I work with make sure that for the first two or three minutes of Reading and Writing Workshop they are watching students read and write by themselves rather than talking with students. Watching students will help you help you assess their strengths and needs so you can effectively plan for the other components of balanced literacy.

Keep in mind that during Reading and Writing Workshop your students will have fewer scaffolds than they do in the other components; therefore, you cannot expect them to perform at quite the same level as they do during the other components. In Part III of this book, I will examine more of the specifics pertaining to minilessons, conferences, and small group work.

PUTTING THE READING/WRITING CONNECTION INTO ACTION

Here are some possible skills/strategies that you might teach during reading and writing workshop.

WRITING WORKSHOP	READING WORKSHOP
How to choose a topic for writing.	How to choose a book for reading.
You use pictures to help you when you write.	You use pictures to help you when you read.
What do you do when you get to a hard word in writing? What strategies can you use?	What do you do when you get to a hard word in reading? What strategies can you use?
What do you do when you think you're finished writing?	What do you do when you think you're finished reading?
You write a variety of forms and genres.	You read a variety of forms and genres.

USING ASSESSMENT TO PLAN THE COMPONENTS OF BALANCED LITERACY

Often when I try to plan for the different components of balanced literacy with teachers, they become overwhelmed. They spend ten minutes coming up with a good idea for Shared Reading, then another ten minutes coming up with an equally good but different idea for Interactive Writing, and then spend yet another chunk of time planning for Shared Writing and so on. They look at me glassy eyed and exhausted. They're frustrated. I'm frustrated. But there really is an easier way.

Plan for what you will teach in the components of balanced literacy by *assessing your students*. Watch them during Reading and Writing Workshop. Look at your running records, your conference notes, and student writing samples. Look also at both your students' strengths and their needs. Then, plan your components alongside your assessments. You can make this planning even more efficient by planning to teach *similar concepts across the reading and writing components*. Next, I want to show you what this looks like.

Ilene Scalon and Jennifer Brady, two teachers from one of my study groups, went into Adele Cammarata's (another member of my study group) kindergarten classroom and assessed her students in order to plan for the components. They watched one student named Tyla in particular because she demonstrated fairly typical kindergarten behaviors (see Figure 5.6).

FIGURE 5.6   When I went to swimming I did lots of swimming stuff.

You might wonder why they decided to base their whole-group instruction on what Tyla needed. Ilene and Jennifer knew that that Tyla represented what many of the students in that class needed, so they used her writing to plan what Adele would teach to her entire class in the different components of her balanced literacy curriculum.

Tyla (as you can see in Figure 5.6) had a lot of detail in her picture. At first she was vague in telling her story, but when Ilene and Jennifer prodded, she was able to tell her story with quite a lot of detail. Those details, however, did not show up in Tyla's words. Tyla listened for beginning and medial sounds for most words; however, she did not consistently listen for the end sounds. Tyla began her writing putting spaces between her words, but as she continued, she seemed to lose her steam and began stringing her words together.

Now I want to show you what we decided to teach based upon our assessments of Tyla. It's interesting to note that looking at Tyla's writing helped us to plan not only what to teach, but also what not to teach. Most of the students in the class were like Tyla in that they were using beginning sounds consistently. Adele no longer needed to conduct Interactive Writing sessions that focused on recording the initial sounds in words. She also no longer needed to conduct Shared Reading sessions in which she focused on getting one's mouth ready for the initial sound. It's also fascinating to see how much curriculum a single piece of writing generated. Tyla's writing helped us plan for Adele's writing components, but interestingly enough, looking at the writing helped us to plan for the reading components as well (see Figure 5.7)

PUTTING THE READING/WRITING CONNECTION INTO ACTION

Align your language across the components so that the connections are explicit. You might say things such as:

- Shared Reading: I want all of you to read along with me and when you see a word that's covered up, we'll try together to look at the picture and get our mouth ready for the first sound.
- Interactive Writing: Today as we write this sign, I'm going to ask you to say the words with me. Listen for the first sound and then we'll write the letter that makes that sound.
- Read-Aloud: I'm going to read aloud and I want you to pay attention to what Peter the character does in this story. We'll pay attention to his actions. We'll stop and talk about that soon.
- Shared Writing: I'm going to write the words, and I want you to help think of what words I should write. Let's write the story of going to Central Park. We were the main characters of that story. What were some of things that we did at the park? What were some of our actions?
- Writing Workshop: Writers sometimes choose familiar topics.
- Reading Workshop: Readers sometimes choose books that contain familiar topics.

FIGURE 5.7   Using assessments to plan for the components of balanced literacy.

- **Shared Writing:** Adele might ask the students to join her in composing a classroom story. Adele would draw the details of the story and ask students to look at those details and then use the details of the picture to retell the story to a partner, deliberately helping students sequence the story by drawing three pictures: the first would be the beginning of the story, the next the middle, and the final the end.

- **Read-Aloud:** Adele might ask students to retell the story she read—deliberately prompting them to retell in order by asking what happened first and then next and then next. She could also have students tell stories from their lives that they were reminded of as they listened to the Read-Aloud. Again, she could make the connection clearer between Shared Writing and Read-Aloud by aligning her language. She might say something like, "In Shared Writing we retold our class story by saying what happened first, and then next, and then next. In Read-Aloud, we can retell the book we read by saying what happened first, and then next and next, just like we did in Shared Writing. In Shared Writing it helped us to remember the whole story. In Read-Aloud it helped us to understand the whole story."

- **Interactive Writing:** Adele might demonstrate how to say a word and then listen for the first sound, and then reread and listen for the next and the next and the next. After Adele demonstrated what it looked like to listen for beginning, middle, and end sounds, she might ask the students to share the pen and join her in listening to the sounds they heard first and then next and then next and then writing the letter that went with that sound. She might help students hear the blends at the beginning of words or help students use sight words more often. Adele might on that day or a different day spotlight putting spaces between words by having a student come up to the front and be the "space maker" by putting two fingers on the chart when the class is about to start writing a new word.

- **Shared Reading:** Adele might ask students to look across words to see if they could find parts of the words they knew to help them read the entire word. She might even purposely choose books and words that has sight words like *sit* or *today* at the end so that the students could clearly see how looking at the end of a word would help them read the entire word. Adele might also cover up the end of a word and have the students look at the picture, and then predict what that word would be by asking themselves what made sense along with predicting what the first and last letter would be. In that way students would be reading trying to make sure that what they read "made sense" and "looked right." She could definitely make the connection between Interactive Writing and Shared Reading clearer if she aligned her language. Perhaps she would say something like, "During Interactive Writing we said the word and listened for the first sound and the end sound. That helped us to write the word. In Shared Reading we can help ourselves read a word by looking at the first letter and the last letter, just like we do in Interactive Writing."

- **Reading and Writing Workshop:** Adele would start to see how students were "putting it all together" during Reading and Writing Workshop. She would notice and note when she saw students read pointing to the words or write using spaces. She would notice and note when she saw students read looking at the last letter and writing listening for the last sound. She would also notice and note how children listen and retell what they read. Could they say what happened in the beginning? in the middle? in the end? Could they retell their own stories, saying what happened in the beginning, the middle, and the end? And could they use the details in their pictures to help them write the details in their words?

FIGURE 5.8   A planning sheet for the components of balanced literacy.

WHAT I NOTICE ABOUT THE STUDENTS' STRENGTHS AND NEEDS 1. *Sources of Information* 2. *Qualities of Writing*	WHAT I CAN TEACH IN SHARED WRITING	WHAT I CAN TEACH IN READ-ALOUD	WHAT I CAN TEACH IN SHARED READING	WHAT I CAN TEACH IN INTERACTIVE WRITING	THINGS TO LOOK FOR IN FUTURE READING AND WRITING WORKSHOPS
Detailed picture. When we prompted Tyla, she retold the story of her picture. Tyla used beginning and medial sounds consistently. She didn't use the details of her picture to help her compose the words. She didn't consistently listen for ending sounds She didn't consistently put spaces between her words.	Looking at the details in the picture to help you tell the details to a partner (beginning, middle, end). Looking at the details to help you write the details (beginning, middle, end).	Listening and retelling the details of a story (beginning, middle, end). Listening and retelling my own story (beginning, middle, end).	Making a word look right by looking at the first and last letters. Pointing to each word as you read.	Making a word look right by listening to the first and last sounds. Putting spaces between your words.	Spacing. Final letter and final sound. Sequencing. Using the picture.

HOW MANY TIMES PER WEEK SHOULD I DO EACH COMPONENT?

I cannot write a chapter on the components of balanced literacy without attempting to answer the question that we all ask: *How often should we do each component?* To answer this question, I want to bring you back to Spiegel's definition of balance: "a decision-making approach through which the teacher makes thoughtful choices each day about the best way to help each child become a better reader and writer" (Spiegel, 1998).

You make decisions about how often to do each component based upon your assessment of your students and what will best help them to become better readers and writers. This will be different across a year and across the grades. In September, for example, if you notice that your students need lots of work in both meaning and structure sources of information, you'll probably do a lot of Shared Writing and Read-Aloud and a little less Interactive Writing and Shared Reading. In this instance, the *balance* in "balanced literacy" will be tipped toward the meaning and structure sources of information.

Perhaps in October you'll see that most of your students need some work in bringing in the visual sources of information and because of that you'll probably do a lot of Interactive Writing and Shared Reading and a little less of Shared Writing and Read-Aloud. There your balance was tipped more toward the visual sources of information. Of course, you're always doing Reading and Writing Workshop so that you can assess the ways in which your students are independently using meaning, structure, and visual sources of information.

Recently, I did a workshop on the components of balanced literacy, and a brand-new teacher followed me out the door and up 120th Street with his notebook opened and his pencil poised. "So when should I do Shared Reading?" He said. When I looked confused, he said, "I should do Shared Reading if I see that my students need . . ." Then he looked at me, hoping I would fill in the blank. He had the right idea. You plan for the components of balanced literacy by assessing your students' strengths and needs. He will decide for himself how many days per week he should be doing each component based again upon the kinds of reading and writing knowledge his students presently need.

Yoga is easier for me these days. I know what I am doing, and why I am doing it. You might say I have cognitive clarity. But it goes deeper than that. I can tell by the rhythm in my body, and the admiring glances I get from my teachers and fellow students, that I've improved. The slowing down, the figuring out why, the understanding of how the poses connect actually transformed my practice. Before long, you'll be once again be planning for the components of your balanced literacy curriculum. Separate each component and find its clarity. Then, blur the lines and bring the components together so that you can make thoughtful decisions about what to teach in each component and, most important, how to connect them across reading and writing. Believe me. It will transform your teaching.

FOR FURTHER STUDY

- Study a class set of writing. Look at both the strengths and needs of your students and plan what you'll teach inside the different components of balanced literacy.

- Study one student's writing to help you plan how you'll teach individuals the components of balanced literacy.

CHAPTER 6

UNITS OF STUDY

*Writing can foster reading competence and vice versa if the learner becomes
aware of the reciprocal nature of these acts.*

—Marie Clay

It's a beautiful October morning as I make my way across Adele Cammarata's kindergarten classroom. I take a quiet moment to look around, and as always it's simply glorious. Groups of students are sitting on the rug, some with arms around one another, some leaning in close, some lying on pillows, but all are happily engaged in reading.

Adele is, of course, sitting among them, watching, listening, teaching, note taking, and if you stick around long enough, laughing at something smart or quirky one of her students has said or done. I make my way over to Mariah and Tyla, who are having a wonderful time reading *The Three Bears.* Tyla is reading and Mariah is leaned in close looking at the pictures and listening. "Once upon a time there were three bears," Tyla begins, with a voice that interestingly enough sounds very much like Adele's teacher Read-Aloud voice. "They lived in a house in the woods. There was a little wee bear, a middle-sized bear, and a . . ."

Mariah can't contain herself any longer. She jumps right in and screams, "A GREAT BIG BEAR!" And then they continue reading and laughing together.

This is a glimpse into Adele Cammarata's Reading Workshop in October. Adele was in the middle of a reading Unit of Study entitled Emergent Literacy. I'll go into more detail about this Unit of Study shortly, but as I watched Mariah and Tyla read, I knew that I was a witness to powerful reading work. All of the students, as a matter of fact, were interacting with the books differently, but everyone was engaged in reading. One of the reasons that this Unit of Study was so successful was that Adele had Read-Aloud all of the books in the study to her students numerous times before she had her students read these books on their own. As I watched her students reading that day, I wondered if it was possible to plan similar Units of Study in both reading and writing in which students would have the opportunity as they did here to be a part of repeated reading activities. I found, of course, that the answer to this question was yes.

This chapter will show you how to spotlight the reading/writing connection while planning Units of Study in three distinct ways. First, I'll suggest that you plan similar types of Units of Study across writing and reading so that the studies can *enhance* one another. Then, I'll show you how to plan the beginning of a writing Unit of Study letting the reading of text *complement* the writing of text. Finally, we'll look at ways to plan reading and writing Units of Study side by side, letting the writing Unit of Study *enhance and complement* the reading Unit of Study and vice versa.

WHAT IS A UNIT OF STUDY?

A Unit of Study essentially is a plan or a roadmap for what you'll teach over a period of time in your Reading and Writing Workshop. This period of time for primary students is approximately three to four weeks. For many of us, organizing our curriculum into particular studies is nothing new especially when it comes to subject areas other than reading and writing. As a matter of fact, I can remember as a first grade teacher planning for Units of Study in both math and science. I did not, however, plan for Units of Study in reading or writing. In these subjects, I assessed my students and then used my assessments to plan my minilessons from day to day. On Monday, for example, I might work with Jose and notice that he needed work on interesting word choice. Because of this noticing, I would do a minilesson the following day on interesting word choice. Perhaps the next day, I would notice while working with Mary that she needed work on recording end sounds in words. I might make a note to myself to do a minilesson that week on hearing end sounds in words.

Assessing my students in this way was certainly helpful; however, because these assessments were not done in conjunction with Units of Study, I never stayed with any one topic long enough for my students to actually learn it. Calkins, talking about the importance of Units of Study, says, "Units of Study allow teachers to plan and organize a sequence of instruction so that over time students successfully tackle new and often increasingly difficult challenges" (2003, p. 19). When we plan for Units of Study in our Reading and Writing Workshop, we are in essence deliberately organizing our instruction so that students are given time to learn complicated concepts just as Calkins recommended here.

Teachers often ask me for a list of reading and writing Units of Study that I recommend for primary students. Although I believe that many of your ideas for Units of Study should come through conversations with your colleagues, I recommend that you read books such as *Units of Study for Primary Writing* (writing Units of Study) by Lucy Calkins and colleagues from the Teacher's College Reading and Writing Project and *Growing Readers* (reading Units of Study) by Kathy Collins. Both of these books are invaluable resources and will provide you with many ideas for Units of Study to do in your classroom.

PLANNING READING AND WRITING UNITS OF STUDY

Research has also shown that repeated reading activities facilitate comprehension and develop story knowledge (Brown and Briggs, 1991; Mason and Allen, 1986; Van Kleeck, 1990). I keep this research in mind when I'm planning for the particular Units of Study that I want to do in my classroom. I deliberately try to plan for Units of Study in both reading and writing that incorporate some sort of repeated reading activity. Often this repetition is in the form of reading and rereading similar types of texts. Many teachers have asked me how repeated reading activities help students increase their comprehension and composition. In Chapter 2, I pointed out that both readers and writers use *meaning, structure,* and *visual* sources of information. When students read and reread similar types of texts they internalize *the meaning and the structures* presented in those texts. This internalization of the meaning and structure helps students to more easily bring in the visual sources of information while reading and writing.

Next, we're going to look at particular Units of Study that you might plan for in both reading and writing that deliberately give students opportunities to read and reread similar types of text. You'll want to be sure that when you do plan for these types of Units of Study, you plan them in both reading and writing. In that way, the rereading that students do in reading will improve the rereading that students do in writing and vice versa.

Emergent Literacy Units of Study.

Elizabeth Sulzby is both a professor of education and a researcher from the University of Michigan. For the past twenty years she has studied the kind of reading and writing work young children do before they read or write conventionally. This phase is often called

Emergent Literacy. She believes that one way to support Emergent Literacy is to read storybooks to students numerous times and then give those same storybooks to the students to read independently. Typically, the students are not actually reading the words of these texts, but rather are looking at the pictures and keeping the story that they heard in their minds.

Teachers observe and then confer with their students in order to build upon the ways they "read" these storybooks. Sulzby (1985) in her research describes different ways that students might "read" these storybooks that range from labeling or responding to the picture with little or no understanding of the entire story, to using literary language, to refusing to read the books at all. At that point, the students have often come to understand that reading also includes the print, and the print in these particular books is at times too difficult for them. This is when Sulzby recommends introducing leveled texts to those students.

Many kindergarten and some first grade teachers plan a specific Unit of Study entitled Emergent Literacy in which they do this type of work with their students. As a matter of fact, that was precisely the study that Adele and her students were doing at the beginning of this chapter. Adele, and other teachers like Adele, not only plan a specific Unit of Study on Emergent Literacy, but also plan for how this work will continue to be a part of subsequent reading Units of Study that they do.

There are two types of repeated reading occurring in this study. First, the students are reading and rereading the same books, thus developing a deeper comprehension with each reading. Also, the students are repeatedly reading stories, thus reading the *same type* of text numerous times. This type of rereading gives students repetition with story structure.

Revision Units of Study in reading.

Revision Units of Study in reading are another great way to help students increase their comprehension. During a revision Unit of Study, students might choose a book (or books) that they have already read but would love to read again. They then read and reread these books, noticing how the rereading brings new ideas to the surface. They might notice, for example, that before the study began they thought a particular character in their book was a good friend, but in the rereading of this book they have revised this thinking. They now have come to believe that although at times he was a good friend, there are also instances when he's not as good as a friend as they once believed. They most definitely during this study would talk about these books with a partner, fully expecting that these conversations would also deepen and revise their comprehension of those texts. In this Reading Unit of Study, the students are getting opportunities to read and reread the same texts.

Series books Units of Study.

A series book Unit of Study is also another great Unit of Study where rereading is incorporated. In a series book Unit of Study, students are asked to read books in a series; that is, they are asked to read books that belong together because there are reoccurring characters. Henry and Mudge, Frog and Toad, and Poppleton are among some of the most popular series for young students. When students read books in a series, their comprehension of these books often grows. With each book they read, they develop a better understanding of the

FIGURE 6.1 Rich storybooks that support Emergent Literacy. These books contain meaningful and familiar topics for most students. They also contain predictable structures that the students can internalize.

The Three Bears by Paul Galdone

A Pocket for Corduroy by Don Freeman

Are You My Mother? by Patricia Eastman

Bunny Cakes by Rosemary Wells

Caps for Sale by Esphyr Slobodkina

The Carrot Seed by Ruth Krauss

The Gingerbread Boy by Don Freeman

Harry the Dirty Dog by Gene Zion

Jamaica's Find by Junaita Havill

Little Engine That Could by Patty Piper

The Little Red Hen by Harriet Ziefert

Little Red Riding Hood by Jacob Ludwig Grimm

The Snowy Day by Ezra Jack Keats

Three Bears by Byron Barton

Three Billy Goats Gruff by Paul Galdone

Where the Wild Things Are by Maurice Sendak

Will I Have a Friend? by Miriam Cohen

characters because these characters are introduced to them repeatedly throughout these texts.

During a series book Unit of Study, teachers might ask students to read, paying attention to a particular character's actions, thoughts, and/or spoken words. Students talk about these books in partnerships, backing up their thinking with evidence from the text. Many of the teachers that I work with also ask students to follow that character throughout the entire series, noticing not only the places where the character acts the way they would expect him or her to act but also the places where the character's actions, thoughts, or words surprise them. Again, more than likely they would be talking about all of this in partnerships. Here, in this study, the students are once again getting repeated exposure this time to the same characters.

Nonfiction Units of Study.

A nonfiction Unit of Study in reading, if planned carefully, also provides many opportunities for repetition. Many teachers that I work with ask students during a nonfiction Unit of

Study to choose a topic they would like to learn more about. Then the students are encouraged to read more than one book on that particular topic. More than likely, they will come across some of the same information across these texts, and this surely will help them internalize that knowledge. Likewise, they'll also come across different and conflicting information, once again deepening and revising their understanding of the topic. In this study, students are getting repeated exposure by reading and rereading different texts that are about the same topic.

Some teachers also conduct nonfiction studies in which students, rather than reading books on one topic, read nonfiction books across a variety of topics. Students will of course receive different types of benefits from this type of Unit of Study. My recommendation is to plan for both types of nonfiction Units of Study in your classroom.

Rereading Units of Study.

So far, we've looked at reading Units of Study, which incorporate some sort of repetition in them. Now, we're going to explore two writing Units of Study—revision and editing—which also include repetition. Once at a workshop Donald Graves remarked that revision and editing in writing were needless activities unless students understood how to reread their writing. I'm embarrassed to think about how many revision and editing Units of Study I have done in the past in which I have never mentioned the word rereading. It's crucial to plan Units of Study where we explicitly teach students how to reread their writing. Revision and editing Units of Study are ideal places to do this.

In a *revision Unit of Study,* students should be rereading their writing in order to improve the content. Often during a revision Unit of Study teachers ask students to choose at least one of their writing pieces that they love and would like to work on more. Then, they encourage students to reread their writing, teaching them specific ways to improve upon their content. In an e*diting Unit of Study,* students should be rereading their writing in order to improve the mechanics of their writing. During an editing Unit of Study, teachers might also ask students to choose a piece (or pieces) of their writing that they would like to work more on. Once again, the teacher would begin by encouraging students to reread their writing. This time, however, the teacher would teach the students specific strategies to improve the mechanics of their writing. In both of these Units of Study, students are having repeating exposure to their own writing, which in turn will help them when it comes to deepening the meaning in their own texts.

"I understand how important rereading is to both revision and editing," teachers will say to me, "but how do I get students to actually reread their writing and see what's missing?" I understand exactly where they are coming from. Everybody struggles with rereading his or her own writing. As I work on this book, as a matter of fact, I'm often shocked by some of the obvious errors I miss when I reread. It's not that I don't know these things. It's just that my mind already has a vision of this book, and when I reread, I often inadvertently reread as if the error is not there. I do this because I am the writer of this text and I know what it should say. In this instance, I am reading my own text as a writer. I do my best revision and editing, however, when I deliberately pretend that my book is a professional book I've picked up in a book store; that is, I try and read my text as a reader, rather than as a writer.

Our students, if we don't show them differently, will reread their writing as a writer, often rereading what their text should say but doesn't yet say. You'll need to teach them during both revision and editing Units of Study how to read and reread their own texts not as the writer of that text, but as a reader of that text. They'll have to ask themselves as readers do if their writing makes sense (meaning), sounds right (structure), and looks right (visual). In Figure 6.2, I've outlined some specific ways that you can, during a revision and editing Unit of Study, teach students to reread their own writing, using meaning, structure and, visual sources of information.

FIGURE 6.2   Strategies to teach students during revision and editing Units of Study.

Rereading Strategies

■ Help students reread their writing *like a reader*. Teach them how to monitor their writing. Have them point at each word while reading their writing, asking, "Does it look right? Does it sound right? Does it make sense?"

■ Help students reread, asking themselves if what they wrote *makes sense*. You can further break this down by having students reread and:
  1. Delete/Change words that don't make sense.
  2. Check the sequence of their writing (beginning, middle, end).
  3. Take out unnecessary parts.
  4. Add necessary parts.
  5. Figure out what to say next.

■ Help students reread asking themselves if what they wrote *sounds right*. You can further break this down by having students reread and:
  1. Omit unnecessary words (*was was*).
  2. Add necessary words (*I to the store.* [add *went*]).
  3. Check the tense (*Yesterday I went to the mall,* rather than *Yesterday I goed to the mall*). Often I ask them if there is another word that would fit.
  4. Check the punctuation.

■ Help students reread asking themselves if what they wrote *looks right*. You can further break this down by having student reread and:
  1. Check the word wall words.
  2. Ask themselves if they just know a word and can write it quickly.
  3. Ask themselves if there are other words that would help them write the word (I know *day;* that would help me write the word *today*).
  4. Write the word a second time and then check to see if it looks right.
  5. Locate the part of the word that doesn't look right. Write the word a second time changing that part.
  6. Stretch the word out one more time.

PUTTING THE READING/WRITING CONNECTION INTO ACTION

Plan for ways to incorporate rereading into every writing Unit of Study.

At times, ask students to begin or end Writing Workshop by rereading. This will help them:

1. Determine if they are finished.
2. Figure out what to write next.
3. Ensure that their writing makes sense.
4. Ensure that their writing sounds right.
5. Ensure that their words look right.

IMMERSION: LETTING READING COMPLEMENT WRITING

So far, I've suggested some reading and writing Units of Study that will provide your students with opportunities to read and reread similar types of texts. Because these Units of Study are similar across reading and writing, you'll also find that you'll be able to let the similarities between these reading and writing Units of Study *enhance* or improve one another. The series book Unit of Study, for example, is bound to improve the revision Unit of Study because the students will use what they learned through repetition in the reading Unit of Study to help them reread and revise in the writing Unit of Study.

Next, I want to show how the reading/writing connection can once again come into play when you immerse students at the start of a writing Unit of Study. Immersion is a structure in which students are asked to read and listen to texts that are like the ones they are going to eventually write. So, for example, if you were doing a nonfiction Unit of Study in writing, you would start that study by first immersing students in nonfiction text and then only after that immersion would you ask students to write nonfiction text. I believe that this immersion structure should be incorporated into the start of every writing Unit of Study.

For a moment, let's think about how students benefit from being immersed in texts at the start of a writing Unit of Study. A reader (as explained in Chapter 2) is introduced to new structures while he reads, while a writer chooses her own structures while she writes. During immersion, students read texts noticing the structures so that they in fact can then use those same structures while writing. Immersion (the reading of text) actually *complements* or adds to the writing of text.

Frank Smith said, "to learn to write, children must read in a special kind of way" (1984, p. 47). Here, Smith is speaking about immersion. Next, we're going to look at a series of immersion lessons that will teach students to read in this special way: specifically, getting them to notice text structures while reading that they can use while writing. This series of lessons are geared toward a nonfiction-writing Unit of Study. My hope, however, is that these series of lessons give you an image of how to immerse students at the start of any writing Unit of Study. Not only will you once again see the lessons but I'll also in italics extrapolate some of the important teaching moves being made (see Figures 6.3, 6.4, 6.5, 6.6, 6.7, and 6.8).

Immersion Lesson 1: Teaching students to notice the structures within texts.

FIGURE 6.3   An immersion minilesson that helps students notice text structures.

Writers, in one week we're going to be writing our own nonfiction books. This week we're going to study some nonfiction books so that we can get ideas for how to write our own nonfiction books.

It's important to let students know why they are looking at these books. Brian Cambourne and Jan Turbill in their research talk about the conditions of learning. They believe that these conditions create optimal learning situations. One of their conditions of learning is expectation. In order for students to learn, they must know they will be expected to try this. Students will obviously notice texts differently if they know there is an expectation that they will write texts like they ones they're studying.

When writers get ready to write nonfiction, they look at nonfiction books and see what they notice about them. First, you'll watch me notice and then you're going to help me. Hmm, what do I notice?

(The teacher is using the book *Pigs* by Gail Gibbons. It is on a transparency.) Oh look, on this first page, the writer puts words in the picture that teach. Look, here it says a pig is also called a swine. I wonder if other nonfiction books will have words in the pictures that teach. (The teacher turns to the next page.) Oh look, here it is again. There are words in the pictures that teach.

It's purposeful that the teacher wonders aloud if there are other books like this one. The teacher wants the students to do the same thing while they're reading their own books. She wants them to wonder if there are other books in the class that share some of the qualities of the book they're reading.

(The teacher reads the next page, but purposely stops on the page with the picture of a pig. She reads the words and then asks the students to stop and talk in partners about what they notice.)

Jose: I notice that it has words around the body.
Teacher: Oh, so you're noticing that some nonfiction books label the parts of something. That is called a diagram. I wonder if other books label the parts of something. I wonder if other books have diagrams. What else?
Samantha: I notice that the pig has a heavy round body.
Teacher: Oh, so you learned about what pigs look like. I wonder if other nonfiction books describe what something looks like. That gives me a great idea for Tony. Tony is always talking about his dog. Couldn't he, when it's time, write a nonfiction book where he describes what dogs look like?

Samantha responded more as a reader when she said pigs have a heavy, round body. She said what she learned from the book rather than what she noticed about how the text was written. The teacher renamed Samantha's readerly comment into a writerly comment. She also reminded the students once again they would eventually be doing this by referring to how Tony might one day try this in his writing.

The teacher had the students notice together before she sent them off to try it on their own. She purposely choose a part of the text that had pictures and words. Some students will notice something about the picture. Some students will notice something about the words. Some students will notice something about both.

(continued)

FIGURE 6.3   Continued

Did you see how much we noticed on just one page? Today I'm going to give you some nonfiction books to look at and read with a partner. You might notice like we did together words in the pictures. You might notice like we did together diagrams—books that label the parts of something. You might notice nonfiction books that describe what something looks like, like we did together. Or you might notice something brand new that we have not even talked about. Your job today is to try and notice lots of things about nonfiction.

Immersion Lesson 2: Teaching students how to internalize the structures within texts.

FIGURE 6.4   An immersion minilesson that helps students internalize text structures.

Writers, you noticed a lot of interesting things in the nonfiction books that we read yesterday. I kept wishing that I had some rubber bands because there were certain books that went together. Let me show you what I mean. Helena and Jordy noticed that these two books needed a rubber band because both of the books give you information about different types of things.

The first book gives you information about different types of houses—see—big houses, little houses, bright houses, and white houses.

The second book gives you information about different types of shoes—see—old shoes, new shoes, just-right-for-you shoes.

Even though this book is about houses and this book is about shoes, the thing that is the same is that both of these books give you information about different types of something.

Here the teacher is demonstrating how to notice books that are not about the same topic, but share the same structure. Hopefully, if the students see the same structure across many texts, they will begin to internalize it and eventually produce it in their own writing. The language "Even though this book is about houses and this book is about shoes, the thing that is the same is that both of these books give you information about different types of something" is important language that you'll hear the teachers in this chapter use over and over again. It is clear and to the point.

Let's try it together. Remember the *Flying Book?* Let's see if this book (the teacher picks up the insect book) should be rubber-banded to *Flying Book.*

(First the teacher reads a page that describes what planes do and then the teacher reads a page that described what insects do.)

Talk to your partners and tell them what is the same about these two books.

The teacher deliberately read a page of a book that describes what insects do and a page about what planes do because she wants them to begin to internalize this structure by seeing it across texts.

I'm sure all of you noticed that both of these books teach you about what a topic does. Even though this book is about planes and this book is about insects, they both teach you what that topic does. Today, as you're studying your own books, see if you think two books need a rubber band and we'll share these at the end.

Immersion Lesson 3: Teaching students how to look at books to get new topic ideas.

FIGURE 6.5   An immersion lesson that helps students come up with topic ideas.

We've been looking at nonfiction books and have noticed quite a bit. Nonfiction books can describe what something looks like. They can have diagrams. They can teach about different types of something. Today, I want to show you how you can look at these same books and also get ideas for what you want to write about.

The students look at the same books day after day. This also happens in emergent reading. We do this because as each minilesson unfolds, students can notice more and more in the texts if they are the same. Students would have a difficult time noticing the sophisticated elements in the texts if they were changing from day to day.

Watch me. Remember the *Pig* book? Well, I am not an expert on pigs, but it reminds that I could write about animals. We have a snail in the classroom. I could make a diagram of a snail. I could describe what snails look like and what they do. Turn and talk. Let your partner know if this book gives you ideas on an animal that you could write about.

The teacher wants the students to realize that the pig book doesn't necessarily have to remind them they could write about pigs, but rather it should remind them that they could write about animals. Her *hope is that through this lesson some students will discover some animals that they are interested in writing about.*

Let's look at the next book, *Where Do I Live?* This author wrote about places he knew a lot about. That reminds me that I know a lot about the grocery store Dagastino's. I go there almost every day. I could write about what different people do at Dagastino's, the different jobs—I could describe what Dagastino's looks like. Hey, I could draw a picture and label the parts—like a diagram. This book gives me ideas on places that I could write about.

Some students will be reminded of animals they know a lot about through looking at the pig book, while others will be reminded of places they know a lot about by looking at Where Do I Live? *The teacher wanted the students to understand that they can get topics ideas from studying text. She also tried to bridge this meaning lesson with the other two structure lessons by modeling how she not only thinks about what topics she's writing about, but also thinks about how she might structure that writing.*

Let's look at the next book. This book is about trucks. It makes me think about transportation. I use the subway for transportation. I could write a book about the subway. I could write about the different types of subways like the A train and the B train. I could make a diagram of the subway. I could describe what the subway looks like. Turn and talk to a partner about what this book gives you ideas for. Did you see how we looked at these books to give us new ideas for our writing? Well, today let's look at the same books again and now let's look to see what new ideas we get for topics that we might write about.

Immersion Lesson 4: Teaching students how to study one particular text structure.

FIGURE 6.6   An immersion lesson that teaches students how to study one particular text structure.

Writers, we are getting closer and closer to writing our own nonfiction books. I want to show you something else that you can do to help yourself get ideas for your own books. You can study one part of a nonfiction book trying to notice a lot about it. Let's try it together. Remember how we have noticed that lots of nonfiction books describe their topics. Let's study the kinds of words they use to describe it. I'm going to read one part aloud and I want you to watch how I study the words—then we're going to try it together. (The teacher takes out the book *Pig* by Gail Gibbons.)

"Pigs have a heavy, round bristly-skinned body with a round flat nose called a snout." The author is describing the pig. Let me try and notice the types of words she uses. Hmm . . . *heavy* and *round. Round* is a shape word. This author describes what the pig looks like by saying its shape. She also uses the word *bristly.* That describes what the pig feels like: bristly. On this page she describes by using shape words and also by describing what a pig feels like. Gosh . . . I wonder if other books will describe their topics with shape words or if they will describe what the topics feel like.

Did you see what I did? Did you notice how I studied the special words that the writer used to describe the topic? Let's try it together. I'm going to read another part of this book and let's see what types of words the author uses to describe the topic.

"Pigs have four toes on each foot. There is a hard hoof at the end of each toe. Only the two long middle hoofs are used for walking. And of course many pigs have wiggly curly tails." What did you notice about how this author described pigs? What special words did she use? Turn and talk to a partner.

> **Jose:**   Hard hoof . . .
>
> **The teacher:**   Oh, she described what the hoof felt like. You know, I was thinking about Billy and how Billy has a cat. If Billy writes a nonfiction book about cats he could describe what cats feel like. He might say, "Cats are soft and furry."

Although afterward the teacher calls on Jose, having students turn and talk is important in that she is engaging her entire class in the question rather than just the one student that she calls on.

Throughout immersion the teacher will imagine aloud what students' topics would sound like if they tried some of the text structures. Katie Wood Ray in her book Wondrous Words *calls this "writing in the air" (1999, p. 127). You don't want them to forget that the reason they're studying these texts is because they're going to make texts like it.*

Today, I've marked the pages in the nonfiction books where they describe the topic. Let's go back and reread only those pages today to study the special words that writers use to describe their topics. I bet you'll get good ideas for words that you can use to describe your topic.

This type of lesson also lets students look closely at word choice in context and will enable them to write envisioning their topic by using more descriptive language. This lesson came toward the end of immersion rather than the beginning. Students at this point should know these books well enough that they can focus in on one single beautiful word like round *or* curly.

FIGURE 6.6   Continued

You want them to now savor the words that they read. The hope is that by admiring these words together students will try them in their own writing when it makes sense to do so.

Some students, hopefully, will write using shape words. Perhaps they might even use words that describe what something feels like. Perhaps someone will use the word bristly. *Perhaps they'll come up with their own.*

Immersion Lesson 5: Teaching students how to produce these structures through talking.

FIGURE 6.7   An immersion that teaches students how produce these structures through talking.

Writers, we're going to start writing our own nonfiction books tomorrow. All of you have come up with topics that you're experts at. Today we're going to look at these books as a way to get ideas on how to write about own topics. Watch me. Remember that one of my topics was snails because we have a pet snail. Watch how I use the pig book to get ideas on how I could write about snails. I turn to the first page. "Many people think pigs are smelly and dirty. They think pigs eats like pigs and aren't very smart. That's because they don't know pigs."

They begin their book with what they think some people think about pigs. They also put words in the pictures. That gives me an idea for how I could start my snail book. I could say, "Many people think snails are a boring pet. They think they sit around and do nothing. That's because they have never had a snail for a pet." Then I could draw a picture of a snail with slime coming out of his body and write words underneath the picture that said when snails move slime falls out of their bodies.

Did you see how I used the pig book to help me practice the words I'll write in my snail book?

Here, the teacher explicitly shows students how to look at the books' structures and then rehearse their writing, imagining what their writing would sound like with those same structures. Modeling how to rehearse writing is essential because it shows students how to rehearse their own writing.

Let me read another page to you and let's think together about other ideas this pig book can give me for my snail book. (She reads the next page. On this page the body parts of the pig are described.) Could you turn and talk to your partner, imagining what it would sound like if we described the snail in the same way they described the pig?

The students turn and talk to a partner. Many students thought that the teacher could describe what the snail's shell feels like or what it looks like.

Did you all see how I used the pig book to get ideas for my own book? Today you are going to look at the same books one last time, and as you read and talk with your partner, see how the book you're reading gives you ideas for the books you are going to write. I'll be around to listen.

Immersion Lesson 6: Teaching students how to produce these structures while writing.

FIGURE 6.8   A writing minilesson that teaches students how to produce these structures while writing.

I know that you have been reading lots of nonfiction and have noticed different things about those types of books. You've been noticing things such as captions. (The teacher points to captions.) You've been noticing that they have information. (The teacher points to the words.) They have diagrams. (The teacher points to the diagram.) We're about to start writing our own nonfiction books, and I want you today and every day to use what you already know about nonfiction to help you write a book that other people could learn from.

The teacher has created a chart that documents everything the students have noticed about nonfiction. You'll notice that she refers to the chart throughout the session.

First, I'm going to show you what that looks like and then we'll try it together. Watch me. I'm going to start writing my nonfiction book about dogs. Watch how I use what I know to help me write a book that others could learn from. Hmmm, what should I try in my book? Captions, maybe. A table of contents. Yes. Let me do that first. (The teacher quickly writes a table of contents.) Hmmm, let me look at the chart to see what else I might do in my book. (She looks at the part of the chart where it says nonfiction books have information.) Oh yes, I'll write information. Maybe on the first page, I'll write some dogs are black and some are white. They are usually soft and furry. They have long pointy tails and a wet nose.

Isn't that a lot? *some of you may be wondering. Wouldn't you just show one structure of nonfiction per day? The teacher has spent a full week immersing students and wants to begin the study by holding the students accountable for what they have already learned during the immersion. By doing this, she has also set up her teaching to meet the needs of a wide range of students. After this big lesson, she will most certainly move into teaching the parts (which you'll see later in the chapter), but starting with this big lesson teaches students to use what they know from reading nonfiction when they write nonfiction.*

(The teacher turns back to the students.) Did you notice how I read the chart and kept asking myself what should I try in my book today that would help people learn about dogs? I decided to try a table of contents (she points to the part of the chart that has a picture of a table of contents and the words) because I knew that it would help someone reading my book learn about dogs.

Okay, now let's try it together. (The teacher pulls out an empty cat book.) Will you read the chart with a friend and give me some ideas on what I should try in the cat book, so that others could learn about cats? (The students stop and talk in partnerships.)

Some of you said we should have a table of contents. Some of you said we should write information about what cats look like. Some of you said we should write information about what cats do. And some of you said we should make a diagram. I could do any of those things in our cat book because they would help people learn about cats. I'm telling you that because, just like I could try these in my cat book, you could try them in your own books. So today and every day as you write, think about what you know about writing nonfiction and use it to help other people learn from your book. Have a great writing time today.

PUTTING THE READING/WRITING CONNECTION INTO ACTION

When you immerse students at the start of any writing Unit of Study you can:
- Teach students to notice how a text is written.
- Teach students how to group texts together.
- Teach students how to get topic ideas.
- Teach students how to study one particular aspect of the text.
- Teach students how to look at texts as way to get ideas for how to structure their own texts.
- Teach students how to use all they have internalized while writing.

PLANNING READING AND WRITING UNITS OF STUDY SIDE BY SIDE

Now that we've examined how to plan a variety of reading and writing Units of Study, I want to explore how to plan one single Unit of Study in writing alongside one single Unit of Study in reading. You see in Figure 6.9 plans for a reading and writing personal narrative Unit of Study. The second grade teachers at PS 261 in Region 8 planned these studies. This was the second personal narrative Unit of Study that these teachers had done both in writing and in reading. The first time their goals were for students to be able use story elements while writing and recognize story elements while reading. This time in writing they wanted their students to be able to use the story elements to reveal the important parts of their text. In reading, they wanted their students to use the story elements to help them understand and determine the important parts of a text. We planned the two Units of Study side by side and found that doing so made our planning both more effective and more efficient. I want to outline what we learned doing this in the hopes that you can use both our plans and our reflections to begin planning your own reading and writing Units of Study side by side.

Plan clear reading and writing goals for both Units of Study.

Although we were planning reading and writing Units of Study side by side, we had to make sure that we had clear reading goals for our reading Unit of Study and clear writing goals for our writing Unit of Study. During our planning sessions, we literally had to ask ourselves, *How would this writing minilesson help our students compose more?* or *How will this reading minilesson help our students comprehend more?* We also found that at times we needed to teach something in writing that didn't have a connected reading piece or vice versa.

Plan to teach reading and writing thinking strategies at similar times.

We also made sure that while we planned the minilessons for our reading and writing Units of Study, we kept in mind how we could connect the thinking strategies across the two subjects. At the start of the writing Unit of Study, we planned, for example, to teach students

FIGURE 6.9   A personal narrative unit of study in both reading and writing.

GOALS:

■ Help students write a focused story that has some main ideas.

■ Help students use the story elements that will help them reveal this idea.

POSSIBLE WRITING MINILESSONS	POSSIBLE READING MINILESSONS	COMMON THINKING STRATEGIES
Each of the ideas below will require more than one minilesson.	*Each of the ideas below will require more than one minilesson.*	
How to start writing a story:	**How to start reading a story:**	Synthesis
You can start your story by introducing the characters and setting. If you find that you don't begin in this way, you can rewrite.	You can start reading by making sure you understand what the setting and who the characters are. If you find that you don't, you can reread.	
Character work:	**Character work:**	Synthesis
If you introduce a character at the start of the story, you need to continue thinking about how to add details to your writing that will build upon that character.	If you are introduced to a character at the start of a story, you need to pay attention to that character throughout the story in order to build your understanding.	
Adding passage-of-time words	**Paying attention to passage-of-time words**	Synthesis
Ask yourself: What is your story mostly about?	**Ask yourself: What is this story mostly about?**	Determining importance
Focus your writing on that part.	Focus your thinking on that part.	
You elaborate on the important parts. You might add:	**You infer at the important parts. You might pay attention to.**	Inference Asking questions
1. Character's actions 2. Character's thoughts 3. Character dialogue 4. Description of scene	1. Character's actions 2. Character's thoughts 3. Character dialogue 4. Description of scene	

how to synthesize in writing, accumulating details about particular characters. Likewise we planned in reading to teach students how to synthesize accumulating details about particular characters. In both reading and writing, we wanted them to understand that the individual details should fit together to create a coherent whole. Later in the both Units of Study, we decided to teach them how to determine importance. We knew that by planning to teach thinking strategies at the same time in both writing and reading, we were setting our studies up so that one would improve the other.

Plan the order of your reading and writing minilessons.

While planning, we discussed how to connect these two Units of Study together. Specifically, we discussed whether we should teach something first in reading, first in writing, or at the same time. We made decisions about this by using what we knew about the similarities and differences between reading and writing. For example, at the beginning of these Units of Study, we decided to teach students how to start a story in writing before we taught them how to start a story in reading. We figured that because they choose their own topics in writing, the setting and the characters in their own stories would be more familiar than the setting and characters in the stories that they read.

Later in the Units of Study, we taught *passage-of-time words* first in reading and then in writing. We figured that because they would be introduced to passage-of-time vocabulary while reading, it would make those vocabulary words more familiar when we asked them to use them while writing. We knew that by making thoughtful decisions about the order of our reading and writing minilessons we were setting our studies up so that the Reading Units of Study would *add to* the writing Unit of Study and the writing Unit of Study would *add to* the reading Unit of Study.

A teacher, after reading this chapter, remarked, "I feel like I could take any of the ideas presented in this chapter and fit them into any Unit of Study that I hope to do." I was thrilled because that was my exact intention: My hope is that this chapter brings power and clarity to your planning of a Unit of Study no matter what the content is. Using the reading/writing connection when planning Units of Study will save you precious time, but most important, it will set up your teaching so that every single student has varied ways to learn the same concepts. What could be more important?

FOR FURTHER STUDY

- Get together with colleagues to brainstorm possible Units of Study. Discuss ways to incorporate repetition into them.
- Study texts in a particular genre with your colleagues. Study the meaning and structure in these texts by asking questions such as:
  1. What kinds of internal structures do I notice in these texts?
  2. Which structures in this text are sophisticated enough to challenge my students but are still within their reach?
  3. Can I find any of these structures across different texts?

- Plan reading and writing Units of Study side by side.
  1. What are my reading goals for the reading Unit of Study?
  2. What are my writing goals for the writing Unit of Study?
  3. What types of thinking will I teach across reading and writing?
  4. Are there times when I'll plan for the reading minilesson to come first?
  5. Are there times when I'll plan for the writing minilesson to come first?

CHAPTER 7

YEARLY CURRICULUM

Units of Study help to set the pace for your workshop. They add quality and consistency that both students and teachers need in a workshop.

—Isoke Nia

In my role as an educational consultant, I not only help teachers plan Units of Study, but I also help them plan their yearly curriculum calendars. In the past, when I had facilitated these planning sessions, we planned our yearly reading curriculum calendar on one day and then, on a different day, we planned our yearly writing curriculum calendar. We planned each curriculum calendar separately, never stopping to think about how these two curriculum calendars might connect. Marie Clay, in her extensive work with schools, noted that teachers often inadvertently hide the reading/writing connection from their students (1998, p. 156). She found that when teachers did this, their students had a more difficult time using writing to inform their reading or reading to inform their writing.

In those early planning sessions we were doing exactly what Marie Clay observed over and over again in schools. By planning our reading and writing curriculum calendars separately, we inadvertently were hiding the connection from our students. Thank goodness, I've learned from my mistakes and now plan reading and writing curriculum calendars side by side, deliberately looking for ways to connect the two.

This chapter will show you how to explicitly plan for the reading/writing connection while creating yearly reading and writing curriculum calendars. You'll see how doing this will set both you and your students up to use the reading/writing connection all year long. Just as you might study one book with your students, noticing every fine detail, we're going to do the same with the following curriculum calendar. Together, we'll study Ilyoung and Lynn's curriculum calendar (see Figure 7.1). Ilyoung and Lynn are both first grade teachers from PS 94 in Queens. Both have been teaching using a Reading and Writing Workshop for four years and collaborate on a regular basis. First, we'll study their curriculum calendar for some general principals about planning curriculum, and then we'll look deeper at how to explicitly plan with the reading/writing connection in mind.

WHAT IS A CURRICULUM CALENDAR?

Sometimes when I've asked teachers to see their curriculum calendars, they'll hand me their grade standards or state mandates. Both of these are helpful tools to use when creating a curriculum calendar, but they are not curriculum calendars. A curriculum calendar should tell the true story of what you plan to teach in the upcoming year. Usually, it is organized by the months of the school year. To begin creating a curriculum calendar, you must start by imagining the future, essentially, where you would like your students to be at the end of the year. You bring it back to the present by making a curriculum calendar that tells the story of how you'll get there.

Although it's helpful to look at examples of curriculum calendars, I do believe that it's crucial that in the end teachers create their own so that they can take their own grade standards and state mandates and put that jargon in their own words to plan meaningful yearlong reading and writing curriculum. Hopefully, by looking at Ilyoung and Lynn's curriculum calendar you'll feel equipped to adapt and/or create your own curriculum calendar that brings together the reading/writing connection in wise ways.

First, let's look at some of the organizational features of Ilyoung and Lynn's curriculum calendar. Reading and writing are purposely put on the same page, so that you see the connection while you plan for the connection. In the first column, Ilyoung and Lynn

FIGURE 7.1   A sample curriculum calendar for both reading and writing.

DATE	WRITING UNIT OF STUDY	READING UNIT OF STUDY	CONNECTION: STRATEGIES, PROCESS	ASSESSMENT	CELEBRATION
September	We write to make meaning.	We read to make meaning.	Activating relevant prior knowledge. Independent decision making. Rehearsal (through talk).	Topic choice. Stamina.	Writing: We tell our story to our partner. Reading: We read a favorite book to our partner.
October	We write in many forms for many reasons.	Beginning reading strategies.	Activating knowledge of print. Monitoring.	Genre choice. Editing.	Writing and Reading: Immediate and informal publishing.
November December	Personal narrative.	Personal narrative.	Synthesis. Determining importance. Asking questions.	Structure. Revision.	Writing: Parents type up and create reading materials for students. Reading: Paint a retelling of your favorite book.
January	Author(s) study.	Comprehension study: Text evidence.	Inference.	Elaboration.	Writing: Read your published piece to fifth grade book buddy. Reading: Discuss your favorite book with your book buddy.
February	Letters.	Nonfiction.	Synthesis. Asking questions. Determining importance.	Structure. Revision. Focus.	Writing: Immediate and informal publishing. Reading: Oral presentation.
March April	Nonfiction. All about. How to.	Comprehension study.	Envisioning.	Descriptive writing.	Writing: Teach what you learned to interested students. Reading: Paint a picture of scene in your book OR dramatize a scene from your book.

FIGURE 7.1   Continued

May	Poetry.	Poetry.	Envisioning.		Reading and Writing: Go to Barnes and Noble and perform a poetry reading. Read a poem that you love and read a poem that you wrote.
June	Fiction.	Reading projects.	Asking questions. Monitoring. Synthesis. Inferring.	Revision. Editing. Structure. Elaboration.	Share your summer plans and bring home your fiction book to read.

used the months of the school year to organize their plan for the year. Some studies were obviously a little bit longer and some were a little bit shorter, but the months of the school year gave them a common reference point and kept both themselves and their students on track. In the next two columns Ilyoung and Lynn noted the particular Unit of Study they would be teaching each month in both reading and writing. The next column records the reading/writing connections they planned on making in the different Units of Study. Then, in the next column, they paired those strategies up with a quality of writing to assess for. Finally, in the last column, they noted the celebration they would have to bring closure to the study. You'll note that some of these celebrations are simple, while others are more complicated.

GENERAL PRINCIPLES FOR PLANNING CURRICULUMS

Isoke Nia, founder of All Write Literacy Consultants, has always been one of my mentors in curriculum planning. She's helped me to develop similar curriculum planning strategies. As you read, you'll note that I do not have one set of principles for planning a reading curriculum and then another set of principles for planning a writing curriculum. I use the same general principles across both reading and writing. We know it's powerful for our students to approach reading and writing in similar ways. It's just as valuable for us as teachers to approach the planning of reading and writing in similar ways.

Curriculum calendars should have some genre Units of Study and some non-genre Units of Study

Cooper Charles, defining the word *genre,* says that genres are "the types of writing produced every day in our culture that make possible certain kinds of learning and social interaction" (1999, p. 25). Ilyoung and Lynn knew that they wanted to teach their students many genres across the year so that they would be aware of the many types of writing available to them. They also knew, however, that it was just as important for them to have time to revisit genres, especially ones they had loved. They tried to create a curriculum calendar that reflected both of these goals. Ilyoung and Lynn, when planning their yearly calendar, planned for Units of Study that were genre based and also planned Units of Study that were non-genre based. In this way, students would be learning new genres in the genre studies and would also be having opportunities to revisit genres in the non-genre studies. Let's look at their calendar to see how they did this.

Ilyoung and Lynn decided to begin the year by having students write in a genre or form of their choice until October. Then in November and December, they planned to study personal narrative. In January, no genre—but rather, an author study and an opportunity for students to choose what genre they would like to write in. In reading, they begin the year with students reading in a genre or form of their choice until October. Then, all of the students would read narrative during the character Unit of Study. In January, they planned a comprehension study rather than a specific genre study. They purposely did this so that students would have an opportunity to choose a genre to read in—perhaps revisiting one that they had already tried.

Planning yearlong curriculums and assessing your students should be simultaneous.

When Ilyoung and Lynn first began teaching using a Reading and Writing Workshop, they did not use a curriculum calendar. Rather, they read their students' writing, watched them carefully, conferred, took notes, and then used all of their assessments to plan their daily teaching. They were relieved the following year to make a plan, because although they found that assessing their students was fruitful, they needed a destination for their teaching.

For the next two years, they created curriculum calendars. Although there were many benefits, they now found themselves looking less and less at their students and their work and focusing more and more on the goals they had designed on their curriculum calendars. "We want to find a way," Ilyoung said, "to have a plan but to let our students reading and writing work affect our plan."

Ilyoung and Lynn, rather than doing one or the other, planned how to do both simultaneously. They planned to assess their students at the start of every Unit of Study, and then use that knowledge to plan the exact content they would teach. For example, Lynn and Ilyoung both planned to teach a "Writing for Many Purposes" Unit of Study in October; both wanted their students at the end of this study to understand that there are many types of writing in the world and that they should keep their readers in mind as they write in these genres. More than likely, however, their Units of Study would look different based upon their assessments.

In Lynn's classroom, signs and cards might become big—perhaps because Lynn's class would have real reasons to write signs and cards or perhaps also because her students might feel more comfortable making those forms. Next door, in Ilyoung's classroom how-tos and lists might become popular for the very same reasons. A curriculum calendar does not tell you what to teach and say each day—that's the job of your students who read and write in front of you day after day in glorious ways. They are your real curriculum.

Curriculum calendars should be used as guides and should be revised and fine-tuned when necessary.

There are certainly benefits to planning curriculum ahead of time. When you do, you can pack your classroom, choose professional literature, and order supplies, all angled toward your plans. Keep in mind, however, that the curriculum calendar you create in June will only reflect what you knew in June. That thinking is bound to improve as you learn more about reading and writing, meet your wonderful students, and watch them read and write. Ilyoung and Lynn made a decision that they would revisit their curriculum calendar and revise if:

> *Their students were interested in a particular study.*

For example, last year in Ilyoung's classroom, the students fell in love with small chapter books such as Henry and Mudge and Frog and Toad. Ilyoung realized that what they had actually fallen in love with was realistic fiction. They kept begging Ilyoung to let them write books like Henry and Mudge and Frog and Toad. She hesitated because realistic fiction was not on her curriculum calendar. In the end, she changed her memoir study to realistic fiction, because she wanted to work with her students' passions rather than against them. She also figured she could teach the same concepts (elements of story) while the students wrote realistic fiction.

> *Ilyoung and Lynn were interested in a particular study.*

Lynn and Ilyoung both attend workshops and read professional literature on a regular basis. They often return from staff development sessions excited about what they had learned. I've always urged them to go ahead and try the new curriculum with their students even if it was not on their original curriculum calendar because I knew that the best teaching often comes from what we are most passionate about.

Keep in mind that too much change isn't beneficial either. You must be careful that you revise your curriculum calendar only when it makes sense to do so. Lisa Burman, an Aussie consultant, says that she suggests that teachers imagine two parrots, one on either side of them, when they are considering changing curriculum. The first is asking, *What is the purpose of these changes?* and the second is asking, *Who will benefit from these changes?* She does this because she believes (as I do) that any changes you make should ultimately benefit your students. Take care when making revisions to your curriculum calendar so that you don't lose the original purpose of creating a curriculum calendar in the first place.

Curriculum calendars should have between eight and twelve studies. Each Unit of Study should last from three to five weeks.

New Units of Study bring communities to life. When the curriculum moves slowly, everyone loses their momentum and production is minimal. In my work with teachers I've noticed several reasons why Units of Study move slowly. One reason is that we match the pace of our teaching to the students who move the slowest. "We can't move on," we tell ourselves, "because Sam is not quite finished yet."

Our pace must be swift so that we keep up with the students who finish quickly, and give a nudge to our students who work more slowly. Make deadlines, knowing that you won't possibly teach everything that you would like to in one Unit of Study. Don't worry. You can fit it in subsequent Units of Study.

The other reason writing studies move slowly is that toward the end of a study we spend too much time conferring with individual writers helping them to fix every error in their pieces. Any of us who have done this with a class of twenty or so students knows how tedious this is and how long it takes.

When I find myself doing this, I'm reminded that showing students seven items to fix up in their writing rarely teaches them much. Usually, when I mention seven things quickly, I never get the opportunity to teach any of them in depth. Limit the amount of new revision and editing strategies you teach in any single Unit of Study. As the students progress through the year and through multiple Units of Study, they will build quite a repertoire of revision and editing strategies. Once you've taught students particular revision and editing strategies, you should hold them accountable to them in subsequent studies. Many schools that I work with often highlight the revision and editing that the students have done so that the outside world understands that although their texts are not perfect, revision and editing is still an important part of the writing process.

Units of Study should build on one another.

Ilyoung and Lynn knew that they wanted October's Units of Study to build into December's Units of Study and so on. Basically, they wanted each study to expose students to new concepts while spiraling back to old ones. Let's take a look to see how they did this in their curriculum calendar.

In Lynn and Ilyoung's curriculum calendar, they planned in September to help students activate relevant prior knowledge through talk. They built upon this in October by continuing to have students talk, activating relevant prior knowledge through talk, but now they highlighted how to encode/decode this knowledge through the print.

MAPPING READING AND WRITING CURRICULUMS TOGETHER

Now that we've established some foundational tips about planning yearlong curriculum calendars, let's look at some of the specific ways that you can connect your reading and writing curriculum calendars. Teachers often ask me if they should plan for connected reading and writing Units of Study side by side on their curriculum calendars, or if one should come before the other. This question of whether a reading Unit of Study should come before a writing Unit of Study reminds me of a similar dilemma: whether students should learn to read first or whether students should learn to write first. Marie Clay, addressing that dilemma, said that "the advocacy of 'writing first and reading later' is as limited as the 'reading first and writing later'" (2001, p. 12).

I believe this is also true when making decisions about how to organize your yearly curriculum calendars. Reading Units of Study should not always come before writing Units of Study, nor should writing Units of Study always come before reading Units of Study.

There will be times when the reading Unit of Study comes first and other times when the writing Unit of Study comes first. And of course, they'll be times when they are happening side by side.

You'll want to connect the Units of Study together in ways that are helpful to both your planning and your students' learning. The answer to this question ultimately lies in both your knowledge of your students and in your knowledge of the reading and writing process. You probably won't make the exact same decisions as Ilyoung and Lynn, nor should you, but I do suggest that your decisions are guided by some of their decisions.

Connect reading and writing curriculums by genre.

The most obvious way to connect your reading and writing curriculum calendar is to plan genre studies at similar times. Let's look again at Lynn and Ilyoung's curriculum calendar to see what they did. They are studying personal narrative *at the same time* (November/December) in both reading and writing. The connection is clear and immediate. That's certainly a valid reason to plan to teach these Units of Study side by side. You read stories and you write stories. It's seemingly simple, but deliberately planning these genres side by side on the curriculum calendar has huge implications for student learning. Some students will be able to use what they're learning about story in reading to help them improve or add to their understanding of story in writing. Other students will use what they're learning about story in writing to help them improve or add to their understanding of story in reading. In essence, you're setting up your year in ways that ensure your students can blur the lines between what they're learning in reading and what they're learning in writing in their own unique, quirky ways.

In February, Lynn and Ilyoung are going to study nonfiction in reading first to set them up to study nonfiction in writing in March. In this case, the *reading came before the writing*. It's often efficient to have the reading Unit of Study come before the writing Unit of Study because by the time the students are writing in the genre, they have become familiar with the genre (and the texts) through being immersed in it during the reading Unit of Study.

Some research, however, suggests that writing in a genre first helps you to later read in that genre. Dorothy Grant Hennings (1984) describes how she approached genre studies in her own class. She begin by first *speaking* the genre with students. Then she asked the students to join her in *writing* in the genre. Finally, she asked the students to *read* in the genre. What she found was that her students' reading comprehension increased when they wrote in the genre before they read in the genre. There is no easy answer. At times in the year you may have students read in a genre first, while other times in the year you might have students write in the genre first. And of course, there will be other times when you do both simultaneously.

Connect reading and writing curriculums by strategies.

Across the year you'll want to bring home the point that good readers and writers think in many different ways at the same time; that is, they don't just determine importance or envision, but, rather, they flexibly think in many different ways in order to compose and comprehend. With this mind, however, you'll also want to plan to highlight different think-ing strategies at different points in the year so that students see clear examples of each of these thinking strategies and in the end can use all of these ways of thinking at once.

It's often helpful to plan to do this at the same time across both writing and reading. Ilyoung and Lynn decided, for example, that in September they would teach their students in both reading and writing how to be *independent decision makers*. They knew they would teach them, for example, what to do when they thought they were done in both reading and writing. In reading it might be reread the book they just read or get a new one. In writing it might be to reread the piece they just did or start a new piece.

In October, Ilyoung and Lynn planned to teach their students how to *monitor* both their reading and their writing. In writing, they planned to teach students how to monitor their writing by rereading and checking to make sure their words made sense, sounded right, and looked right. In reading, they planned to teach their students how to also moni-tor text once again making sure that the words they read in the text made sense, sounded right, and looked right. Again, a seemingly simple idea, but by explicitly planning to work on monitoring in both reading and writing, you are setting your students up to seamlessly blur the lines between reading and writing, letting the monitoring work in reading and writ-ing enhance and add to each other.

Ilyoung and Lynn also paired up a thinking strategy with a quality of writing to look for as evidence of that type of thinking. For example, they know that because they would be working in September on independent decision making, they should expect to see lots of writing (*stamina*). In October, when they are working on monitoring their reading and writing, they should see pieces of writing that have been *edited* in some way.

PUTTING THE READING/WRITING CONNECTION INTO ACTION

You want to ensure that you plan to highlight different thinking strategies across the year. You can pair that thinking strategy with a quality of writing to assess for:
1. Independent decision making. You can pair that up with stamina.
2. Activating relevant prior knowledge. You can pair that up with topic/genre choice.
3. Determine importance: You can pair that up with focus.
4. Inferring: You can pair that up with elaboration.
5. Envisioning: You can pair that up with descriptive writing.
6. Synthesizing: You can pair that up with structure.
7. Asking questions: You can pair that up with revision.
8. Monitoring: You can pair that up with editing.
9. Activating knowledge of print: You can pair that up with spelling/phonics.

Connect reading and writing curriculums by process.

Ilyoung and Lynn knew that their students would internalize the reading and writing process if they planned to teach parts of the process at similar times in both reading and writing. In November, Lynn and Ilyoung planned to teach revision in both reading and writ-ing. They planned in reading to engage students in numerous book talks around familiar texts, showing them how their talk and their rereading could deepen or add to their comprehension. In November, they also planned to teach revision in writing. Here, they planned to have students reread their writing and talk to a partner, noticing how their rereading and their talk helped them to deepen or add to their composition of their own text.

I started this chapter by acknowledging that often we inadvertently hide the reading/writing connection from our students. I want to end this chapter by reminding you of the new worlds of learning you'll open up for your students if you deliberately plan a curriculum calendar that embraces the reading/writing connection. Last year, I did a workshop on this topic and a teacher in the front row stared at me with such intensity that I actually started to blush. "I'm sorry," she said, "but I just can't believe how many new opportunities my students will have if I plan my reading/writing curriculum calendars side by side." When you plan the reading and writing story of your year, include in this story the reading/writing connection. I guarantee your story will have a happy ending!

FIGURE 7.2   **Helpful questions to consider when planning yearly reading and writing curriculum calendars.**

Planning Questions

Can I connect my curriculum calendar by *genre?*

  1. Should I plan to teach the genres at the same time?
  2. Should the reading genre Unit of Study come before the writing genre Unit of Study?
  3. Should the writing genre Unit of Study come before the reading genre Unit of Study?

Can I connect my curriculum calendar by *strategy?*

  1. Should I plan to teach the strategies at the same time?
  2. Should the reading strategy come before the writing strategy?
  3. Should the writing strategy come before the reading strategy?

Can I connect my curriculum calendar by *process?*

  1. Should I plan to teach the processes at the same time?
  2. Should the reading process come before the writing process?
  3. Should the writing process come before the reading process?

FOR FURTHER STUDY

Heidi Hayes Jacobs says, "To make sense of our students' experiences over time, we need two lenses: a zoom lens into this year's curriculum for a particular grade and wide-angle lens to see the K–12 perspective" (1997, p. 3).

In order to get a wide-angle lens you might:

Meet with a different grade (or grades) and share curriculum calendars. You might put the different curriculum calendars on large chart paper so that you can carefully study the details. You could:

  1. Look for places where the curriculum calendars meet (or don't meet) standards.
  2. Look for new places to connect reading and writing curriculum calendars.
  3. Look for new ideas on how to celebrate student work.

4. Look for repetitions and gaps between grades and revise when necessary.

In order to get a zoom lens you might:
Meet with colleagues on your grade. Again, you might put the different curriculum calendars on large chart paper. You could:

1. Align the curriculum calendars across your grade, so that you can plan together throughout the year.
2. Choose celebration days for both reading and writing.

3. Study how people in the world celebrate reading and writing and try some of those ways in your own classroom.
4. Add a new study or take a study out.

Align staff development with curriculum calendars. For example, second grade teachers might want to work with a staff developer during a character Unit of Study because they have never done that kind of study before.

PART **III**

TEACHING

Throughout this book, you've seen countless examples of the reciprocity between reading and writing in action; that is, you've seen reading influencing writing and writing influencing reading. In Part II, I highlighted how this reciprocity had the power to affect your planning in miraculous ways, but the benefits of reciprocity go further than just your planning. The reciprocity between reading and writing also has the power to affect your students' learning in equally miraculous ways every day in your classroom. Unfortunately, though, this is not always the case. All of our students, often without us even being aware of it, benefit from the reading/writing connection; however, some students benefit more than others because intuitively they understand how reading and writing connect and can use that connection to learn more every day. These students often don't need any special kind of instruction from us to use the connection. They learn using the reading/writing connection not because of us, but often in spite of us.

In Part III, "Teaching," I'll show you how to teach in ways that make the reciprocity between reading and writing crystal clear so that all of your students benefit equally from this connection. In Chapter 8, I'll begin by suggesting that in order for our students to effectively learn we must carefully craft all of our teaching in similar ways. In Chapter 9, I'll show you how to make the reciprocity between reading and writing clear in your minilessons. In Chapter 10, I'll highlight how to confer, once again making the connection between reading and writing clear. Finally, in Chapter 11, I will explore how to teach small groups across reading and writing. You'll discover throughout all of these chapters that if you carefully craft your teaching toward the reading/writing connection, you'll open up brand-new learning opportunities for all of your students that you never dreamed were possible.

CHAPTER 8

CRAFTING YOUR TEACHING

When I talk about the craft of teaching, I mean the control of certain things we do, which are similar whether we are conferring with a student about research strategies, leading a discussion about the first five chapters of The Woman Warrior, *or explaining to the class the routine for moving from the minilesson into silent writing. (1995, p. 190)*

—Randy Bomer

I believe that the classroom teacher is the single most important factor in students' becoming lifelong and skillful readers and writers. Because of that, I also believe that it's imperative that teachers pay attention to their methods of teaching. As a matter of fact, The National Research Council, after studying effective teachers, found that "effective teachers are able to craft a special mix of instructional ingredients for every child they work with" (Snow et al., 1998, p. 2). Teachers are often bombarded with the notion that somehow there is a proven program that will magically teach every student to read and write. Although many effective teachers in fact use programs in their classroom, they understand that they must alter and modify their programs to better meet the needs of their students (Allington, 2002, p. 17). These teachers understand that although "proven programs" are at times helpful, ultimately they don't teach students to read and write. They know that they are responsible for that. We're far better off focusing our attention on how effective teachers craft their practice than we are searching for some magical program that will solve all of our students' reading and writing problems.

This chapter will address that very important question: How do we craft our teaching in ways that promote more effective learning? Before we dive into chapters that outline particular types of teaching, I want to explore with you some qualities of effective teaching that you can use to hone all of your teaching practices across both writing and reading. Hopefully, through studying these qualities, you'll start to view your teaching as more like them than different, which in turn will bring greater efficiency to all of the ways that you work with your students.

LISTEN TO YOUR STUDENTS

Walter Dean Myers, the renowned children's poet, recently spoke to a group of teachers at Columbia University. When he finished speaking, he asked for questions. One teacher raised her hand and asked him if he had come from a family of talkers, and if this was the case, did that help him become a writer? He paused for a moment, clearly letting the question sink in.

Finally, he shook his head. "No," he said, "I came from a family of listeners." The entire audience sighed in unison. He reminded all of us about the power of listening. We've already seen how vital it is for our students to listen to one another. I'm not talking here about how our students listen to one another, but rather I'm talking about how *we listen to our students*. We must listen to them in order to effectively teach them. I often watch teachers and revel in how they listen to their students. They not only listen to their words, but they also look into their eyes and listen to their hearts. They listen to their students in ways that perhaps they've never been listened to before. This type of listening makes a difference in student learning.

Renowned educator Herbert Kohl reminds us, though, that listening is more complicated than paying attention to what our students do or say. He reminds us that we can't just listen to our students' words, but we must also "listen to ourselves being listened to" (2002, p. 159). When you teach, you'll want to listen to not only to your students, but also to yourself, understanding that a student is taking in every word that comes out of your mouth. Listening in these ways makes it more likely that you'll teach what it is that your students actually need.

STRUCTURE YOUR TEACHING IN CONSISTENT WAYS

We all know that most young students thrive when there are consistent structures in place. They take comfort in the fact that day after day morning meeting is first, and then Reading Workshop follows it. Many in fact become discombobulated when the schedule is somehow changed or altered. Often the same holds true for our teaching. Most of our students will also thrive if we structure our teaching as we do our schedules in both consistent and clear ways. It should not matter whether it's Monday or Wednesday, Reading Workshop or Writing Workshop, our teaching should unfold in a similar manner. When we do this, it frees both our students and ourselves up to more fully focus on the content at hand. When you organize your teaching in a consistent manner, you can focus more on teaching the content and your students can focus more on learning the content.

As you read on, you'll see two main ways that I tend to organize my teaching. One is the *architecture of a minilesson*. I tend to structure all of my minilessons (Chapter 9) using this architecture. I also use this architecture when organizing lessons for small groups (Chapter 11), because essentially I view small group work as a minilesson for a select group of students. The other structure that you'll see is the *architecture of a conference* (Chapter 10). Both of these structures will be explained in more depth in subsequent chapters; however, what I would like to explore next are the commonalties that both these structures share. In Figures 8.1, 8.2, and 8.3 you'll see examples of a minilesson, a conference, and a small group session. Each of these teaching sessions exhibits the common features that I'm about to discuss. These common features are also noted in sidebar boxes next to each transcript.

Connect the known to the unknown.

"Whenever I sit down with a student," Lester Laminack once said at a NCTE conference, "I always start the same way. I always start by telling that student the smart thing that they have done and then I ask them if I can offer them a suggestion." "The great thing is," Lester said, "No student has ever said no!"

How simple but compelling Lester's words are. Lester brings every student in, by starting with what each one already knows, and then using that as a lead-in to teach the unknown. In my stormiest of days, I've begun minilessons by jumping into the new thing I want to teach or worse yet, telling my students what they don't yet know. The same thing has happened in my one-on-one conferences and my small group work.

Research has shown that expert teachers use knowledge about the students in their classrooms—their backgrounds, strengths and weaknesses—to create lessons that connect new subject matter to students' experiences (Leinhardt, 1989; Westerman, 1991). Our teaching will be better received if we start with the known—the strength—just as this research suggests, and then move to the unknown (what needs to be learned). The strength

FIGURE 8.1   Minilesson.

One teaching point

Unit of Study: Personal Narrative

Teaching Point: You can think about what your character is like and then write words (*character action*) that reveal this (*inferring*).

Connection

Connecting the known to the unknown

I know that all of you have been trying to make your writing sound like stories, like Carol began her story by saying, "One spring day," and that sounded similar to ways that Ezra Jack Keats begins his story. He said "One winter morning." Today I want to teach you something else that writers do when they're trying to make their writing sound like a story. They think about what the characters are like in their story and then they put words that would help someone understand that character.

Teach

Teacher is active

Let me show you what I mean. (The teacher picks up the book *The Snowy Day*. She opens it to the page she has posted.) "Crunch, crunch, crunch, his feet sank into the snow. He walked with his toes pointing out, like this. He walked with toes pointing in, like that." What's Peter doing?

(The students yell out together.)

You're right. Peter is walking with his toes pointing out. Peter is walking with his toes pointing in. Peter, the character, is doing something. That's character action. I bet Peter likes the snow so Ezra Jack Keats wrote what Peter does to help us understand that.

Let's look at another book. (This time the teacher has Elder's book and opens his book to the posted page.) "My uncle said we could go to the movies. I jumped up and hugged him." What's Elder doing?

(The students yell out together.)

You're right. He is jumping up and hugging his uncle. Elder, the character, is doing something. That's character action. Elder, what were you feeling here in the story?

Elder: I was excited.

Do you see what Elder did? Elder put down what he was doing to show he was excited.

Active Engagement

Students are active

Okay, let's try it together. Your teacher told me that yesterday you had a surprise party for the librarian. She told me that you were all really excited right before the librarian got there. I'm going to write the words, but you're going to give me the ideas. Let's try and write it so that we put words down about what you were all doing that would show that you were really excited.

I'll start us off. One Wednesday afternoon we all hid in different corners of the room waiting for Ms. Bishop to come to her surprise party. Could you talk to your partner about what you think I should write, making sure that you use lots of character action that shows how excited you were? (The teacher listens in, record-keeping system in hand.)

Link

I've got lots of great ideas that I'll write when you go to gym today. Samantha said I could write that Tasha and Natalie were giggling by the block area—that's what they were doing, character action—and it shows that they were excited. Jose said that Ms. Demartino smiled and put her finger over her lip—that's what she was doing, character action. It shows that she was excited. So today as you write your stories you'll want to think about what the different characters in your story are like and then use character action to show that. Have a great writing time today.

FIGURE 8.2   Transcript of a conference.

<table>
<tr>
<td>

One
teaching
point

</td>
<td>

Teaching Point: You can determine importance.

Leah: Hi Cassie. How is your writing going today?

Cassie: Fine. I am going to write a story about Christmas Eve with my family.

Leah: If I had not come over, what would you have written?

Cassie: Well, I would have written that I had a very nice Christmas Eve party with my family. Everyone was dancing and I wanted to dance too (Cassie giggles) so I did. And then we played find the candy and then we ate dinner and then everyone went home.

Leah: What's the more important part of your story?

Cassie: The most important part was when we were dancing.

</td>
</tr>
<tr>
<td>

Connect-
ing the
known
to the
unknown

</td>
<td>

Leah: I thought that might be because you were laughing when you told that part. Cassie, can I tell you the really smart thing that you did and then offer you a suggestion?

Cassie: Yes.

</td>
</tr>
<tr>
<td>

Teacher
is active

</td>
<td>

Leah: It's so smart that you had an important part to your story, because I bet you've noticed that most stories that you read have important parts to then. One way that you can help somebody understand your important part is to put a lot of words at that part. You'll write your story telling what happens but when you get to the important part you'll want to slow down and write more. Let's try it with your writing. Because the dancing is the important part, what more might you write there?

</td>
</tr>
<tr>
<td>

Student
is active

</td>
<td>

Cassie: Well, I could say I got to the party and took off my sweater but maybe when I got to the dancing I could say the music was on and everybody was dancing my titi my cousin my sister everybody was dancing. Not regular dancing but fooling around and salsa dancing.

Leah: You did it. You said more at the important part, the dancing. Make sure that today and always when you write you help the reader understand your story by writing more at the important part.

Cassie: Okay.

</td>
</tr>
</table>

might be something our students already know from writing that will help them learn a brand-new writing concept, or perhaps it's something they already know from reading that will help them learn a brand-new writing concept. Lester's words guide all of my teaching these days. Every time I work with students, I structure it by beginning with what they already know and then continue by offering them one suggestion.

Have one clear and brief teaching point.

Reading Recovery teachers dazzle me. I watch them work and admire their clear and straightforward way of teaching only one strategy at a time. Even though they only teach one new strategy per session, the students they work with learn quickly under their tutelage. Sometimes, though, in my own haste to get a lot accomplished I do the exact opposite. I try

One teaching point

FIGURE 8.3   Small group work.

Unit of Study: Author Study

Teaching Point: You can determine importance.

Connection

Connecting the known to the unknown

I know that all of you have been writing about important times in your life and that you have been writing your small story long over pages just like real authors. Look at Jemma's. Jemma wrote her small story long over pages, just like a real author. Today I want to teach you another way that authors help themselves write their small stories long.

Teach

One thing that authors do is they read their writing and ask themselves what their writing is mostly about, then they try and put a lot of words at that part. I want you to watch me. First, I'm going to ask myself what my story is mostly about, then I'm going to talk out my story, trying to put a lot of words at the important part.

Teacher is active

Hmm, I'm working on my yoga story. What's this story mostly about? It's mostly about how embarrassed I was when I fell in class. Okay, if that's what my story is mostly about, I should write it putting a lot of words at the embarrassing parts. Okay, let me try:

> One day I went to yoga. I got into class and looked out the window. There were trees and houses and some children playing outside . . . wait a second. I'm putting a lot of words, but it's not at the important part. Let me try again. One day I went to yoga. I got into class and my teacher was already there. "Okay," she said, "let's begin. Lift your right leg into the air. "Oh no!" I thought, "I hope I don't fall." And before I could stop myself, I fell flat on the mat. My face turned bright red as my teacher screamed, "Are you all right?"

Did you notice how first I read my story and thought about what it was mostly about? I then tried to use a lot of words at the important part. The first time I used a lot of words but they weren't at the important part. The second time I told my story I told my story long and I put a lot of words at the important part.

Active Engagement

I'm hoping you can do the same thing. I'm hoping you can continue writing your small stories long, but that you make sure that you put a lot of words down at the important part. Take a moment to read your writing, asking yourselves what's your piece mostly about.

Students are active

Okay, now tell your partner what your piece is mostly about.

Jemma said her piece was mostly about how excited she was that her grandfather was getting out of jail. Where do you think she should put the most words?

Charlie said his piece was mostly about how his cat and dog were fighting. Where do you think he should put the most words?

Link

So today and everyday as you write make sure that you put a lot of words at the important part. I'll be around to admire your work. (Teacher walks around and coaches into the work.)

to teach my students everything under the sun in just one lesson. My students' minds are of course spinning but, most important, although I have "taught" a lot, my students usually have learned very little.

Whenever you're planning for any sort of teaching, you'll want to start by asking yourself, *What will my one teaching point be?* Whenever you finish a one-on-one conference, you should reflect upon that conference by asking, *What is the one thing I just taught?* Asking yourself these questions sounds small but it's not. It will revolutionize your teaching.

Ensure that both you and your students are active.

I hope that throughout this book I've brought home the point that teaching and learning are not synonymous. Effective teachers must organize their instruction so that not only do they have opportunities to teach, but their students also have opportunities to learn the material at hand. At times, I've begun a minilesson passionate about what I'm teaching. I talked and I talked. My students looked at me with blank eyes and said nothing. I was teaching, but more than likely my students didn't learn. My students definitely would have learned more if I had asked them to engage with the material rather than just listen to me talk. Other times, the exact opposite happens. My students talk and talk and talk during a minilesson. I look at them with blank eyes. They're talking and I'm struggling to get a word in edgewise. Here they are active, but I am not. In this instance they would have learned more if I had asked them to stop talking and listen to what I wanted to teach that day. In the end, our students will learn the most if we structure our teaching so that we get opportunities to teach, and our students get opportunities to engage in our instruction so that they can learn.

TEACHERS TEACH USING THE QUALITIES OF GOOD WRITING AND THE COMMON THINKING STRATEGIES ACROSS READING AND WRITING

In Chapter 3, we explored the thinking strategies that readers and writers use and the qualities of writing that connect to those thinking strategies. It's crucial that you keep both of these things in mind whenever you're teaching. When it's appropriate, you'll want to ask yourself which thinking strategy you're teaching. You'll also want to consider what you can look for in your students' writing as evidence that they are beginning to think in those ways. Figure 8.4 outlines both the thinking strategies that you should be teaching and what you can assess for in student writing.

In Figure 8.1, for example, I was teaching the students how to infer. Specifically, I was showing the students how writers first ask themselves, *What is the character in my story like?* Then, they elaborate on him or her in ways that help the reader better understand that particular character. I taught them the thinking strategy of *inferring*; therefore, I could look for evidence of *elaboration* in their writing. In Figures 8.2 and 8.3 I am teaching students how to determine importance; therefore, I could assess their writing looking for parts that were more *focused*. If I found evidence of focus in their work, I would know that they

FIGURE 8.4 The thinking that you'll want to teach and the qualities of writing to assess for.

WHEN YOU TEACH...	LOOK FOR...
Independent Decision Making ⟶	Stamina
Activating Relevant Prior Knowledge ⟶	Topic Choice/Genre Choice
Determining Importance ⟶	Focus
Inferring ⟶	Elaboration
Envisioning ⟶	Descriptive Language
Synthesizing ⟶	Structure
Asking Questions ⟶	Revision
Monitoring ⟶	Editing
Activating Knowledge of Sounds and Letters ⟶	Spelling/Phonics

were probably determining importance while reading and writing. If I didn't, I would know they probably needed more work on this thinking strategy.

TEACHERS TEACH THE SAME CONCEPT OVER TIME ACROSS READING AND WRITING

Often when we conduct a minilesson on a new topic the same six students understand what we've taught and immediately apply it to their reading and writing. The rest of our students, however, carry on reading and writing. It often seems as if our instruction had minimal impact on them. It's impossible for all of our students to understand a complicated concept in just one short lesson. If we want our instruction to reach all of our students, we need to offer more than just one day's worth of instruction on any one topic. There are many ways that we can do this. One way is to continue teaching the same concept but alter our methods of how we teach that concept. For example, in Figure 8.1, I showed students examples from literature where the author had elaborated. More than likely the students will need more than one minilesson on how to elaborate upon important ideas. I could teach subsequent minilessons where, rather than showing them literature that featured elaboration, I could demonstrate what it looks like when an experienced writer thinks in ways that help him or her to elaborate.

Another way I could extend that teaching is to teach the strategy of inferring in reading as well. Perhaps I could read aloud to the students, asking them to pay attention to the character action in the text and then infer about what they thought those characters were like based upon some of their actions. You can imagine if I taught inferring over time in both writing and in reading all of my students would have a better chance of understanding it.

TEACHERS ASSESS AND REFLECT UPON THE EFFECTIVENESS OF THEIR TEACHING

During my first year of teaching, I learned how to take a running record, and soon I became the running record queen. Every day, during Reading Workshop I assessed my students through running records. When I was finished taking a running record, I would place it into a big file with the previous running records I had taken. I felt very proud, especially when the file was bursting with papers. The problem, however, was that the papers remained in the file and never had much impact on what I taught from day to day. I had assessed my students but I never reflected on my findings. Once, Randy Bomer visited my school and encouraged my colleagues and I to regularly discuss our assessments with one another. What a difference these conversations with my colleagues made to my teaching! Our conversations helped me to use my assessments to develop minilessons, organize for small group work, and prepare my one-on-one conferences.

Sometimes we reflect by having conversations with our colleagues as I did in the previous example, but sometimes we reflect by simply paying closer attention to our students in the midst of our teaching. For example, I can observe my class reading on Monday and notice a particular issue. I might in the midst of this observation reflect upon what I saw and make a note to tweak my lesson on Tuesday. I might notice a look of confusion in a student's eyes during a conference, reflect upon that look, and immediately change my line of questioning. In the end it doesn't matter how or when you assess as long as you pair that assessment up with time for reflection.

At a conference at Lesley College, Barbara Watson recently said, "It's up to us to provide powerful teaching, so that children can move or better yet leap forward." I believe as Barbara believes that in the end it's the way that we craft our teaching that makes the biggest difference in our students' lives. I take enormous comfort in the fact we can craft this teaching in similar ways and then use those same ways over and over, helping our students to leap forward in their development as readers and as writers.

FOR FURTHER STUDY

- Transcribe your teaching (minilessons, conferences, or small group work).
  1. Did you connect the known to the unknown?
  2. Did you have one teaching point?
  3. What was your method of teaching?
  4. Did your student(s) have the opportunity to engage in that teaching point?

Reflect upon your transcripts.
  1. How might you revise your lesson if you were to do it again?
  2. What might you teach next? In reading? In writing?

CHAPTER 9

MINILESSONS

In minilessons we teach into our students' intentions. Our students are first deeply engaged in their self-sponsored work, and then we bring them together to learn what they need to know in order to do that work. This way, they stand a chance of being active meaning-makers, even during this bit of formal instruction. (1994, p. 193)

—Lucy Calkins

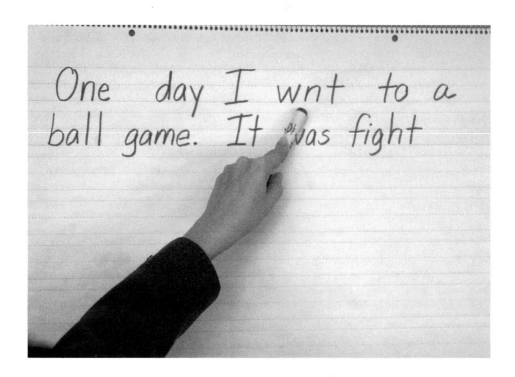

Human beings are always trying to make meaning. It doesn't matter whether we are speaking with a friend, painting a picture, singing, dancing, or writing. Ultimately, what we want to do is to make meaning. It's no different when we conduct reading and writing minilessons for our students. Our goals in these minilessons should be the same: for our students to learn or to make meaning from what we teach. This chapter will outline ways to use the reading/writing connection to help your students make more meaning from your minilessons. First, I'll show you how to align your methods and structures across your reading and writing minilessons. Then, I'll continue to blur the lines between reading and writing by suggesting that you can also align the content across your reading and writing minilessons. All of this will help you continue to bring the reciprocity between reading and writing to life in your classroom.

We'll start by examining both a reading minilesson (Figure 9.1) and a writing minilesson (Figure 9.2), noticing the similar ways that they are organized. Both of these minilessons took place in October of first grade, the reading minilesson occurring one day prior

FIGURE 9.1   Reading minilesson.

Unit of Study: Early Reading Strategies
Teaching Point: You can reread and check what you're read. You can monitor what you read.
Method: Demonstration

Connection

Readers, I've noticed that all of you have been working very hard at tricky words trying to make them look right. That's smart reading work. Keep doing that. I've also noticed that after you do that hard work of making the word look right you're not sure if you figured the word out.

Today I want to teach you something that you can do to check to see if you have indeed figured the word out. You can reread the entire sentence and check the word once again asking yourself three questions: *Does the word make sense? Does the word sound right? Does the word look right?* When you reread and check what you've read, it helps you to make sure you've understood your book.

I'm going to show you what I mean. (The teacher takes out the book *The Carrot Seed* by Ruth Kraus.) I'm going to read *The Carrot Seed* in front of you. You're going to watch how after I work at getting a word to look right, I make sure it's right by rereading the sentence and asking myself three questions: *Does the word make sense? Does the word sound right? Does the word look right?* After you watch me do this, I'm going to have you help me.

Teach

(The teacher begins reading. She models both her reading and her thinking.)

"A little boy planted a carrot seed. His mother said, 'I'm. . .'" (The teacher stops. The next word is *afraid.*)

Here comes a longer word. Let me try and figure out this word. Let me see if I can find a part I know. Hey, I know *aid.* (She points to "aid" inside of the word *afraid.*)

Let me see if I can figure out the word now. I think the word is *afraid.* Let me reread the whole sentence to check if I'm right. After I reread, I'll ask myself those three questions.

(continued)

FIGURE 9.1 Continued

"His mother said 'I'm afraid it won't come up." Does *afraid* make sense? Yes. Does *afraid* sound right? Yes. Does *afraid* look right? (The teacher points to the word *afraid* as she says this.) Yes. I must be right.

Did you see what I did? Did you see how I reread, asking myself three questions? Does *afraid* make sense? I said yes. Does *afraid* sound right? I said yes. Does *afraid* look right? I said yes. It must be *afraid*. Do you see how when I reread and checked my reading it helped me to make sure I understood the book?

Active Engagement

Let's try it together. (The teacher reads on until she gets to the page that says, "Every day the little boy pulled up the weeds around the seed and sprinkled the ground with water." She stops in the middle of the sentence when she gets to the word *sprinkled*.)

Okay, here is a long word. (The teacher points to *sprinkled*.) Let's try and figure it out. Turn to a partner and see if you can find a word inside of this word.

(The students work for a moment in partnerships.)

Okay, I heard some of you say "sprinkled." You found the word *ink* in it. (The teacher points to the small word *ink* inside of *sprinkled*.) Let's check it by rereading the whole sentence. (The teacher points to the sentence and the students read along. After she finishes reading she asks:)

Does *sprinkled* make sense? "Every day the little boy pulled up the weeds around the seed and sprinkled the ground with water." (The students yell out "Yes!")

Does *sprinkled* sound right? "Every day the little boy pulled up the weeds around the seed and sprinkled the ground with water." (The students yell out "Yes!")

Does *sprinkled* look right? (The teacher runs her pointer underneath the word *sprinkled*.)

(The students yell out "Yes!")

Link

What we did together today you can always do when you read. You can reread when you get to a tricky part and check what you've read, asking yourself, *Does it make sense? Does it sound right? Does it look right?* It will help you make sure that you understand your books. Have a great reading time.

FIGURE 9.2 Writing minilesson.

Unit of Study: We write in many forms for many reasons.
Teaching Point: You can reread and check your writing. You can monitor your writing.
Method: Demonstration

Connection

Writers, remember how in reading we learned how to reread, checking our reading by asking three questions: *Does it make sense? Does it sound right? Does it look right?* Remember how yesterday we were reading *The Carrot Seed*. (The teacher holds up the book *The Carrot Seed*.) We got to the word *sprinkled*. The teacher points to the word *sprinkled*. We weren't sure if we had read the word correctly so we went back and reread the whole sentence.

FIGURE 9.2   Continued

We asked ourselves three questions: *Does the word* sprinkled *make sense? Does the word* sprinkled *sound right? Does the word* sprinkled *look right?*

It's very similar in writing. We can reread and check what we've written asking ourselves three questions, just like we do in reading. These three questions will help us check our writing, just like they helped us to check our reading: *Does the word I wrote make sense? Does the word I wrote sound right? Does the word I wrote look right?*

If one of your words doesn't make sense, sound right, or look right you can rewrite so that it does. When you reread and check your writing, you help the person reading your writing understand what you've written.

Sometimes when we read our independent reading books we point to the words. I'm going to do the same thing when I reread my writing. I'm going to point to each word as I read. I want you to notice how I reread and check my writing, rewriting parts that don't look right, sound right, or make sense. First you'll watch me and then you'll help me.

Teach

(Text on the chart says: *I wnt to the ball game. My sister. went too. We both ate a heart dog. It waz fun.*)

(The teacher points to each word as she reads.) I wnt

Hmm . . . "wnt"—that doesn't look right. Let me try and rewrite it so it does look right. (The teacher writes *went* above it.) I went to the ball game. Okay, let me reread and check.

I went to the ball game. Does that sentence make sense?

(The students answer yes.)

I went to the ball game. Does that sentence sound right?

(The students answer yes.)

Does *went* look right? (She is pointing to the word went.)

(The students answer yes.)

Let me keep going. "I went to the ball game. My sister went." (The teacher takes a long pause because there is a period.)

I don't want readers to stop here. That doesn't sound right. I better take away the period. Hmm: "My sister went too." Okay, let me reread and check.

My sister went too. Does that make sense?

(The students say yes.)

My sister went too. Does that sound right?

(The students say yes.)

My sister went too. Do my words look right?

(The students say yes.)

"We both ate a heart dog." "A heart dog"—that doesn't make sense. People don't eat heart dogs. They eat hot dogs. That makes more sense. (She writes the word *hot* above the word *heart.*) Let me reread and check.

We both ate a hot dog. Does that make sense?

(continued)

FIGURE 9.2   Continued

(The students answer yes.)

We both ate a hot dog. Does that sound right?

(The students answer yes.)

We both ate a hot dog. Do my words look right?

(The students answer yes.)

(The teacher stops and now talks to the students.)

Did you notice how I reread, pointing to each word? I stopped here because "wnt" didn't look right. (She is pointing to the word *went.*) I rewrote it so it did look right. Here I stopped because putting the period here didn't sound right. (She is pointing to the place where she took away the period.) I took the period out so it would sound right. And here I stopped because "heart dog" didn't make sense so I rewrote it so it did make sense. (She is pointing to the word *hot.*)

Active Engagement

Let's try it together with this sentence: "It waz fun." (She points as she reads.) Talk to a partner. Is there anything I should change?

After the students talked in partnerships, they changed "waz" to "was" because it didn't look right. Again, they practiced rereading the whole sentence saying, "Does it make sense? Does it sound right? Does it look right?"

Link

The reason why I showed you how to reread and check your writing is because today and every day I want you to reread your own writing just like you read your independent reading books: stopping, checking, and rewriting when things don't look right, sound right, or make sense. This will help the people who read your writing understand it.

Today we're going to practice rereading for the first five minutes of Writing Workshop. You're going to start today by rereading one of your letters. Reread the letter with your finger checking that your sentences and words look right, sound right, and make sense. If you find something that doesn't, rewrite it above. We'll talk about how that went today during share. Have a great writing time.

---

to the writing minilesson. In both minilessons the goal was to help students *monitor* their reading and writing. It's interesting to note that in the writing minilesson the students monitor their writing by reading it. The reading and rereading that these students do adds to or *complements* their writing.

THE PURPOSE OF YOUR MINILESSONS SHOULD BE CLEAR TO YOUR STUDENTS

Minilessons are another important place to teach students specific strategies for how to comprehend and compose. Often, though, we teach students a particular strategy in a minilesson, but we neglect to show them how that particular strategy will help them further comprehend and compose. For example, we might teach students how to connect a book to their lives, but we don't explicitly show them how making this connection will help them further comprehend.

Let's take a look how the purposes in the minilessons in Figure 9.1 and 9.2 are made clear to the students. In the reading minilessons, the teacher clearly lets the students know that rereading and checking what they've read will help them comprehend. She says, "When you reread and check what you've read, it helps you to make sure you've understood the book." In the writing minilesson the teacher lets the students know that rereading and checking what they've written will help the reader understand their writing. She says, "When you reread and check your writing, you help the person reading your writing understand what you wrote."

When planning minilessons, I find it helpful to slow down and literally ask myself, *How will the strategy I taught today help students better comprehend or better compose?* I take my answer and make sure it's tucked inside the start of my minilesson.

THE STRUCTURE OF YOUR MINILESSONS SHOULD BE CONSISTENT

Recently, I worked with a group of teachers helping them to fine-tune their minilessons. We spent a lot of time transcribing the minilessons using a structure that The Reading and Writing Project at Columbia University calls *the architecture of a minilesson.* This architecture was first introduced in Chapter 8. There are brilliant teachers around the world who don't use this particular structure, but I've found that my teaching is more successful when I adapt some type of consistent structure. Figure 9.3 outlines this architecture, explaining the different parts, and also providing helpful language.

The architecture of a minilesson takes into account all of the qualities of effective teaching. This is why I use it whenever I teach a minilesson and I also recommend it to the teachers that I work with. Let's once again look at the same two minilessons in Figure 9.1 and Figure 9.2, but this time let's focus on their architecture and how this particular architecture helps students make more meaning.

The connection.

Everyday in countless classrooms, teachers gather their students together and begin teaching. It happens over and over again. We often do it without thinking—it becomes habitual—but we know that in life and in teaching first impressions matter. The beginning of a minilesson is often called the connection. You'll want to make sure that in your connection you give a good first impression. Pay attention in your minilesson to how your first words will hit your students' ears. Will those words engage and inspire? Will they anger and despair?

It's often inspiring to begin your minilessons by starting with what students already know. Let's take a look at how this teacher begins her minilessons. In the reading miniles-

FIGURE 9.3   The architecture of a reading and writing minilesson.

STRUCTURE	WHY	HOW	HELPFUL LANGUAGE
Connection	To inspire To engage To make use of prior knowledge To connect to previous learning	You can connect to your reading minilesson. You can connect to your writing minilesson. You can connect to another part of the day. You can connect to student work. You can connect to what you have observed by watching your students.	I know that in reading . . . I know that in writing . . . Yesterday Jose did something in his writing that I want to share because it will help all of us. Yesterday when I was watching you read I noticed that . . .
Teach	To focus instruction To equip students to improve their reading and writing	Demonstration. Show and tell (give examples).	Watch me as I . . . Did you notice how I . . . I want to show you a writer who did this . . .
Active Engagement	To help students learn by speaking and listening to one another To provide practice and support	Everyone tries it together on a well-known shared text. Everybody tries it in his or her own reading and writing.	Now we're going to try it together . . . Now you're going to try it on your own for a moment here on the rug . . .
Link	To encourage students to use what they learned on any given day while they read or write on their own	Rename what was taught and let them know they can use that skill/strategy not just today, but every day.	What we just did together you can do all by yourself.

son (Figure 9.1) the teacher uses the strengths she's observed in her students as a lead-in to their needs. She says,

> Readers, I've noticed that all of you have been working very hard at tricky words trying to make them look right. That's very smart reading work. Keep doing that. I've also noticed that after you do that hard work of making the word look right you're not sure if you figured the word out. Today I want to teach you something that you can do to check to see if you have indeed figured the word out.

Note that she made sure that there was a correlation between the strength that she observed and the need that she was about to teach.

In the writing minilesson (Figure 9.2), the teacher inspires her students by showing them what they already know about this writing skill from what they learned previously about it in *reading*. She says,

> Writers, remember how in reading we learned how to reread, checking our reading by asking three questions: *Does it make sense? Does it sound right? Does it look right?* Remember how yesterday we were reading *The Carrot Seed*. (The teacher holds up the book *The Carrot Seed*.) We got to the word *sprinkled*. The teacher points to the word *sprinkled*. We weren't sure if we have read the word correctly so we went back and reread the whole sentence. We asked ourselves three questions: *Does the word* sprinkled *make sense? Does the word* sprinkled *sound right? Does the word* sprinkled *look right?* It's very similar in writing. We can reread and check what we've written asking ourselves the same three questions, just like we do in reading.

Both of these connections (among others listed in Figure 9.3) engage and inspire students and can be used across both reading and writing.

The teach.

Next, we teach one strategy. In both minilessons, the students were taught how to go and back and reread. The teacher deliberately didn't demonstrate how to draw carefully detailed pictures nor did she mention how her story went in sequential order. She didn't mention those things because if she had it would have taken her students' focus off the main teaching point. It's important that we avoid what Lucy Calkins calls the "mentioning curriculum" and instead teach just one thing in each minilesson.

Let's see how this is done. In both minilessons, the teacher teaches by demonstrating the process in front of the students. In both, she sets up the demonstration by telling the students what she would like them to notice. She also let's them know that after the demonstration they will try out what's being demonstrated. For example, in the reading minilesson she says,

> I'm going to show what I mean. (The teacher takes out the book *The Carrot Seed* by Ruth Kraus.) I'm going to read *The Carrot Seed* in front of you. You're going to watch how after I work at getting a word to look right, I make sure it's right by rereading and asking myself three questions: *Does it make sense? Does it sound right? Does it look right?* After you watch me do this, I'm going to have you help me.

In the writing minilesson she says,

> I'm going to point to each word as I read my writing just like we sometimes do when we read our independent books. I want you to notice how I reread and check my writing, rewriting parts that don't look right, sound right, or make sense. First you'll watch me and then you'll help me.

After she sets up her demonstration, she demonstrates the concept by thinking, talking, reading, and writing in front of them. She ends her demonstration by circling back to what she had asked them to look for in the first place. For example, in the reading minilesson (Figure 9.1) she says,

> Did you see what I did? Did you see how I reread asking myself three questions? Does *afraid* make sense? I said yes. Does *afraid* sound right? I said yes. Does *afraid* look right? I said yes. It must be *afraid.* Do you see how when I reread and checked my reading it helped me to make sure I understood the book?

In the writing minilesson (Figure 9.2) she says,

> Did you notice how I reread, pointing to each word? I stopped here because "wnt" didn't look right. I rewrote it so it did look right. Here I stopped because putting the period here didn't sound right. I took the period out so it would sound right. And here I stopped because "heart dog" didn't make sense so I rewrote it so it did make sense.

Note also that this particular teacher set up her *materials* in both reading and writing to match her teaching point. She had already decided which pages in *The Carrot Seed* to stop and pause at and which pages to read quickly. She set up the reading of the book in this fashion so that she could ensure that she stopped only on the pages that best illustrated her teaching point. In writing, the teacher has also carefully set up her materials. She has a chart already written with particular errors to correct. She chose one place where the word *didn't look right,* one place where the sentence *didn't sound right,* and one place where the sentence *didn't make sense.* When you set up your materials in this manner, you help your students learn by not muddling your teaching point with any extraneous information. You also save previous time by getting directly what you want to teach.

I want to talk for a moment about the methods for your teaching. After I finished transcribing the minilessons for the book I coauthored with Lucy Calkins, *Launching the Writing Workshop,* Lucy commented that 95 percent of the minilessons I wrote were demonstration; that is, my main method for conducting minilessons was to ask students to watch me as I modeled the strategy in front of them. I realized from this conversation that demonstration, although not the only method, is a very powerful way to teach young students, because in a demonstration the students are explicitly shown the kinds of thinking that an experienced reader or writer uses while composing and comprehending. Figure 9.3 suggests some helpful language to use while demonstrating. Along with demonstration, I also find myself showing students clear examples in literature of what I'm trying to teach and then talking a little bit about those examples. Figure 9.3 also suggests language you might use when utilizing different teaching methodologies.

The active engagement.

Up to this point in the lesson, the teacher has been speaking and the students have been listening. The active engagement gives the students time to interact with what has been presented and gives the teachers time to coach individuals or groups of students in what they just taught. Sometimes during an active engagement the students try a strategy together on one shared text, while other times the students try out the strategy in their own reading or writing text.

In this particular reading minilesson (Figure 9.1), the teacher has the students engage by monitoring their own reading with a shared reading text. It's the same in the writing minilesson (Figure 9.2). The teacher also has the students engage by monitoring their own writing with a shared writing text. In both active engagements, the teacher listens in, coaches, and records what she notices. Active engagements should be short. It is a time for everyone to simply *try out* what was taught, not to *master* what was taught.

The link.

Just like beginnings matter, so do endings. You want to end your minilesson in a way that shows students how to use what was just taught in their ongoing work. Although it's not essential for every student to put what you taught that day into use immediately (but instead over time), it is essential that you end your minilesson in a way that helps the students to understand *when and why* they might use what was just taught. In both the reading and the writing minilessons, the teacher lets the students know when they should use what was taught and why they should use what was taught. For example, in the reading minlesson she says,

> What we did together today you can always do when you read. You can reread when you get to a tricky part and check what you've read, asking yourself, *Does it make sense? Does it sound right? Does it look right?* It will help you make sure that you understand your books.

In the writing lesson she says,

> The reason why I showed you how to reread and check your writing is because today and every day I want you to reread your own writing just like you read your independent reading books: stopping, checking, and rewriting when things don't look right, sound right, or make sense. This will help the people who read your writing understand it.

Having links such at these in your minilessons help students consider about whether or not they are going to use the strategy presented today. It also gives teachers a chance to assess (and teach into) how students are making their decisions.

CONNECTING THE READING MINILESSON TO THE WRITING MINILESSON

So far, we've connected the reading and writing minilessons by aligning methods and structures. Now, we're going to look at how to align reading and writing minilessons by their content. We'll continue to study the same two minilessons (Figures 9.1 and 9.2). You'll see through these examples that when done carefully the reading minilesson can be a vehicle to teach students more about *both reading and writing,* and the writing minilesson can be a vehicle to teach students more about *both writing and reading.* Hopefully, looking at how to align the content of these two minilessons will help you craft the content of your own minilessons in similar ways.

Just tell the students how the two minilessons connect.

Quite simply, tell your students how what they're doing today in writing is similar to what they previously did in reading. For example, in the writing minilesson this teacher says,

> It's very similar in writing. We can reread and check what we've written, just like we can reread and check what we've read. We can ask ourselves the same three questions to see if we have figured it out.

This is not as easy as it sounds. In order to articulate this, you must plan for *what you'll say* and *how you'll say it.* You'll have to literally ask yourself what you've done recently in reading that is similar to what you're about to do in writing. Then, you'll have to choose the appropriate language to relay this information to your students.

Retell a previous reading minilesson.

If you want students to bring a reading strategy over to their writing, it's helpful to retell a time when they used this particular reading strategy together. For example, in the writing minilesson the teacher retells a time when the class reread and monitored their reading together:

> Remember how yesterday we were reading *The Carrot Seed.* (The teacher holds up the book *The Carrot Seed.*) We got to the word *sprinkled.* The teacher points to the word *sprinkled.* We weren't sure if we had read the word correctly so we went and reread the whole sentence. We asked ourselves three questions: *Does the word* sprinkled *make sense? Does the word* sprinkled *sound right? Does the word* sprinkled *look right?*

Again, this is not as easy as it looks. If you decide to retell a familiar reading or writing experience, you'll want to choose the clearest and most appropriate example and then retell it in a way that's short, but highlights the connection.

Use the same or similar language across the two minilessons.

One way that our students will know that what we're teaching is similar across reading and writing is if we use the same or similar language. Herbert Kohl reminds us that "how you think you are speaking and how your students interpret what you are saying are not necessarily the same" (2002, p.150). We can help to align what we say to what our students hear by choosing our words carefully and then aligning that language across reading and writing. Our most articulate students learn even when we're not consistent with our words, but all of our students will learn more if we use similar language across our reading and writing minilessons. This is especially pertinent to our English language learners.

In both the reading and writing minilesson the teacher referred to the strategy of "rereading and checking." She also referred to the same three questions (*Does it make sense? Does it sound right? Does it look right?*). Her language across reading and writing was exactly the same. Because of this her students would have an easier time understanding that the monitoring they did in reading was in fact similar to the monitoring they did in writing.

Use materials from the reading minilesson in your writing minilesson.

Language certainly helps you to make a reading/writing connection, but it's not enough, especially for our English language learners. When our teaching relies primarily on language, many of our students lose meaning. We need to also use materials in our minilessons that provide concrete examples alongside our language.

In Figure 9.2, the teacher brings the book *The Carrot Seed* to the writing minilesson to remind the students about the monitoring work they had done previously in reading. This book was very familiar to the students, because the class had read it many times. The teacher didn't simply hold the book up, but rather she used it to give a visual aid to her words. She said,

> Remember how yesterday we were reading *The Carrot Seed*. (The teacher holds up the book *The Carrot Seed*.) We got to the word *sprinkled*. The teacher points to the word *sprinkled*. We weren't sure if we have read the word correctly so we went and reread the whole sentence." (She runs her the pointer underneath the entire sentence.)

If the students didn't understand or missed the teacher saying the words "reread and check," they had another chance to make meaning when the teacher pointed to the book or when she ran the pointer underneath the sentence that contained the word *sprinkled*. Obviously, the teacher had to plan for what reading/writing materials she would use and also how she would interact with these materials during the minilesson.

CONNECTING THE WRITING MINILESSON TO THE READING MINILESSON

We just looked at how the reading minilesson can *enhance* or *complement* the writing minilesson. Now, we're going to flip it. We're going to now study two more minilessons, this time seeing how the writing minilesson can enhance or complement the reading minilesson. These next two minilessons (see Figures 9.4 and 9.5) took place in March in a second grade classroom in the midst of a nonfiction study. Specifically, in these two minilessons, the teacher is showing the students how to use the table of contents to plan what they'll write and read. We've talked so far about four ways to use the reading minilesson to teach your writing minilesson.

1. You can simply tell the students how the reading and the writing minilesson connect.
2. During the writing minilesson, you can retell a time when they tried something similar in the reading minilesson.

FIGURE 9.4   Nonfiction writing minilesson.

Unit of Study: Nonfiction
Teaching Point: You can use the table of contents to help you plan what you want to write (Rehearsal).
Method: Demonstration

Connection

Remember, yesterday we looked at the table of contents during reading and we noticed that a table of contents tells us what a particular part of a book is going to be about. (The teacher is pointing to a table of contents in a book as she says this.) It also tell us what page you'll find that part on. (The teacher now points to the page number.) Here in this book you see that on page 6 you'll learn about "What Snails Eat."

Today I want to teach you how to use the table of contents to plan what you'll teach in your writing. First, I'm going to show you what that looks like and then we'll together.

Teach

Watch me. (The teacher pulls out an empty dog book. The book is empty except for the table of contents.) Watch how I use the table of contents to plan what I'm going to write. My table of contents says that page one should be about what dogs look like, so let me turn to page 1. On page 1, I should write information that teaches people about what dogs look like. Maybe I'll write some dogs are black and some are white. They are usually soft and furry. They have long pointy tails and a wet nose.

The teacher turns back to the students. Did you notice how I read my table of contents to help myself plan what I should write? I read the part where it said "What Dogs Look Like . . . Page 1." (The teacher points to the part of the table of contents that says that.) I turned to that page and began my plan. I taught people about what dogs look like. My table of contents helped me to plan what I would teach.

Active Engagement

Now, let's try it together. The teacher pulls out an empty cat book. (The book is empty except for the table of contents.) Will you read the table of contents? Use that to plan what we should write on this first page.

(The students stop and talk in partnerships.)

I heard many of you talking about what cats look like. Some of you said that we should write that some cats are black and other cats are white. Some of you said that we should write that cats have long whiskers and a soft body. Some of you said that we should write that cats have sharp claws. All of you looked at the first part of the table of content to help yourself plan what we should teach on that page. (The teacher points to the table of contents where it says "What Cats Look Like . . . Page 1.) I'm telling you that because you can do the same thing in your own books. You can look at your own table of contents to help yourself plan what you'll teach on each page.

Link

So today and every day as you write, look at your table of contents to plan what you'll teach on each page. Have a great writing time today.

FIGURE 9.5   Nonfiction reading minilesson.

Unit of Study: Nonfiction
Teaching Point: You can use the table of contents to help you plan what you're going to read (Rehearsal).
Method: Demonstration

Connection

In writing, remember how I used the table of contents to help myself plan for what I wanted to write. Remember how I was writing a dog book and I looked at my table of contents to help me plan what to write. (The teacher has her nonfiction dog book with her. She points to the table of contents when she talks about the table of contents.) Remember I looked at the part that said what dogs look like (the teacher points to that part of the table of contents) and then I wrote words that taught people about what dogs look like. (The teacher turns to the page and points to the part where she wrote that.)

It's similar in reading. You can use the table of contents in reading to help you plan what you want to read just like you used the table of contents in writing to help you plan what you wanted to write.

Today, I'm going to read the table of contents from the book *Is It a Fish?* First, you're going to watch me use the table of contents to plan what I want to read and then we're going to try it together.

Teach

(The teacher uses the book *Is It a Fish?* by Brian and Julian Cutting. She has put the pages of the text on overhead transparencies.)

Okay, this book is called *Is It a Fish?* I'm going to learn all about fish. Let me look at the table of contents so I can plan what I want to learn today. (The teacher looks at the table of contents.) What should my plan be today? Well, I think that I should read page 2, "What Is a Fish?" (the teacher points to that part of the table of contents) because it will help me understand everything else I'll learn about fish. Then, I think I want to learn about strange fish. I'm writing a book about fish during Writing Workshop and I would love to put something in there about strange fish. Okay, now that I have a plan, let me start my plan by turning to page 2.

Did you see what I did? Did you see how I planned what I would read by first looking at the table of contents (the teacher points to the table of contents) and then I started my plan by turning to page 2.

Active Engagement

Okay, let's try it together. (The teacher puts the same table of contents on the overhead.) Read this with a partner and talk about what your plan would be if you were reading this book. (The teacher walks around, record-keeping system in hand.)

Link

Tony and Pablo were reading the table of contents in their book. They said they would read page 10 because they would like to learn more about a fish's backbone. Looking at the table of contents helped them to plan what they would learn.

Angela and Samantha looked at the table of contents and when they got to the part that said "underwater animals" (the teacher points to that part on the table of contents), they said that their plan would be to read that page because Samantha wants to write a book about fish and she doesn't know if all fish live underwater.

What we just did together you can do by yourself during Reading Workshop. So today and every day as you read please make sure that you read the table of contents to help you plan what you'll learn that day. Have a great reading time.

3. You can use similar language in both minilessons.
4. You can use materials from reading in your writing minilesson.

We can use these same four techniques when we use the writing minilesson to teach our reading minilesson. In the nonfiction reading minilesson, the teacher first *tells them how this reading minilesson connects to a previous writing minilesson.* She says,

> It's similar in reading. You can use the table of contents in reading to help you plan what you want to read just like you used the table of contents in writing to help plan what you wanted to write.

She also *retells a familiar writing experience during the reading minilesson.* She says,

> In writing, remember how I used the table of contents to help myself plan for what I wanted to teach? Remember how I was writing a dog book and I looked at my table of contents to help me plan what to write. (The teacher has her nonfiction dog book with her. She points to the table of contents when she talks about the table of contents.) Remember I looked at the part that said what dogs look like (the teacher points to that part) and then I wrote words that taught people about what dogs look like.

She uses *similar language,* "plan what you want to write and plan what you want to read," across reading and writing. She brings *materials from the writing minilesson to the reading minilesson.* She brings the dog book from the writing minilesson to the reading minilesson.

Once again these two minilessons exemplify the idea that when you blur the lines between reading and writing carefully you quadruple your students' opportunities to learn complicated concepts. The reading minilesson in Figure 9.5 will not only help students use the table of contents while reading, but it will also add to and improve upon how the students use the table of contents while writing. Likewise the writing minilesson in Figure 9.4 will not only help the students use the table of contents while writing, but it will also add to and improve upon how the students use the table of contents while reading. Figure 9.6 lists some questions to ask while planning and teaching for reading/writing connections.

FIGURE 9.6   Questions to ask while planning and teaching with the reading/writing connection in mind.

1. Is there anything that I have already taught in writing (or reading) that is similar to what I am about to teach in reading (or writing)?

2. What language will I use in my reading and writing minilesson to show the connection?

3. Is there a pertinent reading experience or a pertinent writing experience I want to retell to help my students see the connection? How can I retell this experience in such a way so that it's short but highlights the connection?

4. Are there materials from the reading minilesson (or writing minilesson) that I want to use in my writing minilesson? (reading minilesson?) How will I use these materials during the minilesson to highlight my teaching point?

EXTEND MINILESSONS ACROSS TIME AND ACROSS SUBJECT AREAS

I usually do not recommend that teachers "force" every student to try out what was just taught in any one given minilesson. Teachers often worry when I say this, questioning how they'll know whether a student "gets it" unless they ask him to try it. In the beginning of my career, I had the pleasure of spending nine Thursdays watching Joanne Hindley, author of *In the Company of Children,* teach. One day after doing a minilesson, she turned to me and said, "A good minilesson opens up a problem, it doesn't solve it."

Those words have remained with me. When we teach a ten-minute minilesson, we're kidding ourselves if we think that all of students will actually "get it" in those ten minutes of instruction. Often, I find that if we do in fact ask every student to try the minilesson we end up ignoring the students who we know will get it. We spend all of our time conferring with the other students, and in our efforts to get them to do it, we often do it for them. I worry that in the end nobody is benefiting from this. The question still remains, however: How do we take this problem that we've "opened up" in our minilesson and "solve it" for all of our students?

One way to help all of our students internalize the minilesson is to teach that same material over time in both writing and reading. After we have done this, we most certainly can and should expect our students to use what was taught. Next, we'll look at how a teacher has done this. In Figure 9.7 you see a series of writing and reading minilessons that extend what was taught in the previous table of contents minilessons. These writing and reading minilessons if taught simultaneously have the potential to take the "problem" that was opened up and solve it by giving those students varied instruction over time on the same material.

FIGURE 9.7   Teaching the table of contents across time in both Writing and Reading Workshops.

WRITING	READING
I can use the table of contents to plan (or Rehearse) what I want to write.	I can use the table of contents to plan (or Rehearse) what I want to read.
I can plan to put the important information first in my table of contents. What information should I teach first? (Determining Importance)	I can reread the table of contents and ask, *What's important for me to read first? second?* (Determining Importance)
I can revise my plan and change my table of contents.	I can revise my plan and read new parts of the book.
I can put like things together in my table of contents. (Synthesize)	I can read the table of contents. Which things would make sense to read together? (Synthesize)
I can check my table of contents to see if it matches the text I wrote. (Revise)	Before I start a new book, I can revisit the table of contents to see if I missed anything important. (Revise)

Teaching minilessons across time in the Writing Workshop.

There are two things I want to point out. The teacher purposely began her series of table of contents minilessons with a more open lesson, letting the students know they can use the table of contents to plan their writing. She fully expects that students will use this first table of contents minilesson in a variety of ways. After that, she went to the smaller strategies, specifically teaching the different ways that the students could use the table of contents throughout the process to help them plan their writing.

I believe that when you begin, you must understand where you're going. It's tempting to give students a part, a part, a part, and then wind up with the whole at the end. The problem is that the parts make no sense unless you have a sense of the whole from the very beginning. I tend to begin with the end in mind because I know that it'll be slightly chaotic but informative on that first day. It will also encourage students to become independent. If you give students only the parts, they'll have no choice but to do only the part that you showed them. If they begin also having the end in mind, they're more likely to try out the new concept in new and unexpected ways.

I also often figure out what to teach by observing my students. This particular teacher, for example, noticed that her students made their table of contents haphazardly, not paying attention to what information a reader would need first, second, and so on. Therefore, on subsequent days she decided to teach them how to pay attention to that.

Teaching minilessons across time in the Reading Workshop.

What can we glean from looking at how this teacher teaches the similar concept of table of contents in reading? First, although she blurs the lines between the reading minilesson and the writing minilesson, she is clear on what she is teaching in both reading and writing. In one of the writing minilessons, for example, she teaches the students how to synthesize by putting like information together in their table of contents. She knows this will help them *compose* nonfiction texts. In the reading minilesson, she teaches them to synthesize by reading like information together from the table of contents. She knows this will help them *comprehend* nonfiction texts.

Now that she is clear on what she is teaching in both writing and reading, she can blur the lines. In this particular instance she looked at what she was teaching in writing and asked herself if she could teach a similar strategy in reading. She could have done the exact opposite—that is, she could have looked at what she was teaching in reading and *asked* if she could teach a similar strategy in writing.

SHOULD THE WRITING MINILESSON OR THE READING MINILESSON COME FIRST?

When I taught a course on minilessons at the Summer Writing Institute, one of the participants asked me if I would start by teaching a concept in the reading minilesson first or if I would start by teaching a concept in the writing minilesson first. Her question, as we've seen across this book, is an important one that quite honestly is difficult to answer because, as always, I suggest that you use your knowledge of the relationship between reading and writing to make these important decisions on a minilesson-by-minilesson basis.

Let me show you an example of this decision making in action. Chrissy Koukiotis, a first grade teacher, decided to address the concept of retelling with her students. She began by teaching reading minilessons on this topic, but quickly found that her students struggled with this reading concept. She then tried a different tactic. Rather than continuing to conduct unsuccessful reading minilessons on retelling, she started conducting writing minilessons showing her students how to retell their own stories. Her students seemed to struggle less with this, so for a while she taught retelling through the writing. Eventually, though, she wanted to make the bridge between their success in writing and their need in reading so she had them retell their writing pieces during the reading minilesson. Finally, they successfully started retelling the texts that they read. I love this nugget of teaching because Chrissy began by teaching reading minilessons on retelling, but she quickly realized that she could more effectively teach her students the same skill by conducting minilessons first in writing and then later in reading.

HOW CAN I CREATE USEFUL CHARTS THAT DOCUMENT READING AND WRITING MINILESSONS?

When I taught first grade, I tried to create charts that documented what I had been teaching in my reading and writing minilessons. I did this so that the adults who walked into my classroom would know what I had been teaching. This is of course important, but you also must create charts that not only help adults but also help the students continue to use what you taught in your reading and writing minilessons. When creating charts you want to make sure that:

Your students can read the charts. All students should have access to the information on the chart. You can do this by using neat, bold handwriting with exaggerated spaces. You'll also want to make sure that they are pictures or examples next to all of the print so that students who cannot read the words have a visual reminder. Many teachers also decide to color-code their charts as a way to make them more meaningful for all of the students. For example, Karen Collins, a kindergarten teacher, was doing an author study of Ezra Jack Keats during the Writing Workshop. She put all of the ways he began his stories on purple paper and all of the ways he continued his stories on red paper. She found that by doing this her students could use the charts independently. For instance, she could say to a student, "Go to the red part of the chart to see how Ezra Jack Keats starts his stories" or "Go to the purple part of the chart to see how he continues his stories."

You can create charts that blur the lines between reading and writing. Once at a workshop in Albany a teacher wondered aloud if she could more closely align the reading and writing charts in her classroom: "I have a chart that gives students strategies for monitoring their reading. Shouldn't I organize that same chart so that it also includes strategies for students to use while monitoring their writing?" (see Figure 9.8). As I listened to this woman speak, I realized that she brought up an important

FIGURE 9.8   A reading and writing strategy chart

STRATEGIES TO USE WHILE READING	STRATEGIES TO USE WHILE REREADING YOUR WRITING
Does it make sense?	Does it make sense?
Does it sound right?	Does it sound right?
Does it look right?	Does it look right

point. One way that we can keep the reciprocity in our minilessons alive is to create charts that aren't just about reading or about writing but clearly show the connection between our reading and writing minilessons.

You occasionally make charts without the students. At times, I struggle with making charts in the midst of my teaching. I get into great conversations with my students, but I cut them short so I can make the chart. The making of the chart at times takes me away from building my students' language skills. Many of the minilessons that you conduct in your classroom require you to work hard at drawing language out of your students. This is no easy task especially if you're busy making a neat chart.

Here is what I now do. As students talk, I make a few notes for myself so I will remember what was said and then I make the chart without the students. I show them the chart the next day, and often these charts serve as reading materials for many students in the classroom. If the minilesson is about getting print on the page, then by all means I make the chart with the students so they have a clear demonstration on what this looks like, but if it's not, I'll often make the chart without them.

Making meaning is what it's all about. Yes, your language matters. Yes, your materials matter. Yes, you want to make reading/writing connections. It doesn't matter, though, if your students are not making meaning from your teaching. Choose your words and materials carefully. Use them to create memorable moments for your students.

FOR FURTHER STUDY

■ Transcribe and then study both your reading and writing minilessons.

1. Look for the architecture. Where is the connection? the teach? the active engagement? the link?
2. Discover ways to align the language across your minilessons. Can you revise your language in your writing minilesson (reading minilesson) so that it is the same as your reading minilesson (writing minilesson)?
3. Study the materials that you used during your minilessons. Are there materials from writing (reading) that you could use while teaching reading (writing)?
4. Study your writing minilessons (reading minilessons) as a way to get ideas for possible reading minilessons (writing minilessons). Is there something that you're teaching in your writing minilesson (reading minilesson) that would make sense to teach in your reading minilesson (writing minilesson)?

CHAPTER 10

CONFERENCES

We confer with students to help them become better writers. By "better writers" I mean writers who can do the work we teach them in today's conferences on their own in future pieces.

—Carl Anderson, *how's it going?*

I will never forget my first day of teaching. I took over a class for a third grade teacher one month after school started. Unbeknownst to me, this third grade class had gone through three teachers during the first month of school and fully expected that I would be the fourth. When I made my way up to the classroom with my brand new teaching bag and my mind filled with creative teaching ideas, a teacher stopped me in the hallway and handed me a bottle of Pepto Bismol.® "Last year, I took over a class," she said to me. "I took some of this every morning. It seemed to help."

I thought she was out of her mind, but a half hour later I wished I had taken some. I had thirty third graders who knew in a heartbeat, by my quivering voice and the shake in my hand, that they had a rookie. In the first two minutes a fistfight broke out, and a student got on top of his desk, took off his shirt and started chanting, "We have no teacher! We have no teacher!"

I probably would have left the profession if it weren't for my principal, Leslie Gordon. Every day, she stopped by my classroom to chat. She always began by asking, "How's everything going?" And then she would listen. I remember on one particular day telling Leslie that my students were no longer having fistfights in the classroom (thankfully), nor were they talking back to me. The problem I was now facing, I told her, was that my students wouldn't stop working when I asked them to focus on my directions. It exasperated me, I told her, because they ended up missing most of what I said.

"When they don't listen, what do you do?" Leslie asked.

"I keep going," I replied, "because I don't know what else to do."

"Leah," she said, "It's great that you realize that they should stop, but now let's get them to actually do it. You have a vision for what you want. The problem is that you abandon that vision when the going gets tough. A good teacher has a vision and doesn't deter from that vision. What do you want them to do when you give them directions?"

"I want them to put their pencils down and stop," I said.

"That's your vision," Leslie said. "Don't stop until you have it. I'll go into your classroom next period and show you what that looks like."

A few minutes later, Leslie did come to my classroom, demonstrating what it looked like to wait until every student was listening before you continued. Then she then asked me to focus on that for the week. I did, and to my relief, after a few days, my students were all stopping when I gave them directions. The staff meetings where we gathered as a school community were certainly helpful in the same ways that minilessons are helpful in your classroom. Both imparted a lot of important information to a large group quickly. What I remember most from my first year of teaching, however—and more important, what ultimately improved my teaching the most—were the one-on-one conferences I had with my principal, Leslie Gordon.

Having a vision for my teaching and not deterring from that vision was exactly what I needed in my first month of teaching. This was different than what my more experienced colleagues needed. Her conferences did much more than just help me gain control of my class that year. They are at the cornerstone of my teaching today. Donald Graves often refers to the Writing Workshop as the conference approach to teaching writing. I understand why. A conference is a type of teaching where you listen to one student and then teach that student *exactly* what he or she needs in very much the same way that Lesley conferred with me.

This chapter will begin by showing you how to structure your reading and writing conferences in similar ways so that your ways of teaching across the two can enhance one another. Then, I'll show you how to confer using a student's area of strength to complement his or her area of need.

STRUCTURE OF A CONFERENCE: RESEARCH, DECIDE, AND TEACH

In Chapter 9, I emphasized the importance of structuring your minilessons in consistent ways. The same is true for your conferences. In *The Art of Teaching Writing* Lucy Calkins discusses a structure (research, decide, teach) for conferences that has helped many teachers confer with both rigor and joy (1994, p. 224). Next, we'll examine this structure and the ways in which this structure sets you up to have powerful reading and writing conferences.

Research.

Lucy Calkins reminds us that "the important thing to realize is that our job as teachers is to listen to everything we see and know and hear about a child in order to develop a theory about this particular writer" (1994, p. 225). Lucy is referring here to the importance of the research component of a conference. We can just as easily call this part of the conference *assessment*. It's important during the research/assessment component of a conference to discover what a student knows, and then what might make sense for him or her to understand next, just as Calkins suggested. Remember, though, that you cannot nor should you try to discover everything in one single conference. Odell reminds us that "common sense not to mention theory and research tell us that to understand anything we have to select or pay attention to some things, de-emphasize others and completely ignore others" (1999, p. 8).

We're about to look at some of the ways that you can research/assess your students. Keep Odell's words in your mind as you read on. Each type of research that you'll read about next will provide you with unique information about a student. Each time you confer, you'll want to select from these research techniques, the ones that match the information that you're attempting to discover.

Observation.   One way you can assess a student is through both direct and informal observation. Yetta Goodman (1996) calls this *kidwatching*. Observation is essentially when you watch a student without intervening to teach. Observing a student will give you a specific type of information. I would use observation as my method of research/assessment in a conference if I were trying to notice:

1. How a particular student used the sources of information while reading or writing.
2. A student's stamina for reading and writing: that is, How long of a period of time can he or she sustain reading or writing? *or* How long can he or she sustain working on the same writing piece or reading the same book?

PUT THE READING/WRITING CONNECTION INTO ACTION

Observe your class for the first few minutes of Reading and Writing Workshop. Let them know that you will not be talking with them. These first few minutes can be a valuable research/assessment time.

Look at a student's writing. Ask questions. Listen to a student read. Ask questions. Another way that you can assess/research students is to try to discover the thinking that went along with their writing or their reading. Odell reminds us that when "we assess students' writing, there is a good chance that sooner or later we begin to talk about the thinking that occurred in that writing" (1999, p. 7). The same applies to reading. It's not essential (or helpful) for students to read to you every time you confer with them (their own writing or the text they're reading). If they do, however, you'll want to pair that reading with asking the students questions about their writing or reading. In that way, you'll have a better understanding of the thinking associated with it. I would tend to do this type of research/assessment if I were trying to discover:

1. A student's composing and comprehension strategies (What did you do in your mind to help yourself understand this page? Why did you choose to elaborate on this part in your writing?)
2. A student's attitudes and understandings of the reading and writing process (What does it mean to revise a piece of writing? What do you do when you get confused when you're reading a book?)
3. A student's understanding of both writing and reading content. (Can you retell the chapter that you just read? What happened next when you went to your grandmother's house?)

Figure 10.1 offers some helpful questions to ask students about their reading and writing.

So far, I've outlined ways to research/assess students during the Reading and Writing Workshop; however, your research can happen in other places as well. Next I want to suggest some alternative ways that you might research readers and writers outside of the Reading and Writing Workshop.

Observe a student in another part of the day.   You can also research your students during other parts of the day. Once I observed Fabio during choice time. I watched him build a block city with his best friend Jose. I used this observation later on during Writing Workshop when Fabio cried and said he had no stories to write. During Reading Workshop, I once again used this observation to help him understand that just like he could write stories about buildings, he could choose books to read that were about cities and buildings.

I often observe students in other parts of the day when I'm unsure about how to help them during a reading or writing conference. Often, watching them in art, gym, choice time, and so on gives me a unique perspective on how to help them read and write more effectively.

FIGURE 10.1   Questions that help you discover what strategies a child is using.

How's it going?

What are you working on today as a writer/reader?

Last time, we talked about . . . how is that going?

What do you usually do when you don't know how to spell a word?

What do you usually do when you don't know how to read a word?

What would you do if I weren't here bugging you?

How might you revise this?

What do you do when you don't understand what you're reading?

What might you do next?

How do you use your pictures to help write your words?

How do you use the picture to help you read the words?

Why did you decide to add on here?

Why did you decide to reread here?

Do you ever write about the same topic twice? How does it help you?

Do you ever read the same book twice?

Do you ever read a book in the same series? Why?

How do you help yourself understand the books that you read?

Look at your previous reading and writing conference notes.   Beverly Falk, speaking about effective assessment tools, said, "Assessment that provides an indication of how students have progressed over time offers a clear and more valid picture of achievement than those that focus only on outcomes without regard to students' starting points (1998, p. 61). One way to see how a student is progressing over time is to look back at previous reading and writing conferences notes. Doing this will help you see the growth or lack of growth a particular student is/isn't making.

Many teachers I know create record-keeping systems that help them easily see their students' progress over time. In Figure 10.2, Felicia, a kindergarten teacher, created a record-keeping system that helped her use what she had learned from previous reading and writing conferences. She started each week with a clean form. Before she started conferring each week, however, she reviewed her records from the week before and filled in what she had previously taught on the new record-keeping form. This helped her in two ways. First, looking at her previous notes gave her an opportunity to see how her students were progressing over time. It also helped her when she conferred with students. She now had at her fingertips what she had previously conferred with each student about and she could (if it made sense to) connect her present conference to that.

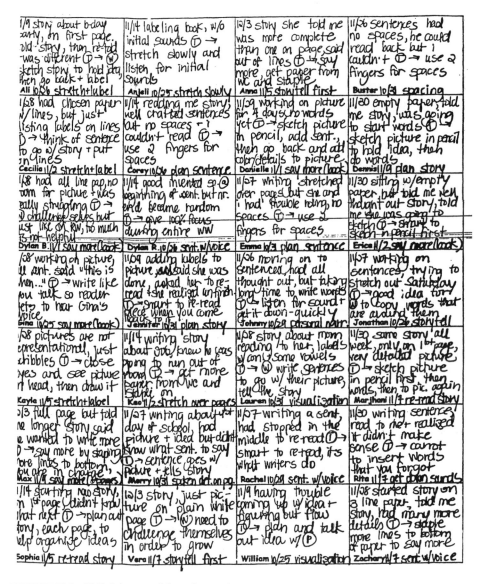

FIGURE 10.2 Felicia's record-keeping system.

Decide

After you've researched a student, you mind is apt to be filled with the many teaching possibilities. When your mind is filled with this many teaching possibilities, you run the risk of not deciding what to teach, but rather trying to teach it all in one conference. This "teaching overload" usually ends up confusing the student and not teaching much at all. When

I'm deciding what to teach, I'll ask myself, *What is the one thing that this particular student needs most right now in order to more effectively compose or comprehend?*

Teach

Then we of course teach. You want to make sure that each of your conferences teaches a student something new, rather than simply assigning a student to do something new in his or her writing. You can make this shift from assigning to teaching by asking yourself, *What method will I use to teach in this conference?* Many of the methods used when teaching whole-class minilessons also work when teaching in a one-on-one conference. Will you demonstrate for students what it looks like when a proficient reader or writer uses this strategy? Will you teach the concept showing them an example from literature?

A teacher recently asked me if I ask students to say back what I taught them at the end of a conference. I understood the question that she was getting at: How do you know that the student understood what you taught during that conference? Primary students often understand what we've taught but cannot articulate it, which it why I would have them try the new concept rather than say it back to me. I tend, as one of my methods of teaching, to actively engage students with what I just taught in very much the same ways that we saw students actively engage with what was being taught during the minilessons in the previous chapter.

PUT THE READING/WRITING CONNECTION INTO ACTION

- Devise systems of record keeping that allow you to see:
  1. A student across time
  2. A student across reading and writing
  3. Your class as a whole
  4. Your class across reading and writing
- When conferring with your students, take care in what you write in your record-keeping forms. You might write:
  1. What you taught
  2. What you didn't teach, but will at a future date
  3. Students' reaction
  4. Language you used to teach in the conference

TYPES OF CONFERENCES

Often we make our teaching harder than it needs to be. We might, for example, come up with six types of reading conferences and then nine completely different types of writing conferences. You can enhance the teaching that you do in one area by teaching in similar ways in another area. Next, we'll study the similar types of conferences that you might con-

FIGURE 10.3   Types of conferences.

TYPE OF CONFERENCE	WHY I WOULD DO IT	TEACHER'S JOB	STUDENTS' JOB	HELPFUL LANGUAGE
Content	To compose more meaning To comprehend more meaning To build classroom community To forge individual relationships To stabilize students with successful reading or writing experiences	Listen for and then highlight significant meaning.	Respond to the teacher. Use talk to support comprehension. Use talk to support composition.	**READING** What do you think? Does that help you understand the book more? **WRITING** Why did you choose to write about that? Can you tell me about one time when . . .? What's the most important part?
Strategy	To teach a students how to integrate new strategies that will help them compose or comprehend in both present and future reading and writing	Discover what the student is presently doing. Teach **one** new skill/strategy.	Talk about strategies they are using. Try out a new strategy with the teacher's assistance.	How's it going? What do you do when you are done? What do you think about when you start your story? How does drawing help your writing?
Coaching	To help students internalize strategies	Observation Offer short quick prompts in the midst of comprehension and composition.	Internalize strategies.	Say the words and write down the sounds you hear. Reread and think about what you want to say next.

duct across both writing and reading, letting your teaching in one area enhance your teaching in the other area (see Figure 10.3).

Content conference.

The main goal of a content conference is to help students compose and comprehend more meaning into texts. During a content conference, I try to intervene in ways that will make the present reading or writing experience a more successful one. Over time students will internalize these successful reading and writing experiences and have them on their own. This is vital. If students repeatedly compose or comprehend in unsuccessful ways, they come to believe that this is what reading and writing are all about. They are not surprised when they read without understanding or write without making sense.

Let's now look at a content conference I had with Amanda during Writing Workshop. I knew from previous conferences with Amanda that she usually had story ideas and wrote them in a sequential manner, quickly telling you a little bit about each part (see Figure 10.4). Based upon this research I wanted to help Amanda have a writing experience where she reflected upon which part of her story was the most meaningful (Determining Importance). I wanted her to then use that reflection to speak and then write more about that part. Let's watch.

> **Leah:**   Hi Amanda. How's it going for you as a writer? Can you tell me about what you're working on today?
>
> **Amanda:**   I'm working on a story about going swimming. Well, first here I am home before I went swimming and then here I'm outside on my way to go swimming and then here is when I got in the pool. (She's pointing to the different pages of her book.)
>
> **Leah:**   So what made you choose this swimming story? What's important to you in this story?
>
> **Amanda:**   This page she says as she points to the page where she is swimming.
>
> **Leah:**   Why?
>
> **Amanda:**   Well, because I had been hot all day long and it felt so good to get in the pool.
>
> **Leah:**   Let me see if I have this straight. (I turn back to the first page.) Here is when you were in the house.
>
> **Amanda:**   I was hot!
>
> **Leah:**   And here is when you were walking to the pool.
>
> **Amanda:**   I was hot and then when I jumped in the pool I felt cool.
>
> **Leah:**   I think I understand now why you wrote this story. Was it because you were hot all day long and then when you got to the pool you were cool? (Amanda nods.) You should add that important part to your story. Let's practice retelling that story so you can imagine what your writing will sound like when you do add that part. I'll start you off. One day I wanted to go swimming because it was hot. (I say this while I'm pointing to the space on the first page where her words are. Then I turn to the next page and look at Amanda.)
>
> **Amanda:**   When I got outside I was really hot but when I got in the pool I was happy because I was cool.
>
> **Leah:**   So now that you've told your story, I want you to take the beautiful words that you said and see if you can get those words down on the page.

It is not my job in a content conference to simply get more content out. I could have done that by asking Amanda what the pool looked like or what she saw on her way to the pool. My job is to listen to find out what Amanda is trying to compose—*what's important*

One sunny day I wonid to o swining!

en I got outsid I xvas rele ot.

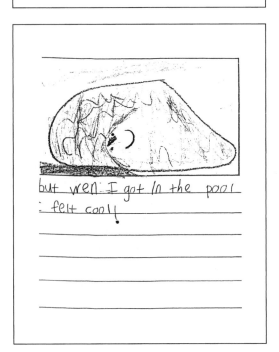

but wren I got ln the pool : felt cool!

FIGURE 10.4   One sunny day I wanted to go swimming. When I got outside, it was really hot but when I got in the pool I felt cool.

or significant in her story—and then become her partner in helping her compose what is in her heart onto the page.

When I asked Amanda why she chose that story, I was prepared for her to say anything. She could have said she chose that story because her best friend was going to be there. That would have completely changed how I helped Amanda retell the pool story. No matter what she said, I knew her answer was a vital part of my research. It would help me to help her determine what was important in her story and then focus her story on the important parts.

When I conduct content conferences during the Writing Workshop, I tend to ask questions such as, *Why did you write this?* or *What's the most important part?* to help me learn what the student is trying to compose. I typically end a content conference by having the student orally rehearse the story with this new meaning tucked into it. Doing this helps the student engage with the new language, which in turn increases the probability that she'll add that new language into her writing. This oral rehearsal also helps you assess how a student tells a story. As I did with Amanda, I'll sometimes collaborate with the student to orally rehearse the story. I tend to orally rehearse the story turning the pages of the student's blank book so he or she can imagine how those words will lie on the page.

Similarly, your role in a reading content conference is to help a student comprehend more meaning from the text he is reading. Let's examine a content conference I had with Michael during Readers Workshop. I already knew from previous conferences that Michael attempted to read activating relevant prior knowledge. He had difficulty, however, in using this prior knowledge to better understand the text. He would connect the book to his life, but would get so caught up in his personal story it was hard to bring him back to the text. I came to this conference knowing that I wanted to help activate relevant prior knowledge to better understand the text. Michael was reading a *Horrible Harry* book. He was reading a chapter when the teacher Miss Mangle is reading the book *Charlotte's Web* to the class. Let's listen in.

Michael: Just like Charlotte died. My uncle died also.

Leah: He did? How does that help you understand the book more?

Michael: Miss Mangle was crying and so was Song Lee. Henry probably felt weird because all these people that he has never seen cry before were are all crying. When my uncle died, I saw my mom and my aunt and my dad crying. It made me feel weird.

Leah: Wow. Let me see if I got this straight. You understood how weird all the students felt seeing their teaching crying because when you saw your aunt and your dad and mom cry it made you feel strange. Did I get that right?

Michael: Yes.

In both reading and writing content conferences, my role as a teacher is to listen carefully trying to determine what is important to the student that will help her more effectively compose or comprehend. In the writing conference, it was the fact that Amanda was hot all day long and then she jumped into the refreshing water. In the reading conference Michael had experienced his own uncle's death and knew what it felt like to see adults cry in front of him. I also want to note that in both situations I asked the students if I had understood them correctly. This is vital. Often we think we understand what a student is saying, but we don't. Asking them enables the lines of communication to be clear between you and your students.

In both the writing and reading content conferences, I got the students *speaking* as a way to help them more effectively compose and comprehend. In the writing conference Amanda used talk as a way to focus her writing on the important parts. Michael's talk in the reading conference help him to activate relevant prior knowledge. I recommend that you conduct content conferences often in the beginning of the year and then do less of them as the year progresses. Content conferences build community and also give students an image of successful reading and writing experiences, which is why these types of conferences are so valuable at the start of the year.

Strategy conference.

Content conferences, like everything in life, have both their strengths and limitations. They give students clear examples of both reading and writing as meaning making activities. This can't be taken lightly. A content conference is limiting, however, because the goal of a content conference is to simply stabilize a student. In neither content conference was I explicit about how they could use what they learned on that day every day. Of course, what I taught them will hopefully stick, but I wasn't explicit about this nor was it my main concern.

In a strategy conference your primary role is to teach the student one skill/strategy, and then be explicit about how that skill/strategy will help him in all of his reading and writing experiences. First, let's look at a strategy conference I had with Sandra during Writing Workshop and then we'll look at a strategy conference I had with Peter during Reading Workshop.

> (I watched Sandra for a while before I approached her. I noticed that she sketched her story first and then went back to add the words.)
>
> **Leah:** How it's going?
>
> **Sandra:** Fine, I am writing a book about riding my bike with my cousin.
>
> **Leah:** Can I take a look? (I read it for a second.) You were looking for your bikes. I'm surprised. You didn't know where your bike was.
>
> **Sandra:** (smiling) At home I know where my bike is but I have a bike at my grandma's house. She is always moving my bike around so I can't find it.
>
> **Leah:** Okay, I get it now. So, Sandra (I turn to her first page), on this page, you and your cousin were looking for your bikes at your grandma's house. She moves them around a lot. That's the setting, your grandma's house?
>
> **Sandra:** Yes.
>
> **Leah:** Can I tell you the smart thing that you're doing and offer you a suggestion?
>
> **Sandra:** Yes.
>
> **Leah:** I see here that you started by saying you were riding bikes with your cousins. It's very smart to begin a story by saying who the characters are. It helps the reader

to understand your story. You'll want to continue beginning your stories like you did here by introducing the characters. Remember how I was confused about why you were looking at your bikes but then when you told me you were at your grandma's house I understood? Just like it's smart to begin your story by saying who the characters are, it's also helpful to begin by saying where you are, the setting. Where were you, Sandra?

Sandra: At my grandmother's.

Leah: What could you add to the beginning of your story that would help the people reading your book understand where you were?

Sandra: I could add on this page. (She points to the beginning.) One day I was at my grandma's house with my cousins. We were looking for our bikes. Grandma moves our bikes around tricking us every time.

Leah: Great! Sandra, today and every day you'll want to begin your stories by letting readers know where the story is taking place, the setting.

Sandra: Okay.

(Peter is reading a Henry and Mudge book. While I observe Peter, I notice that he periodically looks up at me or mumbles to himself predictions such as, "I bet that next Henry is going to . . . I just know that his dad will . . ." I stop Peter to talk.)

Leah: I noticed that when you read you stop a lot and guess or predict about what is going to happen next. Does that help you understand the books you're reading?

Peter: Yes, because when I do that I check to see if I'm right. Sometimes I'm right and sometimes I'm not.

Leah: Peter, can I tell you the smart thing that you did and offer you a suggestion?

Peter: Yes.

Leah: Peter, it is smart to read and think at the same time. You were thinking about what might happen next. That's called predicting. And it's true: Sometimes you're right and sometimes you're not. Predicting and checking your predictions help you understand the books that you read. Keep doing that often. Are there other ways that you think about books besides predicting?

Peter: No, I usually do that one.

Leah: Today, I want to teach you another way you can stop and think about your books. Sometimes you can stop reading after a part and make a picture of that part in your mind. You can ask yourself what that part might look like or sound like. Let's try it together for a second. Let's read the next part. (Peter reads the next part aloud.) What do you see? What do you think it looks like? sounds like?

Peter: Well, I have a picture of the cat in my mind. She has very messy hair and is very skinny. She is probably sitting there quietly wishing someone would take care of her.

Leah: Do you see how making a picture of that part slowed you down and helped you to better understand it? You now understand what the cat looked like when she came to the house. Keep that picture of the cat in your mind as you continue reading and remember that you can always, as you read, stop and make a picture of a part in your mind. I would like you to keep doing that today and every day when you read.

Peter: Okay.

In both of these conferences, I watched the students, first noticing what they were already doing. Sandra was already beginning her stories by introducing her characters and Peter was already predicting. In both, I used the language introduced in Chapter 8: *Can I tell you the smart thing that you're doing and may I offer you a suggestion?* In both I taught them a new skill/strategy that would help them not just on that day but every day. I taught Sandra how to begin her stories with setting and I taught Peter how to make a picture in his mind when he reads. In both conferences I asked the students to try out the new concept with some support.

This is helpful for both you and the students. Sometimes the students will be able to do it with some support but then cannot do it by themselves. I will conduct future conferences differently if I know how/if students were able to utilize the concept with support. In both, I ended by explicitly telling them they could use what I taught them today and every day. This is key.

Most students will not realize this unless you tell them this simply and clearly over and over again in strategy conferences. I tend to do this type of conference throughout the year often and with all students so that they begin to build a repertoire of reading and writing skills and strategies that they can bring to all of their reading and writing encounters. I keep Lucy Calkins's mantra "teach the writer, not the writing, and teach the reader, not the reading" in my mind always when I'm conferring (2001, p. 102). I must make sure that I don't get too caught up in simply improving their reading or writing on any given day. I want to offer reading and writing strategies that they can over time internalize and use automatically.

Coaching conference.

So far, I've given you examples of conferences in which I've asked the students to stop reading or writing and talk. The next conference, the coaching conference, looks quite different in that you don't stop the student from reading or writing. Rather you interject consistent prompts that lift the level of students' reading and writing.

When I think of the coaching conference, I'm reminded of the coaching I received when I trained for the New York Marathon. I hired a coach specifically because my running times were not improving. My coach, rather than holding a seminar about improving times, went out running with me. He was quiet at first, just watching. But after a while he started interjecting quick and concise prompts that didn't take me away from the act of running. "I love the way your arms are moving quickly," he said once. "They are." I remember thinking and I moved them even more quickly. "Head up," he would often say, and I would lift my head remembering that I often lowered it by mistake when I was tired. Other times he said, "Knees up," and again I would remind myself to put my knees up so that I would keep my stride going.

When I ran the New York Marathon, my coach was no longer with me, but I had his voice in my head when I ran. When I got to mile ten, I prompted myself. "Head up!" I said and I did it. Later, at mile eighteen, my knees started to drag. "Knees up!" I said in my mind and I did it. Because my coach prompted me in consistent ways, I no longer needed him. Rather, I had internalized his language and was able to prompt myself in the ways that he once had prompted me.

The teacher's role in a coaching conference is to observe and prompt students to use strategies that, as Vygotsky says, are in their "zone of proximal development" (1962, p. 86). What Vygotsky meant by working within the *zone of proximal development* is ensuring that what you are teaching is not something that your students can already do, nor is it so difficult that they will be unable to do it. The student's role in a coaching conference is to read or write and try the prompts that you offer in the midst of reading and writing. The ultimate goal, however, is for students to internalize these prompts and use them independently while reading and writing. Let's now look at both a writing and reading coaching conference.

Writing coaching conference.

Karen: What's happening in your picture?

Reid: I'm going pumpkin picking. This is the one that my mommy got me. I got five of them. My sister is holding a really big pumpkin.

Karen: I see that you wrote the letters for yours and Jessica's name. That would help someone know that you and Jessica were the people who went pumpkin picking. It would also help if you labeled the pumpkin so that people would know there were pumpkins there.

Reid: I don't know how to do that.

Karen: Sure you do! Remember to say the word slowly and write down the sounds you hear. I'll sit next to you and help. Say the word *pumpkin*. What sounds do you hear?

Reid: Pumpkin. P. (He looks up with a questioning face.)

Karen: I love how you said the word and listened for the sounds. Write that down. (He does.) Say the word again and listen for the next sound.

Reid: C.

Teacher: Good for you! Write that down. Let me ask you a question. You said you needed my help. Who is doing the work: you or me?

Reid: (proudly) ME!

Karen: That's right. You don't need my help. You can say the words and listen for the sounds all by yourself. Good for you.

Reading coaching conference.

(I approached Samantha in the midst of her reading. She is reading the book *My Little Brother Ben* by Karen Cogan.)

Samantha: Ben sat be (She, with her fingers, frames the word *be* inside of the word *besides.* She says "be" a few times and looks up at me hoping that I'll supply her with the word.)

Leah: I love the way you looked for a part of the word that you know. Go back and reread and then look for a part you know.

Samantha: Ben sat . . . (She frames the word *be* again. She continues scanning the word.) beside . . . Ben sat beside me.

Leah: That worked for you. You didn't need my help doing that. Keep reading, Samantha, and don't forget to go back and reread and then look for a part that you know.

There are a few things to note about coaching conferences. First, you want your prompts to be consistent; that is, with Reid I want to always coach by saying, "Say the words and listen for the sounds," and with Samantha I want to always coach by saying, "Reread and look for parts that you know." I can also prompt in consistent ways by aligning the prompts I use across reading and wring.

For example, if a student got to the word *the* in his reading, I might coach him by saying, "You know that word. Read it quickly." Likewise, if the same student was writing "the" I might coach him by saying, "You know that word. Write it quickly." Figure 10.5 offers helpful prompts when coaching readers and writers.

In both of these conferences I coached the students in using the sources of information (meaning, structure, and visual) more effectively. In writing Karen was giving Reid strategies in order to segment sounds in words. In the reading I was helping Samantha cross-check the meaning source of information with the visual source of information. Although you can coach into anything, I tend to use the coaching conference when I am trying to help students learn how to utilize the sources of information. It is vital to coach into strategies that you believe that students could (either at that moment or very soon) use independently. Karen knew that Reid knew a handful of sounds but wasn't stretching words out on his own. She decided to get him to listen to sounds and record letters that he could hear so that he saw he could do this on his own.

If Reid hadn't known those sounds, it would not have made sense for Karen to do that exact conference because he wouldn't be able to continue that work when Karen left his side. You want to be able to end a coaching conference by saying what I was able to say: "Who did the work me or you?" You want the answer to be, of course, the student. Over time you want to hand more and more responsibility to the students. When I coach students over time, I try to prompt less and observe more. In that way, I am handing more responsibility over to the students, helping them to internalize the prompts I've been coaching them on.

One final note: It's important that you use all types of conferences with all students. At times, I'll see teachers conduct only coaching conferences with their struggling readers

FIGURE 10.5   Helpful prompts to use in a writing or reading coaching conference.

If we're trying to get a child to use <u>meaning as a source of information</u>, we might say:

- I like the way you made that make sense.
- Does that make sense?
- Picture it.
- Look at the picture.
- Look at the picture again.
- Reread.
- Stop and think.
- Stop, read, and think.
- What do you want to say next?

If we're trying to get a child to use <u>structure as a source of information</u>, we might say:

- Does that sound right?
- Can we say it that way?
- I like the way you made that sentence sound right.

If we're trying to get a child to use <u>visual sources of information</u>, we might say:

- Does that look right?
- I like the way you made it look right.
- Say that word again.
- Do you hear anything else in that word?
- Look at the picture and the first letter. Then get your mouth ready for that sound.
- Say the word and write down the sounds you hear.
- Do you know a part of that word?
- Do you know that word?
- It's just like _____. (word off the name or the alphabet chart)
- Look at the _____. (ABC chart, word wall, name chart)
- Is there a word like _____?
- I like the way you used (name chart, alphabet chart, word wall) to help you write.
- Say the word and write down what comes next.
- Write it quickly/Read it quickly.
- Do you know _____? Just write it.
- Do you know _____? Just read it.

If we're trying to get a child to <u>self-monitor or cross-check</u>, we might say:

- Is there a problem?
- How can you fix that?
- Reread what you wrote and point to each word.
- Are you right? How do you know?
- Leave a space before you write the next word.

and writers and conduct mostly strategy conferences with their thriving readers and writers. All students need *all* types of conferences in order to grow into well-rounded readers and writers.

CONFERRING ACROSS READING AND WRITING

In Chapter 2, I compared reading and writing, noting both the similarities and differences between the two. We're going to once again use that information to study how to confer with a variety of different students, some of whom are markedly different in their reading and writing abilities. Lucy Calkins once said to me that a student's strength in one area shows the potential for another area. These words stay at the forefront of my mind, especially when I'm conferring with students who are markedly different in their reading and writing attitudes and abilities.

It's easier to chalk up differences in students' reading and writing abilities to individual tastes and personalities. It's more difficult for us to rise to the challenge and say, "Well, if they can do it in writing, it's my job to help them reach their potential and do it in reading, or if they can do in reading, it's my job to help them reach their potential and do it in writing."

Next, we're going to research/assess three prototype students. First I'll introduce you to Angela who is a strong writer but not as strong a reader. I'll suggest some ways that you might confer with students like Angela to help them use their strength in writing to add to their reading. Then I'll introduce you to Tan, who is a strong reader but not as strong a writer. Again, I'll suggest some conferring strategies that would hopefully help students like him use his strength in reading to add to his writing. Finally, you'll meet Tynia, who has similar strengths and needs across both reading and writing. I'll once again suggest conferring strategies for students like her as well. You'll see with all of these students I used my knowledge of both reading and writing and how they are the same and different to speculate on the types of conferences I might have with them in both reading and writing. More than likely you will have an Angela, a Tan, and a Tynia in your classroom. Hopefully, by studying how to confer with each of them you'll feel equipped to confer with students like them in your classrooms.

Angela: Strong writer/not as strong a reader.

Angela is a first grade student from Albany, New York. I spent a morning observing and talking with Angela as she read and wrote. First, I observed Angela reading. She did not seem comfortable with me watching her at all. She looked quietly at the pictures in her book. When I asked if I could read with her, she pointed to the pictures, labeling the pictures with her words. When she got to a picture that she didn't know, she just skipped it. I then asked Angela if she could read the words of that book to me. She told me she couldn't read the words of that book. I then asked her to choose one of her books where she could read the words and she chose a book about farms.

Her reading was choppy and she came upon a lot of unfamiliar language such as *plow* and *tractor*. She also came to words that she simply had trouble reading. In both of these instances she simply skipped the word. Often she stopped and looked at me, hoping that I would supply her with the correct word. When I asked her to get her mouth ready for the word, she would say over and over again, "I can't do it. I can't do it." Lisa O'Brien, her teacher, had confirmed for me that this was typical behavior for Angela during Reading Workshop.

After Reading Workshop, I watched Angela write. She seemed quite content for me to watch her write. Angela wasted no time and wrote a four-page story in the first ten minutes of Writing Workshop (see Figure 10.6). Her story, as you can see, is sequential and tells you in a straightforward manner what happened. I also found, by looking at her writing and watching her writing process, that she knows a lot about words and how they work. She had some sight words underneath her belt (*and, my, had*). She also tried words that she didn't know how to spell, and from her approximations you could see that she knew a lot about sounds and letters (*Hows, levt, thean, choklit*)

When I asked her to read her writing back to me, she did so with great confidence and gusto. When she got to page two she read, "and then we went inside and had hot cocoa." (Her book really said hot chocolate.), I then asked: "Can you go back and read that sentence and make sure all of your words look right?" She reread her writing with her finger. When she got to the word *chocolate* I said, "Can you get your mouth ready for that word?" I watched her mouth form the "ch" sound. She self-corrected and now read her book correctly reading the word as "chocolate" instead of as "cocoa." It's interesting to note that Angela looked at blends while rereading her own writing but she refused to do this while reading her independent books. Angela never once said in writing, "I can't do this," but in reading these words were commonplace.

The first thing I do when assessing students across reading and writing is ask myself, *Why might this student have this discrepancy?* Here is when I use my knowledge of the similarities and differences between reading and writing. Below are some possible reasons why Angela might find writing easier than reading.

- Angela chooses very familiar topics to write about; however, she often chooses books that contain unfamiliar topics.
- Angela has a hard time monitoring the sources of information in reading because she reads books where the meaning inside of them is unfamiliar. Angela has an easier time monitoring the sources of information in writing, because she's writing books where the meaning is familiar.
- When I asked Angela if she liked reading or writing better, she said writing. Perhaps because she liked writing better, she took more care in choosing her topics.

Once I've determined the possible reasons why a student might have this discrepancy I use this research to help me decide what to teach. I speculate some possible ways that I might confer with her in both reading and writing so that the area of strength (writing) complements the area of need (reading). These are simply speculations. As I learn more about Angela, I will build upon these. In the end I want to confer with Angela in ways that show her how to use her strength in writing to help her in reading.

- I might conduct a strategy conference with her in reading, helping her to choose books that contained familiar topics. I might say something like, "Angela can I tell you something smart I noticed and then make a suggestion? It's really smart that you choose writing topics that you know a lot about. I bet it was easier to write the hot chocolate story because you were there and you know what happened. I think that you should do a similar thing in reading. You should at times choose books that are

Oun Day
Me AnD MY
Cusin Went for
a. WoC.

AnD thean We
Want in.
SiD AnD HaD
HotChoKlit.

AnD Thean
MY Cusin
LeVT MY
HOWS.

AnD Thean
I Went to
BeD.

FIGURE 10.6   One day me and my cousin went for a walk. And then we went inside and had hot chocolate. And then my cousin left my house. And then I went to bed.

about topics that you know a lot about. You'll have an easier time reading those books."

- I might conduct another strategy conference teaching her how to do her own book introduction in reading. I might say something like, "Angela, I've noticed that in writing you always tell your partner your whole story before you go and write it. In reading I would like you to always look at the pictures in the books so that you know the whole story before you go and read it."

- I might ask her to read books in a series. Because these books would contain reoccurring characters and/or ideas, the meaning in these books would become more familiar to Angela over time.

- I might conduct coaching conferences asking her to reread her writing using the same prompts that I eventually wanted her to while reading. For example, I might say to Angela while she reread her writing, "Can you find a part of this word that you know?" or "Reread and then get your mouth ready."

- Once she had been doing this for a while in writing, I might conduct similar coaching conferences in reading. I might say, "You're using such smart strategies when you reread your writing. You can use the same strategies when you're reading your independent reading books." I might interject prompts as Angela reads her independent reading books such as, "Can you find a part of this word that you know?" or "Reread and then get your mouth ready."

- We might type up her writing and use that for reading material.

Tan: Strong reader/not as strong a writer.

Now, let's try the same thing with Tan. Tan is a first grade student from Clinton Hill, New York. While Angela was a stronger writer, Tan is a stronger reader. When I read with Tan, he read quickly and fluently. He talked with great gusto about the books he was reading. His teacher Alison informed me that in school he reads a wide variety of genres and topics and is always open to reading something new. On the other hand, when I watched Tan write his process was slow and choppy. He stopped at almost every word, asking me, "How do you spell _____? or "Did I spell _____ right?" I told him to write the words the best he could.

When I returned fifteen minutes later Tan had not gotten much further. Figure 10.7 shows Tan's final piece. Tan started this piece the day I visited his classroom but did not finish this piece for another five days. Throughout those five days, he tried to enlist Alison and the other students in the class to help him spell the words in his writing piece.

Again, just like I did with Angela, first I speculated the reasons why Tan might be a stronger reader. Again, I used my knowledge of reading and writing and how they are both the same and different to help me.

- Tan learned to read by sight and rarely "sounds out" a word while reading. Tan knows what words look like from reading; therefore, perhaps it frustrated him to write because he knew his own words didn't look right.

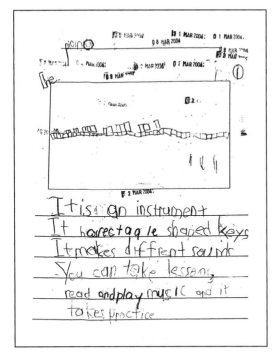 

FIGURE 10.7   It is an instrument. It has rectangle shaped keys. It makes different sounds. You can take lesson, read and play music and it takes practice. Piano is fun. Each key makes a different sound.

- Tan learned to read by recognizing whole words: He didn't seem to sound out. Because of this, sounding out words in writing was foreign and difficult for him and significantly slowed down his writing process.
- Tan might have fine motor issues that also would slow down his writing process.
- Tan enjoyed talking about books with friends. He didn't have this same companionship in writing.
- Tan read books with sophisticated structures and interesting word choices and perhaps this intimidated him.
- Tan read books with sophisticated structures and interesting word choices. Perhaps he didn't realize he could borrow these structures and use them while writing.

Once again, I imagined some of the ways I might confer with Tan across both reading and writing.

- I might conduct a strategy conference showing Tan how to write, spelling the words the best he could and then afterwards circling a few words that didn't look right. He could then either try those words himself or enlist my assistance only after he had written his entire piece. I might say something like, "Tan, because you read so much you can tell when the words in your writing don't look right. I'll be happy to help you with this once you get your ideas down. What I want you to do is to write your piece, spelling the words the best that you can. At the end of writing you can reread your writing and circle two words that don't look right. You can try them yourself or I'll be happy to show you how close you are."

- Rather than walk away from Tan when it's time for him to write "the best he can" I might conduct a series of coaching conferences. As he writes, I might interject prompts such as, "Say the word _____. What sound do you hear first? Write that letter down," or "What do you hear next? Write that down," or "What do you hear at the end? Write that down," or "Say the word. Is there a part of that word that you do know?" Over time, of course, I would want to watch him as he used these prompts independently so that he could develop more fluency in his writing.

- I might conduct a strategy conference suggesting that he partner up with a friend to come up with a writing project. Perhaps they could write a school brochure. Perhaps they could revise their writing together. I might say something like, "Tan, I see that you have so much fun reading with other people. Let's come up with some ways you could work with people in writing and have that same kind of fun."

- I might conduct a few conferences where I dictated Tan's ideas for him, encouraging him to focus on both his word choice and his structures, rather than on his handwriting or his spelling.

- I might conduct a series of strategy conferences in reading where I encouraged Tan to pay attention to the words and structures that he particularly enjoyed and then try them out in his own writing.

Tynia: Similar needs across reading and writing.

Finally, let's look at Tynia, a second grade student from Public School 261 in New York City. I observed Tynia as she read and as she wrote and discovered that she had similar needs across both. I recorded my observations of Tynia's reading in a tool that Marie Clay designed called a running record (see Figure 10.8). Typically, as you can see in Figure 10.8, a running record is used to code and analyze reading behavior. I also recorded Tynia's writing behavior (see Figure 10.9).

Once I've taken reading and writing running records I analyze them so I can assess what a particular student's strengths and needs are. You see through this close analysis in Figures 10.10 and 10.11 that Tynia needed to learn to monitor one source of information against another in both writing and in reading.

I'll now imagine how I might confer with students like Tynia who are very similar across reading and writing.

- I would make sure that my conferences were similar across reading and writing so that conferences I had with her in writing would add and improve her reading and vice versa. For example, I might conduct coaching conferences across both reading and writing helping her to monitor meaning, structure, and visual sources of information at once. In both reading and writing I might coach her by prompting in the exact same way. I might say, "Is there a part of this word that you know? Reread and see if that sounds right. Look at the end of the word. Does it look right? Reread: Does

Fox All Week – Edward Marshal
DRA-16

On Saturday

Carmen called Fox

On the phone.

"Dexter and I are going out

on our skateboards," she said.

"I'll be right over,"

said Fox.

"Not so fast, Fox," said Mom.

"I'm taking the twins to the doctor.

And you must stay with Louise."

"Rats!" said Fox.

"Now, none of that," said Mom.

Fox told his friends

That he could not go out.

"And all because of you,"

he said to Louise.

"Now, don't give me any trouble."

Soon Fox was lost

In his TV programs.

He did not give Louise

Another thought.

All of sudden

There was a loud crash.

It came from the backyard.

"Uh-oh," said Fox.

Louise had taken a bad spill.

"Oh my gosh!" cried Fox.

[handwritten annotations: check marks throughout; "telephone / phone"; "the / our"; "sc / none"; "Teacher told to skip+reread"; "couldn't / could not"; "32"]

FIGURE 10.8   Tynia's running record.

that make sense?" If she's prompted in the same way across the two subject areas, she's bound to become more comfortable with that content faster.

■ I might give Tynia additional phonics support, noting which letters and sounds she knew and which she didn't. I would have to explicitly teach the unknown ones to her and show her how to use them effectively while reading and writing to begin correctly recording beginning, medial, and end sounds in words.

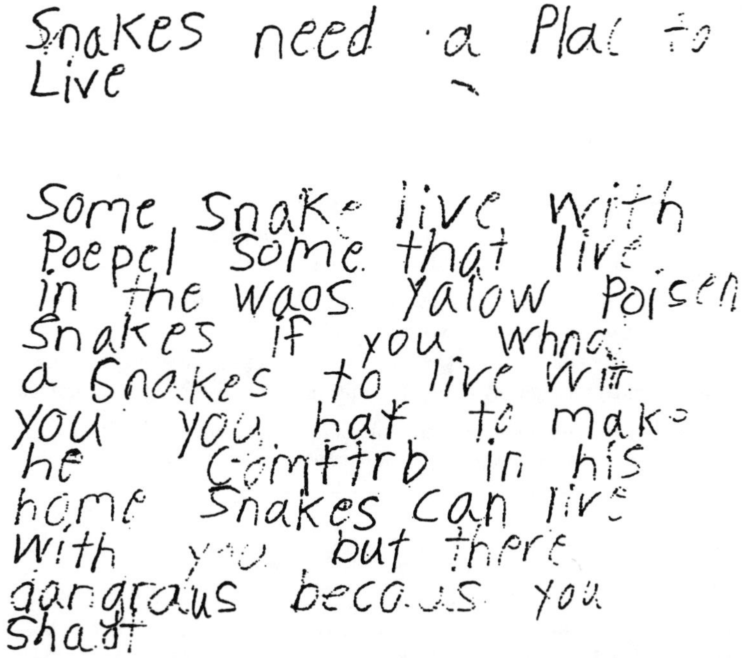

Snakes need ·a Plac̄ t̄o
Live

Some Snake live with
Poepel Some that live
in the waos Yalow Poisen
Snakes if you whna
a Snakes to live Wit
you you hat tc̄ mak̄
he Comftrb in his
home Snakes can liv̄
with you but there
dangraus becaus you
shad

FIGURE 10.9   **Tynia's writing record.**

FIGURE 10.10   **An analysis of Tynia's reading behaviors.**

My Analysis of Tynia's Running Record

At times, Tynia used meaning and structure sources of information but then neglected to use the visual sources of information.

- The sentence read "Dexter and I are going out on **our** skateboards." (Tynia read, "Dexter and I are going out on **the** skateboards.") The substitution of the word *the* for *our* is meaningful. The substitution also is structurally correct but she neglected to look at the *o* and realize that the word didn't look like the word *the*.

In a later first sentence Tynia substituted the word *telephone* for the word *phone*. Again, her substitution made sense and sounded right but it didn't look right.

When Tynia did attempt to use the visual source of information she stopped using meaning and structure effectively.

- For example, the sentence read "'Now none of that.' said Mom." When Tynia got to that sentence, she stuck with the word *none,* trying to figure it out by looking at the letters. She did not, however, ask herself (until I helped her to) what word would not only look right but also sound right and make sense.

In reading, Tynia didn't use meaning, structure, and visual sources of information together, monitoring one source of information against another.

FIGURE 10.11   An analysis of Tynia's writing behaviors.

Tynia used the visual source of information to write entire words by sight and to listen to beginning and end sounds in words. She did not, however, go back and reread her writing making sure that it made sense and sounded right.

■ She wrote words such as *snakes* and *need* without much fuss. Even words like *people* she didn't segment. She is fairly close, which makes me wonder if her strategy for *people* was to try and picture the entire word in her head. She was much more hesitant when it came to listening to the sounds in words and writing those sounds down.

Many times Tynia looked only at the first letter and/or last letter when she used the visual source of information to segment sounds in word.

■ When she wrote "waos" for *was,* she attempted to sound it out and but did the work fairly quickly. It seemed through my observation that she only listened to the first and last sound.

In writing, Tynia didn't use meaning, structure, and visual sources of information together, monitoring one source of information against another.

PUTTING THE READING/WRITING CONNECTION INTO ACTION

■ Study your students across reading and writing as a way to assist you with conferences. You can do this by:
  1. Looking at running records and writing samples side by side.
  2. Observing a student's reading and then observing the same student's writing.
  3. Asking students questions about both their reading and writing processes.
  4. Determining whether reading or writing is the area of strength.
  5. Determining the types of reading and writing conferences that will be most helpful (content, strategy, coaching).
■ Pay attention to the language you use when conferring in one subject area and bring it to the other.
  1. In reading you looked at the pictures to read the words. In writing you should look at your own pictures to write the words.
  2. In writing you choose topics that are familiar. In reading you should choose books that are familiar.

Teachers will often ask me where I learned my techniques for classroom management. My answer is always the same. I learned how to manage a class through my conferences with Lesley Gordon. Leslie certainly knows how to confer because what she taught me almost ten years ago affects the ways in which I teach today. Each conference that we do holds so much promise, so much potential. We have the power to affect our students' reading and writing not just today, but also ten years from today. Sometimes the enormity of this task overwhelms me, and I wonder where I can turn for help. I turn time and time again to the reading/writing connection. It helps me confer in powerful and precise ways.

FOR FURTHER STUDY

- Transcribe your reading and writing conferences.
  1. Where is the research? Where is the decide? Where is the teach?
  2. What type of conference is it? Is it a content conference? Is it a strategy conference? Is it a coaching conference?
- Study a student across reading and writing.

1. Is he or she a stronger reader? A stronger writer? Similar needs across both?
2. Why might they have this discrepancy?
3. How might you confer so that the area of strength complements or adds to the area of need?

CHAPTER 11

SMALL GROUP WORK

I became a teacher only after I learned to listen and watch. I also had to learn to wonder, I mean truly wonder in the absence of a common history, who each child was; why he or she said and did what he or she said and did in the classroom, in the hallway on the playground. Of course it was all so spectacular, I couldn't help but wonder.

—Patsy Cooper

A$_S$ I continued to learn more about the reading/writing connection, I searched for new places in my teaching where this connection could work its magic. I was always overjoyed when I saw the reading/writing connection making an impact upon my students, which is why I became increasingly uncomfortable when I discovered that I wasn't making reading/writing connections in my small group instruction. During Reading Workshop, I conferred one on one with students and also worked with them in small groups. During Writing Workshop, however, I found that I only conferred one on one with them.

I thought that perhaps I was the only one, but as I spoke with my colleagues, I realized that many of them also used small group instruction while teaching reading, but not while teaching writing. Small group instruction was a powerful structure in my teaching of reading. I wondered if I could enhance and add to my small group work in reading by also conducting small group work in writing. The answer to this question was a resounding yes.

This chapter will tell you the story of a class of kindergarten students and their teacher, Shawn Brandon. Through this story I hope to show you how small group work in writing can not only be a successful structure to teach writing strategies, but also can also be an additional avenue to teach reading strategies. Through this story, you'll see how Shawn and I assessed her students and then used those assessments to form writing groups. Then, you'll see how those groups moved between reading and writing so that the students could once again have multiple opportunities to learn similar concepts.

"Small group work," some teachers will say to me. "Do you mean guided reading and guided writing?" Other teachers think that what I mean by small group work is book clubs or literature discussion groups. There are many different reasons why you might group students together; however, all small group work should in some way guide readers and writers. You'll see this in action as Shawn and I guide her students in different ways based upon their particular strengths and needs.

WHAT ARE THE BENEFITS OF SMALL GROUP WORK?

Sometimes when I suggest small group work to teachers, they'll tell me that they prefer working one on one with their students. I understand what they are saying. There are many reasons why you might decide to work one on one with a student rather than in a small group, as discussed in Chapter 10, but now I would like to talk about the benefits of small group work.

First, small group work is efficient. Often, I confer with a student on a strategy only to find myself conferring with another student across the room on that same strategy a few minutes later. I clearly would have saved time if I brought both of those students together and taught that strategy in a small group, rather than in a one-on-one conference.

Small group work also strengthens relationships among students. When you bring together small groups of students for reading, you build a community of readers who have a shared reading history. Over time, they will have read common books. Likewise, when you bring together small groups of students for writing, you are building a community of writers who will have a shared writing history. They will write some texts together, and will get to know each other's favorite topics and genres.

Another benefit of small group work is that it gives you opportunities to group different students together for different reasons. Later on in the chapter, you'll see that Shawn and I didn't form a low group, a medium group, and a high group of writers and readers. The groups, we found, were constantly shifting and changing as we continued to assess and reflect upon their progress. Usually we found ourselves putting students together because they had similar strengths and needs; however, at times we also put very different writers and readers together so that one could support the other.

Lastly, we found that planning for small group work became another excellent opportunity for us to carefully *assess* our students. It not only required us to have strong assessment tools, but it also required that we *reflect* upon our assessments. When we assessed the students in order to form groups, we looked at our reading and writing conference notes, writing samples, and running records to ensure that we grouped students together in wise ways.

THE STORY BEGINS: ASSESSING WRITERS

We'll begin this story by meeting the main characters: the students in Shawn's classroom. On the day that I visited in May, Shawn had conducted a simple minilesson reminding her students that they could write in a variety of genres and forms. Once the students began writing, we circulated from table to table watching and talking with the students. Afterward, we looked at their writing samples and then used our assessments to group the students together.

We assessed her students in two distinct ways. First, we observed them in the process of writing. Through these observations, we were able to see whether they were using meaning, structure, and visual sources of information simultaneously; that is, we were able to see how/if they were *monitoring* their writing. The second way that we assessed her students was through their actual writing samples. These writing samples provided us with tangible evidence of some of the deeper ways they were thinking in order to compose their texts (see Chapter 3).

Students are able to think in these complex ways when they are using the meaning, structure, and visual sources of information appropriately; however, different types of thinking required students to lean more heavily on different sources of information. For example, when students envision in order to write with descriptive language, they lean more heavily on the meaning and structure sources of information (although they also use the visual sources of information appropriately). When they activate their knowledge of letters and sounds, they lean more heavily on the visual sources of information (although they of course still use the meaning and structure sources of information appropriately). Figure 11.1 outlines not only the thinking strategies and qualities of writing that we assessed Shawn's students for, but also the sources of information that those students were probably leaning more heavily on in order to think in those ways.

For the purposes of this chapter, we assessed ten of her students that spanned the range of her classroom. In that way you'll get sense of how to assess and form groups across a wide range of abilities. Whenever I assess students, I make sure that I understand what they wrote. I also jot down *what I noticed* and *what I said*. I also write down any *questions I still have*. You see this in action as you read on and meet the students and see both Shawn's assessments and mine (see Figure 11.2).

FIGURE 11.1   The thinking strategies and qualities of writing that you can assess for and the sources of information that students lean on in order to think and write in these ways.

THINKING STRATEGIES TO ASSESS FOR	QUALITY OF WRITING TO ASSESS FOR	SOURCES OF INFORMATION USED
Making decisions independently	Stamina	Meaning, structure, and visual
Activating relevant prior knowledge	Topic choice	Meaning and structure
	Genre choice	
Determining importance	Focus	Meaning and structure
Inferring	Elaboration	Meaning and structure
Envisioning	Descriptive language	Meaning and structure
Synthesizing	Structure	Meaning and structure
Asking questions	Revision	Meaning and structure
Monitoring	Editing	Meaning, structure, and visual
Activating knowledge of letters and sounds	Spelling/phonics	Visual

FIGURE 11.2   An assessment of Shawn Brandon's kindergarten students.

NAME OF STUDENT	WHAT HE/SHE WROTE (TRANSCRIPTION)	WHAT I OBSERVED/ WHAT I SAID QUESTIONS I HAVE
Lenny	Me and my friend Jon and Caitlyn. We got ice cream one for Jon and one for Caitlyn and one for me. We got Tweedy and Caitlyn and me. The eyes were blue and they were bumble guys. Then my aunt picked me up from school I went into the car. My mom picked Caitlyn up from school. And my dad said yes and we screamed and we said hooray to the ice cream.	Lenny needed assistance in telling his story in order. His writing is not structured in order, which reveals that he needs to work on synthesizing. **Questions I have:** Would it help Lenny to synthesize his story if he drew his pictures first?

(continued)

FIGURE 11.2   Continued

NAME OF STUDENT		WHAT HE/SHE WROTE (TRANSCRIPTION)	WHAT I OBSERVED/ WHAT I SAID QUESTIONS I HAVE
Ariel		Me and Jesse went to the movies Me and Jesse drank soda	Ariel said each word and pointed to the page each time he said a word to signify where he would write that word. Ariel typically did not listen to and then record the letters in a word. Rather, he tended to use words that he already knew how to write. My observation revealed that he needed to work on activating his knowledge of letters and sounds.
Jade		I was riding my go-cart. It is fast. Hair blowing, shining in your face. Go-carts are cool.	Jade used some interesting structures for her poem by writing poetic phrases such as "hair blowing" and then ending her piece with a summary. Her piece reveals that she has synthesized—that is, she put the parts of her poem together to create a coherent whole. **Questions I have:** Would Jade be interested in studying some other structures of poetry (perhaps repetition)?
Suzanne		Birds fly Birds walk wobbly. Some birds swim and it eat worms	Suzanne was writing a poem. Her descriptive language reveals that more than likely she envisioned. I might want to work with her more on that.

FIGURE 11.2 Continued

NAME OF STUDENT		WHAT HE/SHE WROTE (TRANSCRIPTION)	WHAT I OBSERVED/ WHAT I SAID QUESTIONS I HAVE
Grace	 	Once there was a butcher. In that butcher there was a lady. She said no one is coming. She was tired of working. She ran out of the store without closing it. Someone came in and took her job. She was soo happy	Her story is in order, which reveals that she synthesized. She resisted revision, which reveals that she is not asking questions while she writes.
India		White skin, Black skin Skin that has hair like bears	India has descriptive language, which reveals that she envisioned. My observations of India revealed that she used meaning and structure sources of information while writing but struggled more with using the visual sources of information.
Peter		Dear Mom, May I get the incredible hulk movie and all the movies that we rented? Please, thank you.	Peter started with a reason to write, which reveals that he activated relevant prior knowledge. He resisted revision, which revealed that he wasn't asking questions while writing.

FIGURE 11.2   Continued

NAME OF STUDENT	WHAT HE/SHE WROTE (TRANSCRIPTION)	WHAT I OBSERVED/ WHAT I SAID QUESTIONS I HAVE
Jesse 	Me and dad go to the movies. We was pokeyman. We eat popcorn and we drink soda	My observation revealed that Jesse did not monitor his writing. Although many of his words looked right, he did not go back and reread to see if his writing made sense and/or sounded right.
Ginnah 	Me and my mom went to Central Park with my favorite ball. My friend was waiting for me on the horse and then . . . I went on a merry go round and my tummy was hurting. And we played with my favorite ball. They went all the way up and then we went home.	When I spoke with Ginnah, I discovered that her story was mostly about playing with her favorite ball. I encouraged her to focus on that part. She then inserted the words *my favorite ball*. Although Ginnah can determine which parts of her story are important, she struggles more with how to elaborate on those important parts.
Bennie 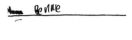 	Vampires suck blood and they have very sharp teeth. They bite hard. They leave the holes open.	Lenny's writing is hard to read because he has not activated enough knowledge of letters and sounds. He is, however, using meaning and structure sources of information.

THE STORY CONTINUES: FORMING GROUPS

Once we assessed Shawn's students, we reflected upon our assessments by forming groups (see Figure 11.3). You'll recognize many of the students in these groups because you've just seen their writing samples and our assessments of them. Others, however, are students that you did not meet, but are in Shawn's classroom and have similar strengths and needs to the students that you did meet. We often placed students in more than one group. India, for example, is in two groups. She was placed in Group 4 to further her knowledge of poetry, but she was also placed in Group 5 to help her record more than one sound in a word.

DECIDING ON METHODS OF TEACHING

Once we formed these groups, we needed to provide the types of instruction that would best support each of them. In Chapter 6, I discussed the components of balanced literacy. I showed you how different components highlighted or taught into different sources of information. We're going to once again look at the components of balanced literacy, but this time we're going to look at them as possible methods for our small group instruction.

The students in Group 3, for example (see Figure 11.3), needed work activating their knowledge of letters and sounds. In order to do this, they need to use visual (or graphophonic) sources of information. Since we already know that Interactive Writing is a component that primarily supports the students in learning more about the visual sources of information, our method of instruction for this group might very well be Interactive Writ-

FIGURE 11.3   Forming groups.

NAMES OF THE STUDENTS	WHY THEY ARE GROUPED TOGETHER	METHOD OF INSTRUCTION
GROUP 1 Grace, Peter, Tyler, Brianna	Asking questions/Revision	
GROUP 2 Grace, Chanelle, Danielle, Kevin	Elaboration/Inferring	
GROUP 3 Ariel, Lenny, Chanelle, Benny	Activating knowledge of letters and sounds/Phonics, Spelling	
GROUP 4 Suzanne, India, Jade, Jose	Synthesizing/Different ways to structure poetry	
GROUP 5 India, Danielle, Benny	Activating knowledge of letters and sounds/Phonics, Spelling	
GROUP 6 Ginnah, Grace, Tony, Juan	Inferring/Elaboration	

ing. If we wanted to teach this group from the reading angle, we might use Shared Reading as our method of instruction, since we also know that Shared Reading supports students in learning more about the visual sources of information.

The students in Group 6 needed work on elaborating in their writing. In order to do this, they need to lean more heavily on meaning and structure sources of information. We already know that Shared Writing supports students in learning more about the meaning and structure sources of information; therefore, when I work with the students in Group 6, I'll probably use Shared Writing as my method for instruction. Again, if I wanted to teach this group from the reading angle, then I might use Read-Aloud as my method of instruction, since I already know that the Read-Aloud is a good place to teach students more about the meaning and structure sources of information.

Figure 11.4 shows you not only the groups that we formed, but also the method of instruction we planned to use with each group. Of course, the components of balanced literacy are not the only methods for small group instruction, but it is helpful to consider the idea that you can use these components not only with your entire class, but with small groups as well.

TEACHING SMALL GROUPS

Now that we've looked at how to form groups and what methods would best suit particular groups, we're going to look more closely at the actual teaching that took place with the students in Group 3 and Group 6. Group 3, as seen in Figure 11.4, is working on activating

FIGURE 11.4   Forming groups and deciding on a method of teaching.

NAMES OF THE STUDENTS	WHY THEY ARE GROUPED TOGETHER	METHOD OF INSTRUCTION
GROUP 1 Grace, Peter, Tyler, Brianna	Asking questions/Revision	Shared Writing/Read-Aloud
GROUP 2 Grace, Chanelle, Danielle, Kevin	Elaboration/Inferring	Shared Writing/Read-Aloud
GROUP 3 Ariel, Lenny, Chanelle, Benny	Activating knowledge of letters and sounds/Phonics, Spelling	Interactive Writing/Shared Reading
GROUP 4 Suzanne, India, Jade, Jose	Synthesizing/Different ways to structure poetry	Shared Writing/Read-Aloud
GROUP 5 India, Danielle, Benny	Activating knowledge of letters and sounds/Phonics, Spelling	Interactive Writing/Read-Aloud
GROUP 6 Ginnah, Grace, Tony, Juan	Inferring/Elaboration	Shared Writing/Read-Aloud

knowledge of letters and sounds, specifically listening and recording sounds in order. Group 6 is working on elaborating, specifically writing more at the important parts of their texts. First we'll look at the transcripts, and then I'll extrapolate some of the important features (Figure 11.5 and 11.6).

Small groups should teach a strategy that some but not all students need.

Sometimes, teachers will tell me that they use small group instruction to reteach the minilesson they just did. There may be times when this is appropriate; however, it should not be the primary reason you form small groups. If it is, you probably need to restructure your minilessons so that they teach a wider range of students. The majority of your small groups should be formed because of a specific strength/need that some but not all students have.

The students in Group 3, for example, had a specific need (segmenting sounds). Most of the students in the classroom were already doing this; therefore, it made more sense to do it as a small group rather than as a minilesson. The students in Group 6 also had a specific need that some but not all of the students had (elaboration). Most of the students in Shawn's classroom were still trying to retell and write their stories in sequential order. Clearly, in these instances we did not simply reteach the minilesson. What both of these groups needed was not likely to come up in whole group instruction, which is why we knew they would benefit from receiving some small group instruction on these topics.

Small group instruction should be structured in ways similar to your minilessons.

In Chapter 9, we looked at the architecture of a minilesson and saw the impact that this architecture had on student learning. I use the same exact architecture when I pull small groups of students together for instruction. As you see in Figures 11.5 and 11.6, I start by *connecting* to what they already know. I continue by *teaching* them one new idea or concept. I ask them to practice that concept during the *active engagement* and then I *link* what I just taught to their ongoing work. I also used the components of balanced literacy as methods for my instruction as I also often do in my minilessons.

BLUR THE LINES: MOVING SMALL GROUPS BETWEEN WRITING AND READING

As Shawn and I worked with these groups, we realized that they needed more instruction on the same concept. After all, we had only met with them once. We realized, though, that we had options on how to continue supporting these students. We could continue with each group by providing them more small group instruction in writing; however, we could also enhance and add to this work by offering them similar small group instruction in reading. Next, I want to share some of the additional teaching that we did with both groups. Some

FIGURE 11.5   Small group writing instruction helping students to activate their knowledge of letters and sounds.

Members in Group: Group 3: Ariel, Lenny, Chanelle, and Benny
Working on activating knowledge of letters and sounds: Segmenting sounds
Method of Group: Interactive Writing

Connection

I know that in writing all of you have been listening to the sounds you hear and then writing down the letters that match those sounds. That is such smart work. Today I want to teach you one more thing that writers do when they're writing their words so it's easier to go back and reread.

Writers say the word and write down what they hear first. Then they say the word again and write down what they hear next. They keep saying the word until they don't hear any more sounds. Then, they know the word is over and they leave a space. First you're going to watch me, and then you're going to help me.

Teach

Today I thought that we could make a sign to put next to the math games. So we need to write two words: *math games*. Math—hmm . . . what do I hear first? M—that is an *m*. (The teacher puts her finger underneath the *m*.)

Math—let me say it again: aaa. I hear an *a*. (The teacher again puts her finger under the *ma*.)

Let me say it again. Ma*th*. (The teacher highlights the *th* sound.)

I hear "th." That is *t-h*.

Did you notice how I said the word and wrote down the letters that matched what I heard? Then I reread (I point to the word) and wrote down the letter that matched what I heard next. And then (I point again to the word) I reread again and wrote down what I heard at the end. I didn't hear any more sounds. That's the end of the word. We need a space. Benny, can you be our space maker?

Active Engagement

Let's try it together with the word *games*. Say the word *games*. What do you hear first?

(They all say the word *games*.)

Ariel: I hear a gggg. That letter is *g*.
Leah: Great, Ariel, can you come up and make the letter *g*? Benny, can you make sure that Ariel leaves a space?
Leah: Let's say *games* again. (Leah points to the *g*.) What do you hear next?
Lenny: I hear an *a*.
Leah: Great, come put that down.
Leah: (Lenny comes to the front and writes the *a* down.)
Leah: Let's say it again.
Leah: (Leah points to the letters *ga*. *Games*—what do you hear next?
Chanelle: I hear an *m*.
Leah: Great, come write it down.
Leah: (Chanelle comes to the front and writes the *m* down.)
Leah: At the end of this word there is a silent *e*. We have more than one game, so I'll add an *s*.

FIGURE 11.5   Continued

Link

What we just did together you can do always when you write. When you go back to your own writing today say the words and write down what you hear first and then next and then next. When you don't hear any more sounds, you know it's the end of the word. You'll make a space just like we did together. Have a great writing time.

FIGURE 11.6   Small group instruction on elaboration.

Members in Group: Group 6: Ginnah, Grace, Tony, Juan
Working on Elaboration
Method of group: Shared Writing

Connection

I know that all of you have been working on writing stories when you say what happened first and then next and then next. Putting your story in order helps people to understand it. Today I want to teach you another way to help people understand your story. You can think about which part of the story is most important and then put a lot of words at that part. First you're going to watch me, and then you're going to help me.

Teach

I've got the story we wrote the other day about going on the field trip to Central Park. Remember we all decided that the most important part of this story was when we couldn't find the lunch basket. We should put more words at this part because it's important.

What could we say? We could say what the different people in the story were doing when they couldn't find the lunch basket. Nobody knew what to do. Pam's mom looked in the playground. Sandra's mom looked on the bus. (The teacher jots what she wanted to add to the story in her notes.)

Did you see what I just did? Did you see how I put more words at that part because it is important? What else could we put?

Active Engagement

Grace: We could say that the whole class was worried. We thought that we would starve.
Leah: Oh yes, you're right: We could also say how everyone was feeling. Ginnah, what else could we write if we were going to put more words at the important part?
Ginnah: You could say that you called the school on your cell phone.
Leah: You're right. We could add more words about what the people, the characters, were doing.

Link

Did you all see how we put more words at the important part? This is something that you can always do. Today as you write I want you to think about which part of your own story is the most important and then put more words at that part. You might put down words that describe what the characters were doing like we did when we said Pam's mom looked in the playground. You might put down words that describe what the characters were feeling like Ginnah when she said everyone was worried. You might put down different words, but remember to put down a lot of words at the important part.

of this additional teaching took place in small groups during Writing Workshop, while some of it took place in small groups during Reading Workshop.

Continuing with Group 3: Small group instruction in both writing and reading.

We wanted the students in Group 3 to activate their knowledge of letters and sounds while writing. We continued to use Interactive Writing with this group, but we watched them as they wrote and addressed some of the issues that arose. We found that sometimes the students couldn't activate their knowledge of letters and sounds because they didn't know what some letters looked like. We extended their instruction in writing by meeting with them again, but this time helping them use the alphabet chart. We showed them how to locate the picture that made the same sound of the word they wanted to write. This way they could independently discover what a particular letter looked like. Another time, we met with them and gave them additional strategies for activating their knowledge of letters and sounds. We showed them how to ask themselves questions such as, *Is there a part of this new word that I know?* We also showed them how to reread, asking themselves if the words they wrote "looked right."

Shawn and I decided to add to Group 3's understanding of activating knowledge of letters and sounds by working with them in small groups during Reading Workshop as well as during Writing Workshop. We helped them in reading to locate parts of the word that they knew in order to help them read a new word. We used Shared Reading as our method of instruction (see Figure 11.7). Finding a part of a word that you know is of course a good reading strategy, but it's also a good writing strategy and will reinforce the writing work that this small group has already done.

Just as we knew that one small group in writing would not be sufficient, the same was also true for reading. We also met with this group over time in reading. We taught them how to use the same strategies that they used in shared reading books with the books that were at their instructional level. We introduced these books to them. After we introduced these books to them, we coached them while they read. We tended to say things such as, "Get your mouth ready for that word," and "Is there a part of that word that you know?" As you can see, the prompts that we taught in reading were very similar to the prompts that we taught them in writing.

Continuing with group 6: Small group instruction in both writing and reading.

The students in Group 6 needed further small group work in writing that would show them specific ways to elaborate upon the important parts of their stories. We continued using Shared Writing as our method of instruction but now we wrote stories together, writing words at the important part that told what the characters were doing (character action). We also met with them, helping them to put words down at the important part about what the characters were thinking. Other times, we focused on what the characters actually said (character dialogue). Figure 11.6 shows you some of that work.

FIGURE 11.7   Small group instruction that focuses on activating knowledge of letters and sounds.

Members in Group: Group 3: Ariel, Lenny, Chanelle, and Benny
Working on activating knowledge of letters and sounds (visual sources of information)
Method of Group: Shared Reading (*Animal Feet* by Carolyn MacLuLich)

Connection

I know that in writing we worked on listening to all the sounds in a word. We listened to the beginning sound, the middle sound, and the end sound. Today I want to show you how in reading you can look at all the parts of the word to help you figure it out, just like you listened to all the parts of a word while writing. And when you figure out the word, you'll understand the story more.

Teach

We've already read this book many times. We're going to read this book again. I've put some sticky notes on some of the words. When we get to those words, I'll take the sticky notes off. Then you'll see if you can find parts of the words that you know to help you read the new word. First you're going to watch me, and then you're going to help me.

(The teacher reads until she gets to a sticky note. The word is *horse*.) Hmm. Let me look to see if there is a part of this word that I know. Hey, I know the word *or*. Let me reread to see if that helps me. They are the feet of a h-*or*-se. That makes sense: It sounds right and it looks right. Yes, it did help me to find a part of the word that I knew.

Did you see how I used a part of the word that I knew to help me read the whole word?

Active Engagement

Okay, let's try it together. Let's keep reading until we get to a sticky note. When we get to one, you'll check to see if there is a part of that word that you know that will help you read the whole word.

(They keep reading until they get to the word *stands*.)

(The teacher takes off the sticky note.) Hmm, look to see if there is a part of this word that you know.

Ariel: and

(The teacher frames the word *and* with her hand.) You're right. We do know the word *and*. Let's look at that word together.

Now, let's go back and reread and use that word to help us read this new word: "These feet are soft with five toes, so the animal can balance when it st-*and*-s upright." Does *stands* look right?

(The students answer yes.)

Let's reread and make sure that *stands* makes sense and sounds right: "These feet are soft with five toes, so the animal can balance when it stands upright." Yes, it does make sense and it does sound right.

Link

What we just did together you can do by yourself with your own books. When you get to a tricky word, you can look to see if you know a part of the word. Then, you can reread and use what you know to help you read the new word, just like we did together today. Have a great reading time today.

In Figure 11.8 you see that we also worked with the students in Group 6 on the similar concept of inferring during small group instruction in reading. We continued this work in reading in similar ways to how we continued with this in writing. We showed them how to pay attention to what the characters in the story were doing, saying, and thinking. We also asked them to not only use the text evidence to infer but also use their own experiences to help them think about what the characters in the story were like.

FIGURE 11.8 Small group instruction in reading that focuses on inferring.

Members in Group: Group 6: Ginnah, Grace, Tony, and Suan
Working on Inferring
Method of Group: Read-Aloud (*The Snowy Day* by Ezra Jack Keats)

Connection

I know that you've been writing books and have trying to put a lot of words at the important part. We've tried to write words that show what the characters are doing, thinking, and saying. Today I want to teach you how you can help yourself understand a book by paying attention to what the characters are doing, thinking, and saying just like you do when you're writing. I'm going to read *The Snowy Day* to you again. As I read, I'm going to stop at different points for you to think about what Peter the main character is like. Pay attention to Peter's actions, his thoughts, and his words. First you're going to watch me do it, and then you're going to try it.

Teach

(The teacher reads about four pages.) Hmm . . . Peter is walking with his feet pointing in all different ways and then he's dragging a stick. His actions tell me that he must like playing in the snow.

Did you see what I did? Did you see how I read paying attention to Peter's actions? It helped me to understand the kind of person Peter is.

Active Engagement

Let's try it together. (I read on to the end. I stop and let the students talk.) What do you think Peter is like and how do you know that?

Ginnah: Well, I think that Peter is scared of the big kids because the books says that he thought it would be fun the join the big boys in their snowball fight, but he knew that he wasn't old enough.
Grace: Yeah, he made snow angels all by himself.
Teacher: So you could tell by those two parts that Peter might be scared of the older kids?
Grace: Yes.

Link

What we just did together with the Read-Aloud you can do by yourself when you read. You can read and pay attention to what the character does like I did when I said Peter must like the snow because he was walking in all different directions in it. You can read and pay attention to a character's thoughts like Ginnah did when she said that Peter might be scared of the big boys because he thought about playing with them but then decided he wasn't old enough. You might pay attention to something else, but remember to keep asking yourself, *What do these words teach me about the character?* Have a great reading time.

PUTTING THE READING/WRITING CONNECTION INTO ACTION

Examine your small group instruction in reading. Is it possible to enhance or add to that work by conducting similar small group instruction in writing?

Examine your small group instruction in writing. Is it possible to enhance or add to that work by conducting similar small group instruction in reading?

How do we best help our students progress in both reading and writing? As a first grade teacher, I agonized over my struggling readers. I met with them in small groups for reading both in school and after school. I met with them in reading over and over again, even when I wasn't seeing progress. I naively thought that the more small group instruction that I did in reading the faster they would grow.

The National Reading Panel suggests that we don't need to treat students' reading difficulties as evidence that "they need more of the same type of instruction that they have been receiving" (National Institute, 2000, p. 2.138). You can help your students read with clarity and skill by placing them not only in small groups for reading, but also in small groups for writing. Likewise, you can help your students write in clear and co-herent ways by placing them not only in small groups for writing, but also in small group work for reading.

The answer to how we help our students progress is not more small group work in reading, nor is it small group work in writing. It's a thoughtful combination of both.

FOR FURTHER STUDY

- Assess your students in order to form small groups. Observe them and look at their writing samples.
- Group students together based upon similar strengths and needs.
- Decide on your method of teaching (Components of Balanced Literacy).

- Plan small group instruction using the architecture of a minilesson.
- Plan additional small group work on the same strategy in writing.
- Plan additional small group work on the same strategy in reading.

CHAPTER 12

FINAL THOUGHTS

To find new things, take the path you took yesterday . . .
—John Burroughs

In the Preface to this book, I quoted Marie Clay when she said, "The reading/writing connection has the pleasant ring of a 'two-for-one bargain'" (2001, p. 11). As we approach the end of this book, I want to return once again to those powerful words, because what she says truly gets to the heart of what it means to teach using a reading/writing connection. In every chapter throughout this entire book, you saw this "two-for-one bargain" in action. You saw different ways that you could deliberately *blur the lines* between reading and writing, letting reading affect writing and writing affect reading, thus that powerful "two-for-one bargain" in action.

I took this same path throughout the entire book in the hopes that in the sameness you would make brand-new discoveries about what it means to assess, plan, and teach using the reading/writing connection to assist you. And now as we approach the end of this book and I get ready to leave your side, I would like to offer you some suggestions on how to keep these powerful "two-for-one bargains" alive and well in your classroom. (After all, who gets tired of a bargain?) In that way you can continue inventing brand-new ways to let reading and writing affect one another.

BLUR THE LINES IN YOUR METHODS AND STRUCTURES OF TEACHING

When you keep your teaching simple and predictable across reading and writing, you can use one area of teaching to enhance and improve the other area of teaching. Marcy Mattera, a second grade teacher at PS 261, for example, recently told me that her reading minilessons were clear, but her writing minilessons were not. "What makes your reading minilessons clear?" I asked her. "I demonstrate my reading process," she told me. "I tell them what I'm thinking while reading." "Why not do the same with your writing?" I suggested. "Demonstrate your writing process. Tell them what you are thinking while writing." The next day when she conducted her writing minilesson, she demonstrated what she thought about while writing in very much the same way that she was already demonstrating what she thought about while reading. Here, Marcy let her teaching methods in reading improve upon her teaching methods in writing. She received a "two-for-one bargain" by using demonstration not only as a method of teaching reading but also as a method of teaching writing.

It makes so much sense, doesn't it? But I've found as I've examined my own teaching and the teaching of the teachers that I work with that it's not always the case. Is the architecture of your writing minilessons the same as the architecture of your reading minilessons? What about your conferences? Do you conduct similar types of conferences across reading and writing? What about your methods? Are they similar across reading and writing? Search for places in both your teaching and planning where you can align both your methods and structures of teaching across reading and writing.

BLUR THE LINES IN YOUR PLANNING AND YOUR ASSESSMENTS

One fall morning I walked into a classroom in the midst of a teacher's minilesson. The teacher was using the book *Night Owl* to teach her students how to predict by looking at the title and cover. My mind was whirling as I watched her, not just with ideas on what she could do next in reading, but also with what she could teach next in writing. I was wondering if her students would benefit from a reading minilesson on doing their own "picture walk." I was also wondering if her students would benefit from a writing minilesson on composing titles and covers for their own stories that would assist the reader. Once again, I got a "two-for-one bargain." I was planning, at the same time, reading and writing mini-lessons—both of these minilessons would help students understand similar concepts.

Later on in the day I conferred with one of her students. He read carefully, but at times got bogged down in the minutiae without getting the gist of what mattered in the book. As I conferred with him, I was thinking about what I could say to him right there in the midst of the reading conference, but at the same time, I was wondering if he also got bogged down in the details in his writing without getting to the gist of what truly mattered. I was getting another one of those wonderful "two-for-one bargains." Maybe his reading and writing were similar. Maybe they weren't, but my assessment of him in reading would certainly add to my assessment of him in writing. What can you do to keep the two-for-one bargain alive in your planning and your assessments? Can you create record-keeping systems that allow you to assess more easily between reading and writing? Can you also plan your reading and writing curriculum side by side, rather than separate them?

BLUR THE LINES IN YOUR STRENGTHS

Elizabeth Sulzby's research in Emergent Reading had a powerful effect upon my teaching. It helped me understand the power of rereading similar types of text. It became even more powerful, though, when I took what I learned from Emergent Reading and used it to add to and improve my teaching of writing. I used my newfound understanding of rereading similar types of texts to plan immersion lessons for the teaching of writing. Here, I used my strength in reading to add to and improve my teaching of writing.

Chrissy Koukiotis, who's teaching graces the pages of this book, did something very similar. She knew that she was adept at teaching her students how to read in a variety of genres. She wondered how she could use this strength to enhance and add to her teaching of writing. She decided to teach her students how to write in a variety of genres and forms, in the same way that they already read in a variety of forms and genres. Her strength in teaching reading became even more powerful when she used it to enhance and add to her teaching of writing.

Sometimes the strength starts in reading as it did with both Chrissy and myself, but sometimes the strength starts in writing. Recently, a teacher told me that she had taught her second grade students how to reread their writing. They did this beautifully, she said, but they struggled to reread their independent reading books. She realized they struggled because she had never taught them how to do this. So she then taught her students how to reread their independent reading books in very much the same way that she had taught them to reread their own writing. This teacher took her strength in the teaching of writing and used it to enhance and add to her teaching of reading.

Make a list of your strengths in the teaching of reading and writing. Can you take the strength you have in one area and turn it into new and powerful curriculum for the other area?

BLUR THE LINES IN YOUR MATERIALS

When you know your materials well, you can move these materials more easily between reading and writing. Many teachers I know select books for each writing Unit of Study they do. They carefully study these books in order to find the ones that they can use to add and improve to their students' writing skills. These teachers studied reading materials and turned them into powerful writing materials. You also study writing materials and turn them into reading materials. For example, many teachers also study their students' writing. They use their writing samples to teach reading strategies. Just recently I watched a teacher use a student's nonfiction writing piece during a reading minilesson. The teaching was particularly powerful, because the students were learning how to comprehend a diagram by reading a classmates' writing. The lesson wouldn't have been nearly as powerful if the teacher hadn't studied her students' writing carefully and then chosen an appropriate selection to use in her reading minilesson.

How can you become more familiar with the materials in your classroom? Can you study children's literature with your colleagues, carefully choosing the books that will affect your student's writing? Can you study your students' writing samples, choosing pieces that will affect your students' reading? When you approach the end of the school year, why not set aside books that you'll use the following year to teach writing? And while you do that, you'll also want to read and then make copies of student work that you know will help you in the future to teach reading.

BLUR THE LINES IN YOUR PROFESSIONAL READING

You can also get a "two-for-one bargain" in your professional reading. Last year, I was lucky enough to spend the year studying the reading/writing connection with ten brilliant teachers. We read Debbie Miller's book (among others) *Reading with Meaning* with a double lens. First, we talked about how this book would affect our teaching of reading, and then we talked about how this book would affect our teaching of writing.

For example, one of her chapters examined the comprehension strategy of envisioning. We talked about not only that comprehension strategy, but also how we could pair that comprehension strategy with descriptive language in writing. We considered how and when we might teach both. We also thought about how the teaching of one might affect the teaching of the other.

At the end of that year, Eileen Scanlon, a member of this group, wrote in her reflection journal, "Since being in this group, I can't look at professional texts in the same way. Whenever I read a professional book about reading, I'm always thinking about its teaching implications for writing. Whenever I read a professional book about writing, I'm always thinking about its teaching implications for reading." I hope that you also can now read professional literature and attend staff development sessions differently. View them as Eileen did, with a double lens, one for its implications for the teaching of reading and the other for its implications for the teaching of writing.

It's time for me to leave your side. I hope that I've nudged you to grab a colleague and to continue studying the reading writing connection. Barbara Kingsolver in her wonderful book *Small Wonders* talks about reading being not a chore but rather a *life raft*. The reading/writing connection is a life raft for my teaching and I hope it becomes one for you. I hope that it helps you teach with greater joy and focus in on what matters most, the students in front of you! Most important, I hope that this book has inspired you to continue studying the reading/writing connection so that you can take the same path as you did yesterday but discover something new every single time.

RECOMMENDED PROFESSIONAL LITERATURE

Throughout this book I've examined many topics through the lens of the reading/writing connection. Below is a list of professional books that you can refer to if you're looking for a more comprehensive look at any of the topics.

THE COMPONENTS OF BALANCED LITERACY

1. *Interactive Writing* by Gay Su Pinnell (for Interactive Writing)
2. *Read It Again* by Brenda Parkes (for Shared Reading)
3. *Foundations of Literacy* by Don Holdaway (for Shared Reading, Chapter 4)

READING AND WRITING WORKSHOP

1. *The Writing Workshop: Working through the Hard Parts (And They're All Hard Parts)* by Katie Wood Ray with Lester Laminack
2. *About the Authors: Writing Workshop with Our Youngest Writers* by Katie Wood Ray with Lisa B. Cleaveland
3. *The Art of Teaching Reading* by Lucy Calkins
4. *The Art of Teaching Writing* by Lucy Calkins
5. *Units of Study for Primary Writing: A Yearlong Curriculum* by Lucy Calkins and colleagues from The Teachers College Reading and Writing Project
6. *. . . And with a Light Touch* (2nd edition) by Carol Avery
7. *Writing through Childhood: Rethinking Process and Product* by Shelley Harwayne (Chapter 4)
8. *In the Company of Children* by Joanne Hindley
9. *Growing Readers: Units of Study in the Primary Classroom* by Kathy Collins

CONFERENCES

1. *The Art of Teaching Writing* by Lucy Calkins (Chapter 14)
2. *The Writing Workshop: A World of Difference* Lucy Calkins (Chapter 7)
3. *Writing Workshop: The Essential Guide* by Ralph Fletcher (Chapter 5)

4. *Writing Teachers and Children at Work* by Donald Graves (Chapters 10–14)
5. *how's it going?* by Carl Anderson
6. *The Writing Workshop: Working through the Hard Parts (And They're All Hard Parts)* by Katie Wood Ray with Lester Laminack (Chapter 14)
7. *Writing through Childhood: Rethinking Process and Product* by Shelley Harwayne (especially Chapters 4 and 6)
8. *In the Company of Children* by Joanne Hindley
9. *Conference and Conversations: Listening to the Literate Classroom* by Douglas Kaufman

SMALL GROUP WORK

1. *Guided Reading* by Irene C. Fountas and Gay Su Pinnell
2. *The Foundations of Literacy* by Don Holdaway
3. *Talking about Books* by Kathy Short
4. *What Really Matters for Struggling Readers: Designing Research-Based Programs* by Richard Allington
5. *Starting Out Right: A Guide to Promoting Reading Success* by M. Susan Burns, Catherine E. Snow, and Peg Griffin.
6. *The Art of Teaching Reading* by Lucy Calkins
7. *On Solid Ground* by Sharon Taberski
8. *Reading Instruction That Works* (2nd edition) by Michael Pressley

TRANSCRIPT OF REHEARSAL AND REVISION IN READING

REHEARSAL

The Teacher: Readers, this book is called *Sunrise*—that means the sun is coming up. What do you think this book is going to be about?

Isaiah: I think a rooster because—look—there is one. (He points to the picture.)

The Teacher: You're right. There is a rooster. This book is about different animals, and it's sunrise—the sun is coming up—and it is time for all the animals to wake up. On every page a different animal says it is time to get up. Let's look at some of the pictures to see which animals need to wake up. (The teacher opens up the book, while the other students sit in a circle around her.)

Evan: Oh look, a lizard has to wake up.

Sam: Oh, on that page a cow is waking up. (The teacher continues to turn the pages of the book.)

REVISION

The Teacher: Tell me about the book you're reading.

Taisha: I just love this book. I'm thinking about Little Bear. (The class was studying characters.) Little Bear is always sad, because no one remembered his birthday. He is always sad!

The Teacher: You're right: Little Bear does seem like a very sad character, but sometimes when you read more you change your mind. As you read today, see if Little Bear is always sad, or just sometimes sad. You never know, you might change your mind as you read.

(And sure enough, by the time Taisa had finished the chapter her mind had been changed: She had found places at the end where Little Bear was quite happy.)

STRATEGIES TO TEACH MEANING, STRUCTURE, AND SOURCES OF INFORMATION

STRATEGIES TO TEACH MEANING AND STRUCTURE

EMERGENT WRITING STRATEGIES	EMERGENT READING STRATEGIES
We speak and draw to compose meaning into text (Meaning, Structure).	We speak and look at pictures to compose meaning from text (Meaning, Structure).

- We choose stories to tell in lots of different ways (books we know give us ideas, school stories, home stories, ordinary events, extraordinary events).
- We can build more meaning into what we write by talking. We can:
  - Tell our story over and over, each time adding more story element words (*where, what happened, who*), etc.
  - We can share what we know about a topic (snakes) over and over, each time remembering something that we know.
- We can also build more meaning into our drawing by adding more story elements to the illustration, such as more illustrations that show story elements (*where, what happened, who*), etc.
- We can also build more meaning into our drawing by adding more information about what we learned.
- We can build more meaning into our drawing by adding pages to show the passage of time.

- We choose books in lots of different ways (topics we love or topics we know well, books we love or we already know well, books we just instantly connect with).
- We can build more meaning into the books we read by reading them over and over again, each time adding more story element words (*where, what happened, who*)

- We can build more meaning into the books we read by looking at the pictures very closely.

- We can build more meaning into the books we're reading by saying more about what we are learning each time.
- We can build more meaning into the books we're reading by connecting one page to the next page.

STRATEGIES TO TEACH WHEN YOU'RE ADDING ON VISUAL SOURCES OF INFORMATION

WRITING STRATEGIES	READING STRATEGIES

We speak, use pictures, and use words to compose meaning into text (M, S, V).

- We use the letters of the alphabet when we write.
- We write from left to right, top to bottom.
- We say words slowly and listen for sounds (any sounds).
- We say words slowly and listen for the first sound, and then the next, and the next.
- We have other strategies for spelling words, such as, *Is there a word like this word that would help me? Do I just know this word? Is there a part of this word I know?*
- We solve problems and use resources around the room independently.

We speak, use pictures, and look at the words to compose meaning from the text (M, S, V).

- We use the letters of the alphabet when we read.
- We read from left to right, top to bottom.
- We think about what would make sense, and we get our mouth ready for the first sound.

- We have other strategies for reading words, such as, *Do I know a word that would help me read this word? Can I just read this word quickly? Is there a part of this word I know?*
- We solve problems and use resources around the room independently.

THINKING STRAGEGIES THAT READERS AND WRITERS USE

THINKING STRATEGIES THAT READERS AND WRITERS USE	QUALITY OF WRITING THAT REVEALS THIS TYPE OF THINKING	HELPFUL LANGUAGE
Readers and writers *make decisions independently*.	*Stamina:* Students have the ability to write independently for a sustained period of time. Students have the ability to stay with one writing piece for an extended period of time.	What can you do to solve this problem without me?
Readers and writers *activate relevant prior knowledge*.	*Topic Choice:* Students choose to write about familiar topics. Students choose to write in familiar genres and forms.	What topics do you know a lot about? What types of writing do you see in the world? How does this book connect to your life? How does that connection help you understand your book?
Readers and writers *determine the important themes and ideas* in text. They use evidence from the text, their knowledge, and their beliefs.	*Focus:* Students choose to include some details, while not including others.	What is the most important part of your writing (or your reading)? Can you tell me about one time when . . .? Why did you write this?
Readers and writers *infer*. They use their prior knowledge and textual information to draw conclusions and form unique interpretations from the text.	*Elaboration:* Students expand upon the important parts.	Could you say more in your writing? What were you doing in your story? What were you thinking in your story? What did you say in your story? What do you think the character in this book is like? Can you find places in the book that prove that?
Readers and writers *envision*. They create images using visual and other sensory information from and into text during and after reading and writing.	*Descriptive Language:* Students include visual and other sensory images in their text.	What does it look like? What does it sound like? What does it smell like? What does it taste like? What does it feel like?

THINKING STRATEGIES THAT READERS AND WRITERS USE	QUALITY OF WRITING THAT REVEALS THIS TYPE OF THINKING	HELPFUL LANGUAGE
Readers and writers *synthesize.* They order, recall, retell, and recreate into a coherent whole.	*Structure:* Students organize their writing. It could be organized sequentially. It could be organized to support an idea. It could be organized through knowledge of genre.	What happened first (in your story or the story you're reading)? What happened next? What happened at the end of your story? How does this part of your writing fit with the rest of your writing? How does this part of the book that you're reading fit in with the rest of the book? What do you know about nonfiction that could help you write your own nonfiction book? What do you know about nonfiction that could help you read this nonfiction book?
Readers and writers *ask questions* of themselves and of the readers and writers.	*Revision:* Students add or take away details, keeping both their vision and their audience in mind.	*Questions that readers ask:* What is the writer trying to tell me in this text? What does this part mean? What significance do I see in this text? *Questions that writers ask:* What will my readers need to know in order to understand my writing? What am I really trying to say here? What is significant?
Readers and writers *monitor.* They read, reread, and rewrite using one source of information against another.	*Edit:* Students improve the mechanics of their piece. This includes: Spelling Conventions Grammar	Does it make sense? Does it sound right? Does it look right?
Readers and writers *activate their knowledge of letters and sounds.*	*Spelling/Phonics:* Students encode print, matching letters to the appropriate sounds. Students spell words they know correctly.	What do you hear first? What do you hear next? What do you hear at the end of the word? Get your mouth ready. Find a word inside the word that you know. Look at the end of the word. Does it look right?

PLANNING SHEET FOR THE COMPONENTS OF BALANCED LITERACY

WHAT I NOTICE ABOUT THE STUDENTS' STRENGTHS AND NEEDS 1. SOURCES OF INFORMATION 2. QUALITIES OF WRITING	WHAT I CAN TEACH IN SHARED WRITING	WHAT I CAN TEACH IN READ-ALOUD	WHAT I CAN TEACH IN SHARED READING	WHAT I CAN TEACH IN INTERACTIVE WRITING	THINGS TO LOOK FOR IN FUTURE READING AND WRITING WORKSHOPS

PLANNING A UNIT OF STUDY

Unit of Study: _____

Method: Demonstration and Show and Tell

GETTING READY FOR THE STUDY:

- Look at student work and watch students in the midst of reading or writing. Determine their strengths and needs and angle your study toward them. Lay out three to four goals.
- Determine the length of the study.
- Gather the books needed for the study and read through them. Choose a few touchstone texts.
- Look through past notes and plans and alter if necessary.
- What new tools will you introduce?
- What will the final pieces look like?
- How will you celebrate?

IMMERSION

Purpose: To build meaning and structure in the particular genre or form being studied

1. What will your minilessons be for immersion?

WRITING

Beginning Minilesson

Purpose: To help students become more independent

Other Minilessons

Purpose: To address students' strengths and needs

REVISION

EDITING

PLANNING READING AND WRITING UNITS OF STUDY

Name of Study: _____

Goals:

POSSIBLE WRITING MINILESSONS	POSSIBLE READING MINILESSONS	COMMON THINKING STRATEGIES

PLANNING A
CURRICULUM CALENDAR

DATE	WRITING	READING	CONNECTION *Strategies* *Process*	ASSESSMENT	CELEBRATION

SAMPLE CURRICULUM CALENDARS

Mapping Curriculum (Half-Day Kindergarten)

DATE	WRITING	READING	CONNECTION *Strategies Process*	ASSESSMENT: QUALITIES OF WRITING TO LOOK FOR	CELEBRATION
September/ October	Building a community of writers	Building a community of readers	Independent decision making Activating prior knowledge Rehearsal	Stamina Topic choice	Classroom celebration
November/ December	Personal narrative	Emergent Reading storybooks	Synthesis	Structure	Read aloud to other classes
January/ February	We write for many reasons	Nonfiction	Determining importance Activating knowledge of print Asking questions	Focus Print strategies	Share what you learned with your book buddy
March/April	Nonfiction	Comprehension strategies	Activating prior knowledge	Topic choice	Parent celebration
May/June	Revision	Revision	Monitoring Asking questions	Editing Revision	School celebration

Mapping Curriculum (Grade 2)

DATE	WRITING	READING	CONNECTION *Strategies Process*	ASSESSMENT: QUALITIES OF WRITING TO LOOK FOR	CELEBRATION
September	Writerly life	Readerly life	Independent decision making Activating prior knowledge Rehearsal	Stamina Topic choice	Read and/or write with an upper-grade buddy.
October	Personal narrative	Partnerships	Using character and plot Determining importance Rehearsal (talk) Revision (talk)	Focus	Bind into books for classroom library.
November	Revision	Character	Determining importance Inference	Elaboration	Process celebration with parents.
December	Conventions	Nonfiction	Asking questions Monitoring Editing	Revision Editing	Process celebration with partners. Teach a partner what you learned about nonfiction.
January	Nonfiction	Nonfiction	Synthesis	Structure	Teach something about what you learned.
February	Launching writers' notebooks	Setting	Asking questions Envisioning	Revision Descriptive writing	Museum Share: The class walks around and admires the notebooks.
March	Poetry	Reading series books	Monitoring Asking questions Envisioning	Editing Revision Descriptive writing	Create a poetry reading at a local book store.
April	Realistic fiction	Mystery	Synthesis	Structure	Bind into classroom books.
May/June	Writing projects	Reading projects	Asking questions	Revision	Parent celebration.

TRANSCRIPT OF A CONNECTED READING AND WRITING MINILESSON

READING MINILESSON

Unit of Study: Launching the Reading Workshop
Teaching Point: You can look at your picture to help you read your words.
Method: Demonstration

Connection

Yesterday when I was watching all of you read, I saw Julia doing something that was so smart that I wanted to share it with the class. Julia was reading the book *Time to Get Up*. In the middle of the book she got stuck on a word. (The teacher opens up to the page where Julia got stuck.) Julia looked at the picture of the cow and that helped her to read the word *cow*. When Julia looked at the picture, it helped her to understand what was happening in the story. Today I want to teach all of you how to do what Julia did. I want to teach you how you can look at the picture to help you understand what's happening in your book. First, you're going to watch me use the picture to help me understand what is happening and then we're going to try it together.

Remember *The Little Mouse, The Red Ripe Strawberry, and THE BIG HUNGRY BEAR*. (The teacher has this story in a big book, so that students can follow along.) Well, today I'm going to read in front of you and I want you to watch me as I look at the picture. (The teacher points to the picture.) And then look at the words. (The teacher points to the words.)

Page 1: Hmm . . . let me look at the picture. Hello, little Mouse. What are you doing? (Because the picture on this page isn't incredibly supportive, she makes a point of looking at the picture, but then quickly moves on.)

Page 2: Hmm . . . let me look at the picture. (She turns the page and looks at the picture.) Oh, there is that big red ripe strawberry and there is the mouse. He is about the pick the red ripe strawberry. Okay, I looked at the pictures. Now, let me read the words. Oh, I see. "Are you going to pick that red ripe strawberry?"

Did you notice how first I looked at the picture? Like on the first page I looked at the mouse and that helped me understand what was happening in the story. On the second page, I looked at the big red ripe strawberry and the mouse and that helped me to understand what was happening.

Active Engagement

Let's try it together. I'm going to read part of this to you. You can read along if you like and then we'll get to a page where I'll stop. When I stop, you're going to look at the picture first, and then you're going to read the words with a partner. (The teacher reads on until she gets the page where the strawberry is disguised.)

Okay, turn to your talk partner, look at the picture together to figure out what's happening, and then try and read the words.

Today I saw Jose looking at the picture and how the strawberry had glasses and that helped him understand that the strawberry was disguised, and then he was able to read the words.

Link

What we just did together you can do by yourself always during Reading Workshop. Today remember that you can look at the pictures to help you understand what's happening in the books that you're reading. Later on, we'll share how this helped you read. Have a great reading time.

WRITING MINILESSON

Unit of Study: Launching the Writing Workshop
Teaching Point: You can look at your picture to help you write your words.
Method: Demonstration

Connection (1–2 minutes)

We already know that one way to help ourselves understand our books in reading is to look at some or all of the pictures. Remember yesterday when we read *The Little Mouse, The Big Red Ripe Strawberry, and THE BIG HUNGRY BEAR* together. (The teacher held up the book *The Big Red Ripe Strawberry.*) We looked at the pictures first, and then we read the words. It helped us understand the book. (As the teacher says this, she points first to a picture in *The Big Red Ripe Strawberry,* and then to the words.)

I saw Jose reading a book called *Going to the Circus.* (The teacher held up Jose's book.) He looked at some of his pictures first, and that helped him understand his book. It also helped him when he got to tricky words. The pictures helped him to read the words. (As the teacher is saying this, she is again pointing first to the picture in Jose's book and then to the words.)

It's similar in writing. You can help other people understand what's happening in your story by first looking at what's happening in your picture and then writing your words. Today I want to teach you how in writing you can look at your picture first to help you write your words, just like you look at the picture first to help you read the words. First you're going to watch me, and then you're going to help me.

Teach (5-6 minutes)

Remember my story about running. (The teacher has her story about running on the easel. All of her pictures are already completed.) Well today, I'm going to first look at my picture (she points to her picture) to help me write my words (she points to the empty place where her words will go).

Hmm . . . let me look at my picture. (The teacher pauses and looks.) Oh, I know what I will write. One day I was running in the park. (As she says this, she points to the trees in her picture.) I was really happy. (As she says this, she points to the expression on her face in her picture.)

Okay. Now that I've looked at my picture, let me write my words. (She quickly writes her words, not enlisting any help from the students. She also writes the words conventionally.)

(She turns to the next page.) Let me look at my picture. (The teacher pauses and looks.) Oh, I know what I will write. All of the sudden I saw a puddle. I was worried. *Don't slip in the puddle,* I thought. (Again, as she says this aloud as she points to the parts in her picture.)

Okay. Now that I've looked at my picture, let me write the words. (She quickly writes the words.)

Did you notice how I first looked at the parts of my picture, like the tree (she points to the tree) and that helped me remember to write that I was in the park, and then I looked at my happy face, and that helped to remember to write, "*I was really happy.*" I'm telling you that because you can do the same thing. You can look at your pictures to help tell us what happening in your story.

Active Engagement (2 minutes)

Okay, let's try it together. Remember yesterday how we went to the assembly to watch the fifth graders dance. Well, I drew the pictures of that story. Turn to your talk partner. Partner one, you go first. Look at the picture and tell partner two what words you might write. Then partner two, tell partner one what words you might write. I'll be around to listen.

(The teacher is walking around, record-keeping system in hand.)

Today I saw Julia looking carefully at the picture. She looked at the fifth graders dancing and laughing on stage and thinks we should write "One day we went to an assembly. We walked in, and the fifth grade kids were dancing and laughing on the stage." Julie looked at the faces in the picture, just like I did in my picture and it helped her to tell what happened. (As the teacher says this, she points to the picture and then to the empty space where later she would write the words.)

Link

What we just did together when we looked at the picture to help us decide what to write is something that you can always do by yourself during Writing Workshop. Many of you have worked hard on your pictures and are ready to write your words. If so, you might want to look carefully at your pictures today to help you write your words. If you are not ready to do this, put the idea in your pocket and use it later on. Thumbs up if you think you'll be trying this today. Have a great writing time.

CONFERRING WITH STUDENTS ACROSS READING AND WRITING

Name of Student: _____

Research the Student:

- Watch him/her in the process of reading and/or writing
- Previous reading and writing conferences
- Writing products
- Watching students in other parts of the day

Stronger Writer _____
Stronger Reader _____
Very similar across reading and writing _____

Why might this be the case?

Possible conferences in writing:

Possible conferences in reading:

Marcy's Writing Conference Notes

Aaliyah	Amanda	Androcles	Cesar
Diamond	German	Hope	Isaiah
Kalifia	Kani	Lamar	Melanie
Michael	Patricia	Rahan	Rudolph
Tamara	Taylor		

Marcy's Reading Conference Notes

Aaliyah	Amanda	Androcles	Cesar
Diamond	German	Hope	Isaiah
Kalifia	Kani	Lamar	Melanie
Michael	Patricia	Rahan	Rudolph
Tamara	Taylor		

STUDENT'S NAME	DATE	STRONGER IN READING	STRONGER IN WRITING	HOW TO TEACH TO STUDENT'S STRENGTHS	TEACH IN MINILESSONS OR CONFERENCES

READING WORKSHOP	**WRITING WORKSHOP**
Focus: _____	Focus: _____
Language Used: _____	Language Used: _____
_____	_____
Introduction _____ Applying _____ Mastery _____	Introduction _____ Applying _____ Mastery _____

SMALL GROUP WORK
PLANNING SHEETS

NAME OF STUDENT	WHAT HE/SHE WROTE	WHAT I OBSERVED WHAT I SAID QUESTIONS I HAVE

NAMES OF STUDENTS	WHY THEY ARE BEING PUT TOGETHER	METHOD OF INSTRUCTION

Adams, Marilyn Jager. 1990. *Beginning to Read: Thinking and Learning about Print.* Cambridge, MA: The MIT Press.

Afferback, P.P., and P.H. Johnson. 1986. What do expert readers do when the main idea is not explicit? In J.F. Baumann, ed., *Teaching Main Idea Comprehension.* Newark, DE: International Reading Association.

Allington, Richard. 2001. *What Really Matters for Struggling Readers: Designing Research-Based Programs.* Boston: Addison-Wesley.

Allington, Richard. 2002. *Big Brother and the National Reading Curriculum.* Portsmouth, NH: Heinemann.

Allington, Richard, and Patricia Cunningham, 1996. *Schools That Work: Where All Children Read and Write.* New York: Longman.

Anderson, Carl. 2000. *how's it going?* Portsmouth, NH: Heinemann.

Anderson, R.C., and P.D. Pearson. 1984. A schema-theoretic view of basic processes in reading. In P.D. Pearson, ed., *Handbook of Reading Research.* White Plains, NY: Longman.

Avery, Carol. 2002. *. . . And with a Light Touch.* Portsmouth, NH: Heinemann.

Barone, Diane M., and Lesley Mandel Morrow, eds. 2003. *Literacy and Young Children: Research-Based Practices.* New York: Guilford Press.

Baumann, J.F. 1986. The direct instruction of main idea comprehension ability. In J.F. Baumann, ed., *Teaching Main Idea Comprehension.* Newark, DE: International Reading Association.

Baumann, J.F., and G. Ivey. 1997. Delicate balances: Striving for curricular and instructional equilibrium in a second-grade literature/strategy-based classroom. *Reading Research Quarterly 32,* 244–275.

Bomer, Randy. 1995. *Time for Meaning.* Portsmouth, NH: Heinemann.

Bomer, Randy, and Katherine Bomer. 2001. *For a Better World: Reading and Writing for Social Justice.* Portsmouth, NH: Heinemann.

Brown, D.L., and L.D. Briggs. 1991. Becoming literate: The acquisition of story discourse. *Reading Horizons 32*(2), 139–153.

Butler, Andrea, and Jan Turbill. 1987. *Towards a Reading-Writing Classroom.* Portsmouth, NH: Heinemann.

Calkins, Lucy. 1994. *The Art of Teaching Writing.* Portsmouth, NH: Heinemann.

Calkins, Lucy. 2001. *The Art of Teaching Reading.* New York: Longman.

Calkins, Lucy, and colleagues from The Teacher's College Reading and Writing Project. 2003. *Units of Study in Primary Writing: A Yearlong Curriculum.* Portsmouth, NH: Heinemann.

Cambourne, Brian, and Jan Turbill. 1991. *Coping with Chaos.* Portsmouth, NH: Heinemann.

Cary, Stephen. 1998. *Second Language Learners* (pp. 53–57). York, ME: The Galef Institute/Stenhouse Publishers.

Clay, Marie. 1975. *What Did I Write? Beginning Writing Behaviour.* Auckland, NZ: Heinemann.

Clay, Marie. 1977. *Write Now: Read Later: An Evaluation.* Auckland, NZ: International Reading Association.

Clay, Marie. 1998. *By Different Paths to Common Outcomes.* Portland, ME: Stenhouse.

Clay, Marie. 2001. *Change over Time.* Portsmouth, NH: Heinemann.

Collins, Kathy. 2004. *Growing Readers: Units of Study in the Primary Classroom.* Portland, ME: Stenhouse.

Cooper, Charles R. 1999. What we know about genres, and how it can help us assign and evaluate writing pages. In Charles R. Cooper and Lee Odell, eds., *Evaluating Writing.* Urbana, IL: NCTE.

Cooper, Patsy. 1993. *When Stories Come to School.* New York: Teachers and Writers Collaborative.

Cunningham, Patricia. 2003. Speech at Teacher's College Reading and Writing Project, Columbia University, New York.

Edwards, Sharon, and Robert Maloy. 1992. *Kids Have All the Write Stuff.* New York: Penguin Books.

Falk, Beverly. 1998, September. Focus on research testing the way children learn: Principles for valid literacy assessment. *Language Arts 76.*

Fitzgerald, Jill. 1999, October. What is this thing called "balance"? *The Reading Teacher 53*(2), 100–106.

Fletcher, Ralph. 1992. *What a Writer Needs.* Portsmouth, NH: Heinemann.

Fountas, Irene, and Gay Su Pinnell. 1996. *Guided Reading: Good First Teaching for All Children.* Portsmouth, NH: Heinemann.

Fountas, Irene, and Gay Su Pinnell. 1998. *Word Matters: Teaching Phonics and Spelling in the Reading/Writing Classroom.* Portsmouth, NH: Heinemann.

Garner, R. 1987. *Metacognition and Reading Comprehension.* Norwood, NJ: Ablex.

Gibbons, Pauline. 1991. *Learning to Learn in a Second Language.* Portsmouth, NH: Heinemann.

Gibbons, Pauline. 1991. *Scaffolding Language, Scaffolding Learning: Teaching Second Language Learners in the Mainstream Classroom.* Portsmouth, NH: Heinemann.

Goodman, Yetta. 1996. *Notes from a Kidwatcher.* Portsmouth, NH: Heinemann.

Gordon, Thomas (with Noel Burch). 1974. *T.E.T.: Teacher Effectiveness Training.* New York: David McKay Co.

Graves, Donald. 1985. The reader's audience. In Jane Hansen, Thomas Newkirk, and Donald Graves, eds., *Breaking Ground: Teachers Relate Reading and Writing in the Elementary School* (pp. 193–199). Portsmouth, NH: Heinemann.

Graves, Donald. 1994. *A Fresh Look at Writing.* Portsmouth, NH: Heinemann.

Graves, Donald, and Jane Hansen. 1984. The author's chair. In Julie M. Jensen, ed., *Composing and Comprehending* (pp. 69–76). Urbana, IL: ERIC Clearinghouse on Communication Skills.

Hansen, Jane. 1987. *When Writers Read.* Portsmouth, NH: Heinemann.

Harwayne, Shelley. 2000. *Lifetime Guarantees: Toward Ambitious Literacy Teaching.* Portsmouth, NH: Heinemann.

Hemming, Heather. 1985. Reading: A monitor for writing. In Jane Hansen, Thomas Newkirk, and Donald Graves, eds., *Breaking Ground: Teachers Relate Reading and Writing in the Elementary School* (pp. 53–59). Portsmouth, NH: Heinemann.

Hennings, Dorothy Grant. 1984. A writing approach to reading comprehension schema theory in action. In Julie M. Jensen, ed., *Composing and Comprehending* (pp. 191–200). Urbana, IL: ERIC Clearinghouse on Communication Skills.

Hiebert, E., and J. Colt. 1989. Patterns of literature-based reading instruction. *The Reading Teacher 43,* 12–20.

Holdaway, Don. 1979. *The Foundations of Literacy.* Gosford, NSW: Ashton Scholastic.

Holt, Suzanne, and Joanne Vacca. 1984. *Reading with a Sense of Writer: Writing with a Sense of Reader.* Urbana, IL: ERIC Clearinghouse on Communication Skills.

Jacobs, Heidi Hayes. 1997. *Mapping the Big Picture: Integrating Curriculum and Assessment K-12.* Alexandria, VA: Association for Supervision and Curriculum Development.

Jensen, Julie M. 1984. Introduction. In Julie M. Jensen, ed., *Composing and Comprehending* (pp. 1–5). Urbana, IL: ERIC Clearinghouse on Communication Skills.

Keene, Ellin Oliver, and Susan Zimmermann. 1997. *Mosaic of Thought.* Portsmouth, NH: Heinemann.

Kohl, Herbert. 2002. Topsy-turvies: Teacher talk and student talk. In Lisa Delpit, ed., *The Skin That We Speak* (pp. 147–161). New York: New Press.

Lamont, Anne. 1994. *bird by bird.* New York: Random House.

Langenberg, D.N., ed. 2000. *Report of the National Reading Panel: Teaching Children to Read.* Washington, DC: U.S. Department of Health and Human Services.

Leinhardt, G. 1989. Math lessons: A contrast of novice and expert competence. *Journal for Research in Mathematics Education 20*(1), 52–75.

Lyons, Carol, and Gay Su Pinnell. 2001. *Systems for Change in Literacy Education: A Guide to Professional Development.* Portsmouth, NH: Heinemann.

Mason, J., and J.B. Allen. 1986. A review of emergent literacy with implications for research and practice in reading. *Review of Research in Education 13,* 3–47.

Miller, Debbie. 2002. *Reading with Meaning.* Portland, ME: Stenhouse.

Moffett, James, and Betty Jane Wagner. 1983. *Student-Centered Language Arts and Reading, K-12: A Handbook for Teachers.* 3d ed. Boston: Houghton-Mifflin.

National Institute of Child Health and Human Development. 2000. *Report of the National Reading Panel: Teaching Children to Read.* Reports of the Subgroups. NH Publication N. 300-4754. Washington, DC: U.S. Government Printing Office.

Nia, Isoke Titlayo. 1999. Units of study in the writing workshop. *Primary Voices 8*(1), 3–9.

Nickel, Jodi. 2002, November. When writing conferences don't work: Students' retreat from teacher agenda. *Language Arts 79*(2), 136–147.

Odell, Lee. 1999. Assessing thinking: Glimpsing a mind at work? In Charles R. Cooper and Lee Odell, eds., *Evaluating Writing* (pp. 7–22). Urbana, IL: NCTE.

Olson, Carol Booth. 2003. *The Reading-Writing Connection: Strategies for Teaching and Learning in the Secondary Classroom.* Boston: Pearson Education.

Owocki, Gretchen, and Yetta Goodman. 2002. *Kidwatching: Documenting Children's Literacy Development.* Portsmouth, NH: Heinemann.

Peterson, Ralph. 1992. *Life in a Crowded Place.* Portsmouth, NH: Heinemann.

Pressley, M. 1998. *Reading Instruction That Works: The Case for Balanced Teaching.* New York: Guilford Press.

Raphael, T.E., and P.D. Peterson. 1997, November. *Balance in Reading Instruction: Deconstructing a Complex Notion.* Paper presented at the California Reading Association's Research Conference, San Diego, CA.

Smith, Frank. 1983. *Essays into Literacy.* Portsmouth, NH: Heinemann.

Smith, Frank. 1984. Reading like a writer. In Julie M. Jensen, ed., *Composing and Comprehending* (pp. 47–56). Urbana, IL: ERIC Clearinghouse on Communication Skills.

Smith, Frank. 1985. *Reading Without Nonsense.* New York: Teachers College Press.

Snow, C.E., M.S. Burns, and P. Griffin. 1998. *Preventing Reading Difficulties in Young Children: A Report of the National Research Council.* Washington, DC: National Academy Press.

Snowball, Diane, and Faye Bolton. 1999. *Spelling K-8: Planning and Teaching.* Portland, ME: Stenhouse.

Spiegel, D. 1994. Finding the balance in literacy development for all children. *Balanced Reading Instruction 1,* 6–11.

Spiegel, D. 1998. Silver bullets, babies, and bath water: Literature response groups in a balanced literacy program. *The Reading Teacher 52,* 114–121.

Squire, James. 1984. Composing and comprehending: Two sides of the same basic thought process. In Julie M. Jensen, ed., *Composing and Comprehending.* Urbana, IL: ERIC Clearinghouse in Communication Skills.

Sulzby, Elizabeth. 1985. Children's emergent reading of favorite storybooks: A developmental study. *Reading Research Quarterly 20,* 458–481.

Sulzby, Elizabeth, and W.H. Teale. 1991. Emergent literacy. In R. Barr, M.L. Kamil, P. Mosenthal, and P.D. Pearson, eds., *Handbook of Reading Research* (pp. 727–757). New York: Longman.

Tierney, R.J., and J.W. Cunningham, 1984. Research on teaching reading comprehension. In P.D. Pearson, ed., *Handbook of Reading Research*. White Plains, NY: Longman.

Tierney, Robert, and David Pearson. 1984. Towards a composing model of reading. In Julie M. Jensen, ed., *Composing and Comprehending*. Urbana, IL: ERIC Clearinghouse in Communication Skills.

Van Kleeck, A. 1990. Emergent literacy: Learning about print before learning to read. *Topics in Language Disorders 10*(2), 25–45.

Vygotsky, L.S. 1962. *Thought and Language*. Eugenia Hanfmann and Gertrude Vakar, ed. and trans. Cambridge, MA: The MIT Press.

Warner, Sylvia Ashton. 1963. *Teacher*. New York: Simon & Schuster.

Westerman, D.A. 1991. Expert and novice teacher decision making. *Journal of Teacher Education 42*(4), 292–305.

Winograd, P.N., and C.A. Bridge. 1986. The comprehension of important information in written prose. In J.F. Baumann, ed., *Teaching Main Idea Comprehension*. Newark, DE: International Reading Association.

Wood Ray, Katie. 1999. *Wondrous Words: Writers and Writing in the Elementary Classroom*. Urbana, IL: National Council of Teachers of English.

Wood Ray, Katie, with Lester Laminack. 2001. *The Writing Workshop: Working through the Hard Part (And They're All Hard Parts)*. Urbana, IL: National Council of Teachers of English.

INDEX